Fortune in My Eyes

For Liz—
Best wishes to you!
Dick Rosenberg

Fortune in My Eyes

A Memoir of Broadway Glamour, Social Justice, and Political Passion

David Rothenberg

APPLAUSE
THEATRE & CINEMA BOOKS

An Imprint of
Hal Leonard Corporation

Published in 2012 by Applause Theatre & Cinema Books
An Imprint of Hal Leonard Corporation
7777 West Bluemound Road
Milwaukee, WI 53213

Trade Book Division Editorial Offices
33 Plymouth St., Montclair, NJ 07042

Unless otherwise credited, all photos are from the author's collection.

Printed in the United States of America

Book design by Lynn Bergesen

Library of Congress Cataloging-in-Publication Data

Rothenberg, David, 1933-
    Fortune in my eyes : a memoir of Broadway glamour, social justice, and political passion / David Rothenberg.
        pages cm
    ISBN 978-1-55783-926-8
1. Rothenberg, David, 1933- 2. Rothenberg, David, 1933—Friends and associates. 3. Theater—New York (State)—New York—History—20th century. 4. Theater—Production and direction—New York (State)—New York—Biography. 5. Publicity—New York (State)—New York—Biography. 6. Broadway (New York, N.Y.)—History—20th century. 7. Fortune Society (New York, N.Y.) 8. New York (N.Y.)—Biography. 9. Political activists—United States—Biography. 10. Social justice—United States—History—20th century. I. Title.
    CT275.R7948A3 2012
    974.7'1044092—dc23
    [B]
                                            2012030166

www.applausebooks.com

To the many men and women at the Fortune Society,
whose stories are sprinkled through these pages.
I am grateful and honored to be a part of your lives.

Contents

Acknowledgments

My thanks to...

Julia Lord, friend and literary agent, in that order, who told me, "Stop telling those stories and write them down." That's the push and support needed for anyone who presumes to share their life story. That's where my thanks begin.

Greg Norris, whose computer skills were far superior to my plumed pen, transforming my tales into a readable manuscript. His teaching background provided editorial guidance, but most important, he always provided support.

And Carol Flannery at Applause, who gave encouragement that transformed my approach from presumption to pride.

Fortune in My Eyes

ONE

Attica

It was Danny Hogan even more than Attica that politicized me—no, radicalized me—about the criminal-justice system.

Don't misunderstand me: Attica had a profound effect. In September 1971 I was one of three dozen men called to that upstate New York prison, which was in the midst of the most notorious and violent uprising in American history. It left thirty-nine men dead, inmates and guards, with hundreds of others severely wounded.

We were ushered into the yard after being flown to Buffalo, and state troopers rushed us into the prison. I had received a call from a staff member of state representative Arthur Eve informing me that I was on the short list compiled by prisoners for observers to be in the yard during negotiations with the state. Inmates had taken over at Attica, holding two dozen guards hostage. They were making serious demands about conditions in the oppressive prison complex near the Canadian border. Before they offered their list to Commissioner Russell Oswald, the inmate leaders called for outsiders to witness the negotiations. It was clear that they had little trust in traditional corrections leadership, though Russell Oswald, who had recently been head of parole, was a more progressive voice in the field. In fact, in the early days of his parole administration, Oswald had reached out to the Fortune Society to establish some new ground rules. We were a newly founded organization created by and for the formerly incarcerated, and Oswald, in an unprecedented move, had met with us and changed some of the repressive parole restrictions.

When I received the summons to go to Attica, I quickly said I wouldn't go alone and asked permission to bring Kenny Jackson and Mel Rivers, two key men at Fortune, both of whom had done time. It was agreed, and when we arrived at the prison, Russell Oswald, exhausted and beleaguered, welcomed us in the waiting room before we entered the yard, where one thousand inmates and their hostages were making worldwide news. Oswald greeted us: "At last, some friendly faces." That was probably the last time he viewed us with that perspective.

As we entered the yard, you could cut the upstate air with a knife. The tension was unbearable. Mel whispered into my ear, "I smell death." We were aware of the hostage guards sitting in improvised tents close to the table where the Attica observers had been placed alongside the men who had authored the list of demands being submitted to the Department of Corrections. We could also see the armed soldiers patrolling catwalks that hovered over the yard.

The air was steamy. It was late summer in upstate New York, with threats of an autumn chill as morning approached. We were seated at picnic tables pressed against the wall. There were more than thirty of us, the observers, sitting among the inmate leaders of the uprising. Two inmates, Roger Champen and Herbert X. Blyden, introduced themselves to me. I had been in correspondence with both men; perhaps that is how my name landed on the list of civilians requested by prisoners to be observers. In detailed letters they had alerted me of the threatening atmosphere in Attica.

After the August killing of celebrated California prisoner-author George Jackson, activists in many institutions across the country engaged in sit-downs and hunger strikes. The political and social campaigns of the late 1960s had penetrated the prison walls, and Attica was a particularly political hotbed. The words and passion of Dr.

Martin Luther King Jr. and Malcolm X were well cited in this bastille. Roger Champen's letters revealed a deep political sophistication. Attica inmates were reflecting a growing awareness of the communities in which they had been raised, in which prison was an inevitable conclusion. They quoted Frantz Fanon and Che Guevara to highlight the persecution and expendability of poor and black people.

In decades past, prison riots had always been blunt actions demanding better food and less brutality. My own frame of reference was old movies. I recalled Burt Lancaster in *Brute Force* leading the turmoil in the yard, yelling "ya ya" at the sadistic warden, Hume Cronyn.

Attica, on September 9, 1971, was a long way from a Hollywood version of a prison protest.

Through the long night we listened to a variety of speeches—some politically brilliant and others disjointed harangues. Then the observers were asked to give some words to the prisoners and the hostages, who were huddled in quickly made tents nearby the observers' tables.

I can't recall a word I said when Brother Herbert X. Blyden handed me the mike. I do know that when he introduced me, he said that I was the founder and executive director of the Fortune Society and that I had produced the off-Broadway prison play *Fortune and Men's Eyes*. Years later, when I saw Brother Herbert in New York City after he assumed civilian status, I commented that I was probably the only person in penological history to be introduced during a prison riot with his theatrical credits. He laughed and told me that the prisoners tried to stay informed. I pointed out that my theater credits were much longer than he had suggested in the introduction, and that he'd best go back to the drawing board. We had a good laugh at that.

After the second day of negotiations and machinations between the protestors and the state, the observers took a break and went back into the administration-held portion of the prison. We agreed that our observers' group was too large, too cumbersome, and that we should select a smaller team to represent us, pending prisoner approval. Attorney William Kunstler, *New York Times* columnist Tom Wicker, Congressman Herman Badillo, and State Senator John Dunne were chosen, and the rest of us left the prison.

Outside, townspeople from Attica and nearby towns were holding vigil. Many of them were relatives of the hostages. We were immediately fed rumors that busloads of black people were heading for Attica, and they were arming up for war. Of course, no such thing was in formation, but the fears and rumors enflamed the frightened.

Kenny, Mel, and I went back to New York City, and on that fateful Monday, with a host of friends at Fortune, we listened to the reports and heard the guns going off—weapons that killed many of the men we had just met. Governor Nelson Rockefeller had made the decision to send in troops and take over the yard. He could have maced the place and sent in gas-masked troops, but his decision instead was to shoot to kill. Keep talking, the observers had urged Rockefeller. Congressman Badillo, pleading with the governor for more time, had stated that there was always time to die.

Tom Wicker, quoting Badillo, would title his book on Attica *A Time to Die*.

The state lied about the dead hostages, claiming they had been stabbed to death by prisoners, but a Wyoming County coroner later contradicted the front-page headlines of the previous days. He reported that the dead hostages had all been shot by state troopers. He eventually lost his job, but the Attica Observers Committee uncovered many missteps by the state.

The Observers Committee began meeting weekly at various sites, including the home of Attorney Kunstler. Eventually, we all appeared before the McKay Commission, whose task was to examine the causes and decisions that led to all that was Attica. It became clear to me that Rockefeller's decision to send in troops had had little to do with the conflict at hand. The Attica decision was part of the political reconstruction of the governor, who still had presidential aspirations and was viewed as a liberal easterner by hardcore Republican conservatives. His infamous and draconian drug law, the one bearing his name, was another sign of his political transformation.

Rockefeller's drug law altered New York dramatically. The prison population escalated from thirteen thousand in 1967 to seventy-seven thousand in the late nineties. More prisons were built, and his drug law was emulated by states all over the country. It created the prison industrial complex, making it fiscally impossible to discuss problem solving and crime fighting when so many corporations had an investment in the increase of prisons and prisoners.

At point of arrest, conviction, and sentencing, the drug laws were racially selective. White people with drugs often ended up in community treatment, with reduced sentences, an option less often afforded to people of color. As a result, more than 90 percent of the men and women doing time under the Rockefeller drug law in New York State were black and Hispanic—a pattern that was repeated around the country. The drug laws destroyed not only families: entire inner-city communities were thrown a beanball. Subsequently, many states implemented voting restrictions based on past felony convictions, a policy that altered voting patterns dramatically, undoing almost all of the efforts of Dr. Martin Luther King Jr. to register black voters. This factor leaped into the limelight in Florida in 2000, when America became aware of the systematic exclusion of African Americans from voting. A racial disparity in arrests, convictions, and sentencing had a rippling effect and determined who would be president of the United States.

The great irony, of course, was that Rockefeller's law had no impact on drug use or sales. The big wheeler-dealers were protected;

they avoided street contact and were shielded by a fleet of attorneys. Meanwhile, there were always another hundred mules, poor kids from the streets who were recruited for fast, big money and, of course, nabbed by the police in inner-city sweeps. This was nothing new in criminal-justice history, where poor people are still left to the overworked, understaffed legal-aid attorneys. The guys at Fortune often said, "Money talks and big-timers walk."

I came to understand what I had witnessed and heard in Attica was political and had to be fought on political terms.

Four of the slain prisoners were unclaimed. The Fortune Society took the responsibility for their funerals. We had a funeral procession following a rally and led the wooden coffins to a potter's field burial. At our small midtown office we notified families of inmates of the status of their loved ones. The Department of Corrections, refusing to talk to the families, consented to give us the list of the dead and wounded so we could make the emotional calls to the parents, wives, and children of the assaulted.

After the state took over the prison and killed inmates and hostages, there was little reason to believe that officials would reach out to the families of inmates. If the prison were filled with sheep instead of men, they would have run the institution in the same fashion. You don't call anyone when a sheep is wounded or killed.

In 1971, advocacy for prisoners was in the embryonic stage. Prison administrations assumed little or no responsibility or accountability to the public. The men who ran the institutions had been born and raised in prison towns, and their job was to keep the prison secure. When Attica jumped into the headlines, they were suspicious of the press. The air was filled with rumors. At one point, when we had departed from Attica prison, the townspeople were reporting that buses of black people were heading to Attica from

Harlem and Bedford-Stuyvesant—and they were armed. The people in the town of Attica were mostly relatives of prison personnel, some of whom were being held hostage.

For years people have asked me about sitting in the yard at Attica: What were my emotions? What was I thinking? It is like those television interviewers insisting that someone—anyone—who has endured a headline-making event be able to reenact their thought process. I have attempted to recreate an image, giving dramatic interpretation to my role in this historic event.

In fact I was but a speck on the stage of a national drama, which had the world's eyes focused on it. I couldn't imagine that anything I said would alter the conflict—I was more concerned that something I uttered might exacerbate the hostilities. I was an advocate for prisoners, but a few years earlier I had been a Broadway press agent and a producer of an off Broadway prison drama. My recent writings, critical of prison policy, placed me among the very few voices in the prisoners' corner, and so desperate were they for sounds of support that my literary outbursts earned me a role in the Attica uprising as an observer.

In the yard I was numb—frightened would be a more accurate description—realizing that I could die in the middle of a state-versus-prisoner conflict. I felt less than heroic as I realized I had left the comfort zone of social critic and had entered the battlefield of social and racial strife that was erupting in an upstate New York prison.

My role in Attica was insignificant.

What I took away from it was vast.

This all took place in 1971, and when I run into a few of the still-remaining Attica brothers or other observers, we recall it in detail. It was a life-changing experience and one that made clear to me the lengths the state will go to protect image, reputation, status quo... even if lives have to be unnecessarily sacrificed.

Nelson Rockefeller's political ambition was the determining factor in Attica decisions, at least in my eyes, and that is enough to politicize and radicalize any thinking, caring person. Attica had its impact. But it was Danny Hogan who provided the final notes in this unfinished symphony.

Two

Danny Hogan

Danny Hogan, a skinny, nineteen-year-old Irish kid from Paterson, New Jersey, looked like he weighed about a hundred pounds. He came to visit me at the Fortune Society and said, "I witnessed the murder of Richard Speller in the Vroom Building. He was killed by the guards there."

The Fortune Society, an organization I had begun in 1967 to advocate for prisoners and the formerly incarcerated, was in its infancy. I was a newcomer to the field of criminal justice, and Danny Hogan's story was my coming of age in that arena. It was a time when those of us who responded to the real and human needs of individuals in and out of prison also realized that there were political aspects, and the terrain could often be serious and dangerous.

Danny informed me that he had been sent to the Vroom Building from the Passaic County Jail, where he'd been awaiting trial. Vroom, infamous in New Jersey history, was a state hospital for prison inmates in Trenton. It was the place where inmates were sent for mental observation but, more accurately, were abused and/or ignored. One man told me, "If you didn't have head problems when you got there, you would when you left."

Danny was sent back to the county jail after observation and was bailed out by his family, awaiting disposition of his drug-related case.

Here's the background on what Danny knew:

Wilfred Hardman was thirty-two years old when he died—January 27, 1972.

R. Merrill Speller was thirty-four years old when he died—March 16, 1972.

Apparently, the two men never met, though each spent the last day of his life in the Vroom Building.

Mr. Speller, the autopsy states, took his own life.

Mr. Hardman, the autopsy states, died of a brain tumor.

There is something that links the deaths of these two men. Before each man died, the Fortune Society received word that his life was in danger.

Mr. Hardman's mother, a registered nurse, called on January 20 to inform us that she had protested to officials in the state prison in Trenton that her son was showing signs of having been drugged with Thorazine. In a letter to Governor Cahill, Mrs. Hardman wrote, "My son was seated on a stool, swaying back and forth, so sedated he could hardly raise his eyelids. I went out to the other room and asked to see a doctor. One of the guards told me to go into the deputy's office—A Mr. Drisbe…who had 'Chief Deputy' on his name pin. I asked him what was wrong with my son, that I was a registered nurse and that it was very obvious to me that he was heavily drugged. Mr. Drisbe became very indignant and said, 'If he is drugged, he got it from another prisoner.' I answered, 'That is unlikely; my son has not been involved in drugs.'"

Later she was told that her son was "emotionally disturbed" and had been "trying to eat garbage." Mrs. Hardman questioned how her son could get garbage in his cell and insisted that he be treated. She was informed that her son would see a psychiatrist, a decision she protested because she felt he was too drugged for a psychiatric evaluation to be valid.

Mrs. Hardman called the Fortune Society and said that her son was being moved to the Vroom Building after this visit. On the morning of January 28 she left a message with the Fortune Society's answering service: "My son was found dead in his cell last night."

Around the same time, an inmate named R. Merrill Speller wrote the Fortune Society from the Vroom Building. In my reply to him, I stated that the Fortune Society was acquainted with the conditions and atmosphere of the Vroom Building and had just learned of the questionable death of Wilfred Hardman.

In response to that, R. Merrill Speller wrote, "I'm writing to let you know that I fear your mention of the patient that died here last month caused the people here to reevaluate their plans on what they intend to do with me. Suddenly (after your letter) I found that I was soon to be iced." He closed with, "One attendant came to my cell and said he was the executioner and asked if I wanted it in the front or the back." A PS written in pencil on the front of the letter stated, "I was severely beaten about the head and body with clubs right after writing to you."

A letter from another inmate to the Fortune Society stated: "Things are getting worse. This morning they (the officers) almost killed a prisoner. They brutalized him with sticks and kicked him in the face and all over and this act of animalism continued for about fifteen minutes. I told them to stop and they said, 'You shut your mouth you little bastard or you'll get it worse than he did if you get someone to come up . . .' His name is Richard M. Speller. . . ."

In late February, the Fortune Society contacted the public defender's office, and attorneys went into the Vroom Building to see Mr. Speller. We also contacted the governor's office and stated our concern for Mr. Speller's safety. I wrote to Mr. Speller on February 24 and asked that he write weekly to "assure us that your health and personal well-being are okay." Speller gave reports of his physical state in letters on March 3, March 7, and March 12. On March 17 his sister called the Fortune Society and stated, "My brother died last night. He told us that if anything happened to him we should contact the Fortune Society."

Officials at the Vroom Building told Speller's family that he had taken his own life.

I told Danny Hogan that he had explosive information and that, based on what he had observed, he should immediately get a lawyer for his protection. We urged him to stay in contact with us and said that if he didn't have an attorney, we would contact the ACLU of New Jersey on his behalf.

A week later, Danny's mother called me at his request. She informed us that Danny had been suddenly brought to trial, convicted, and sentenced to five years. Shockingly, he was immediately sent to Trenton State Prison, an infamous bastille that housed lifers and violent offenders. Most teenagers with a drug bust would have been sent to Jamesburg or Leesburg. Danny's quick trial, sentencing, and delivery to Trenton indicated that all facets of the system were working together: the courts, the prisons, and the police.

I called Anne Klein, a woman who had been recently named as commissioner of corrections in New Jersey. She was a former state legislator, progressive in her views about the prison system and determined to make some changes. She was also the first woman to head the department in New Jersey and faced immediate opposition from the machismo-dominated power structure in the New Jersey Department of Corrections. I informed Anne that I was concerned about the safety of Danny Hogan, and that his being sent to Trenton was a travesty and a signal he had been fingered as a witness of a crime at the Vroom Building.

On New Year's morning, I turned on the radio to hear reports of the holiday celebrations around the world. The first bulletin I heard was that an inmate at Trenton State Prison had been scalded to death when his toilet backed up, hit the boiling radiator, and killed him. I knew immediately that Danny had been murdered. Moments later my phone rang. It was Anne Klein confirming that Danny was dead, scalded to death in his Trenton cell.

Over the years, released Trenton prisoners have told me that they heard the screaming of Danny Hogan through the New Year's Eve night.

Back in the early seventies, it was well known in New Jersey corrections that I had been in contact with Wilfred Hardman's mother and had received kited letters from R. Merrill Speller, and that Speller's family was threatening to sue the state of New Jersey. And it was public knowledge that I was an advocate for Danny Hogan, who had informed me that he'd been witness to a murder.

The Mercer County grand jury was convened to consider Danny's death, and I was brought to Trenton to testify. It was my first appearance before a grand jury and was nothing like you see on *Law and Order*. It was closed—no outsiders, including the press, were in attendance—and orchestrated by the district attorney. The DA ran the show.

From the outset, it was clear to me that the district attorney was not seeking the truth, and that in fact he was part of the machinery to protect the misdoings of the Department of Corrections. I never got to talk about the letters from Richard Speller or the observations of Wilfred Hardman's mother. At a grand jury hearing, you are alone. You are not allowed legal representation. The DA threatened me that perjury could prompt imprisonment. He would not let me talk about the warnings related to Danny Hogan, to say nothing of Speller and Hardman.

I recall my train trip back from Trenton to Manhattan. I wasn't depressed, but I had an overwhelming sadness—I was sad about the needless death of three young men and sad because my faith in the system had been totally shattered. I had grown up in suburban New Jersey, had saluted the flag with pride and read the Constitution and the Bill of Rights; I believed in the grandeur of America down to my core.

I had never met Speller, although we had corresponded. I had never met Wilfred Hardman, though his mother had told me a great deal about him. But Danny Hogan was a real person whom I had met and talked with—a simple, confused, but nice kid who had been caught up in drug use. He didn't deserve to die.

I recalled having read Anne Frank's *The Diary of a Young Girl*. All the statistics of the Holocaust were too overwhelming to absorb. But Anne Frank I understood, and one life became six million.

I have had trouble understanding the counterproductive, often evil aspects of the prison system. The stories are too numerous and overwhelming to grasp. But I saw and knew Danny Hogan. He was real, and I can't get him out of my head.

THREE

The Theater

Reflective in my senescence, I have begun to diagram how my life took the turns it did, going from a successful career in the theater to finding myself comfortable working with men and women who have been behind bars.

Over the years I have discovered that most civilians will listen endlessly to my stories of Elizabeth Taylor, Peggy Lee, Charles Laughton, Eartha Kitt, or any of the other luminaries who crossed my path. Yet when I begin to discuss my concerns about the prison system and the people who have changed my life, there is a pulling away, a look that suggests the listener doesn't want to hear about those who have been incarcerated. There is great interest in the details of the crime but not the cause and effect that led to it or the conditions of punishment that exacerbate alienation.

So how did I come to walk a different path ... at war with the dinosaurs?

In the 1960s everything was unlikely. Andy Warhol's cultural nihilism and voyeurism flourished amid civil rights and antiwar demonstrations. Americans because acquainted with political assassinations. Every ethnic and religious group boasted visible militants. It was an era that nurtured protest and ferment. The unrest was threatening to some, exhilarating for others.

No collection of disenfranchised people had a more convoluted beginning than the Fortune Society, which came right off the stage of an off-Broadway prison drama, *Fortune and Men's Eyes*, authored by a Canadian ex-convict, John Herbert. I was restless with the theater when the script of the play arrived and excited me. It was socially provocative and dramatic, challenging of hidden social mores, but at its core a triumphant depiction of man's ability to survive adversity.

When you work in the theater, it isn't often that you develop a life-altering passion for a play. It certainly wasn't always that way for me.

I arrived in New York City in 1958, after my release from the U.S. Army. Two years in Georgia in the peacetime military and I was ready for any reasonable challenge. It was my intention to work in the theater, but, predictably, there was an assortment of jobs before I got my foot in the door. I had no aspirations to be an actor or a playwright...so where would I fit in?

I think my motivation came from Joseph Mankiewicz's dialogue in the movie *All About Eve*, which I had seen on a Friday night while in high school. I was so fascinated with the quick banter that I went back to see the movie a second night and declared to myself that I wanted to live in the world that Margo Channing and Bill Sampson inhabited. They snapped hilarious one-liners at each other. The conversation was not only brittle but reflected an awareness of the politics and culture of the time. It was clearly not the conversation you heard around Teaneck High School, which was typical of suburban America. The relationship between Bette Davis (playing a Broadway star) and Thelma Ritter (her dresser, a sharp-tongued former vaude-villian) was one I would recognize in the theater years later. The humor in the movie was rich and topical, with layers of irony. There was also trust and acceptance. I knew instinctively that there was something for me in the theater world. A friend of mine once commented, "David, half your lines are right out of *All About Eve*," and I responded, "And the other half?"

Perhaps what I appreciated most about the dialogue was that it revealed the characters. They weren't serving up gags with punch lines but evoking laughter that emerged from the situation.

If anyone had told me that I would be working with Bette Davis, the cinematic Margo, within ten years, I would have considered him nuts.

I was sharing an apartment on Manhattan's Upper West Side with an army pal and began a series of typing jobs with ad agencies and book publishers. My top salary was sixty-five dollars a week. Methodically, each week, I mailed letters of introduction to every theatrical producer, agent, and press agent listed in the yellow pages of the Manhattan directory. With equal consistency, I responded to all classified ads in the *New York Times* listed under "show business." From the start, I knew the theater was the world where I belonged.

The first and only real response to any of my pleading letters came from a theatrical press agent, Max Eisen. The call came at home on a Saturday night. That should have been the first warning. He invited me to his office for a Sunday morning interview. Max was located in the Sardi Building, and I knew enough to recognize that this location was the real thing. I was one of two dozen young and eager would-be theater dynamos who had responded to the *Times* ad. Eisen, we discovered, was going to hire five of us as stringers at five summer theater tents he represented. It was an eight-week gig and would pay sixty-five dollars a week.

My interview was brief, and Max gave me the famous words: "I'll let you know." I called conscientiously for the next five days before his assistant finally told me, "Listen kid, you're persistent. Come in and talk to me." After my workday concluded, I returned to the West Forty-Fourth Street office and met Bob Larkin, who informed me that Max had already hired the five guys and didn't know how to tell me no. "But," Bob added, "I'm overworked and need help, and I'm going to tell Max that I need you." Larkin called later that night and told me it would be six days, sixty dollars a week, and I would be typing, stuffing envelopes, and answering phones. "You start on Monday."

I was in show business, working for Max, a man who screamed and insisted that I work every other Sunday. There was always another envelope to stuff.

I once heard someone on a radio interview program say, "If you want to work in a particular field, get your foot in the door any way possible and make yourself indispensable. Learn everything, remember everyone's name, and in a few weeks they won't be able to function without you." It is advice I have always passed on, and it has only occasionally been heeded.

At Max's office, I listened and I learned. It wasn't difficult in a three-man operation. In no time he had me covering interviews with actors at radio and TV stations. I would take Charles Nelson Reilly to Jack Silverman's International to be interviewed by Bea Kalmus at midnight and get to the office next morning at ten a.m. before anyone arrived. The mystery of the business was unveiled to me. It was about tenacity and remembering. The fact that I was starstruck didn't hurt. Suddenly I was meeting performers whose names I had seen on marquees. I was calling people who were major players—actors, directors, and producers. They talked to me like a peer. They were relying on my knowledge or information about their specific appointments.

In reflection, it is interesting to realize that the stars of yesterday who most impressed me are virtually unknown to most people decades later. Doretta Morrow, Hal LeRoy, and Bert Wheeler were all legendary show-business personalities I met and worked with while at Max's office. The unknowns of the time would be remembered today. An off-Broadway show, a revival of Jerome Kern's *Leave It to Jane*, had a moderate success. One of the young girls in the chorus, a statuesque high school senior, was Lanie Kazan, and the youthful juvenile lead was George Segal. Max worked on several off-Broadway shows with stars-in-the-making like James Earl Jones and Cicely Tyson.

One of the summer touring shows Max was representing was an edition of the hit Broadway musical *Jamaica*. I was asked to cover a photo session in which the star, Abbey Lincoln, who was playing the part created by Lena Horne, was to be photographed. Max told me that some dancer from the cast was directing the touring package and I should meet him at the photographer's studio. I knew nothing about photo shoots but was told that the director would set up the pictures. I was just covering for the office.

The dancer-actor-choreographer of that production was to become my first friend in the theater. I arrived at the photo studio and saw this imposing, almost intimidating man. Later I would describe him as having "a dancer's carriage." I introduced myself, and he told me his name was Alvin Ailey. He patiently set up the various pictures with his star. I was impressed with his energy and his command of the situation. He also revealed an impish humor and quiet intelligence. After the session, we went for lunch. He told me of his plans in the world of dance and was equally curious about what paths I would be taking.

A year later, he invited me to a rehearsal of his young troupe of dancers. I had run into Alvin on West Forty-Sixth Street and Seventh Avenue in front of Howard Johnson's. It was a hot morning, and Alvin declared, rather sheepishly, "I started a dance company. We're having a rehearsal this afternoon. Would you come up and watch?" I was hesitant—I knew little or nothing about dance—but I didn't want to offend him, so I agreed.

It was a humid August day in an era before air-conditioning. I ventured into a studio inhabited with dancers who had been rehearsing all day. I was the only audience. Then Alvin told me he was recreating a piece from the Bible, and I thought to myself, "Well, this is the final nail in the coffin." I was an audience of one watching sweaty dancers in torn leotards dancing from the Bible in an over-heated rehearsal hall. And that is where and when I discovered genius can surface in the most unlikely locations.

Alvin called his dance *Revelations*. It would become his signature piece and be celebrated around the world in later decades.

Being a press agent in the theater meant establishing credibility, meeting people, knowing where to place a good idea, timing, and recognizing what the media need would be. During the summer, I met another theatrical press agent, Bob Ullman, who told me that he had a show opening, and that if it received the kind of reviews it deserved, he would need help. The job would pay eighty-five dollars (twenty-five more than I was earning), and I would only have to work a five-day week. Unlike Max, he would let me go out for lunch and be home for dinner. I saw freedom on the horizon. The off-Broadway musical was *Little Mary Sunshine*, and after the rave reviews were published, Bob called me, shouting, "Help!" I gave Max two weeks' notice, and he didn't talk to me for two years.

My real theatrical apprenticeship was with Bob Ullman. He taught me, introduced me to people, and had confidence in me, allowing me to create on my own. It was a time when I began to feel comfortable about my vocational potential. I was becoming a theater pro.

Bob sponsored my apprenticeship in ATPAM (the union for theater press agents and managers) and arranged for me to spend my summers as the press rep in warm-weather theater houses. I spent the summer of 1960 at the Lakewood Theatre in Skowhegan, Maine. In addition to seventy-five dollars a week, I had my own lakefront cottage and three meals a day at the theater's adjoining first-rate restaurant.

I was right where I wanted to be. Touring shows played at Lake-wood for a week or two, and it was my assignment to alert the Maine media about the upcoming attractions. Citizens of Portland, Augusta,

Waterville, and Bangor were dependent on my information for their summer theater treats.

The stars passing through Lakewood included Darren McGavin (TV's Mike Hammer), Tom Poston, Eve Arden, Oscar winners Joan Fontaine and Shirley Booth, and TV personality Henry Morgan, who appeared in an old chestnut, *Accent on Youth*.

It was with Henry Morgan that I established myself as an inventive young person in the theater. I had read that the neighboring town of Waterville was planning summer Dollar Day sales on the day before Henry was to open at Lakewood. I contacted the town's chamber of commerce and suggested they have a Dollar Day parade with Morgan as the grand marshal, concluding with the mayor presenting him the key to the city. Every store advertising their sales included a "Welcome Henry Morgan" box in the local newspaper ads, accompanied by a picture of the TV star. Henry, who was working for a percentage of the gross at Lakewood, had given me the go-ahead for the plan.

On the day of the parade, the Waterville streets were lined with thousands of people. News estimates were that the town tripled in population for the day. Henry, at that time, was a panelist on the popular TV game show *I've Got a Secret*. He and his lady friend, opera singer Joanna Simon, and I were placed in an open convertible, following the high school band and preceding a bevy of floats and local booster organizations.

Henry was presented with the key to the city in the town square. He was to mingle among the throng and give away fifty silver dollars. What was not anticipated was a crowd swelling that got out of control. Police protection was provided, and Morgan, Ms. Simon, the mayor, and I were ushered into a local bank for safety. We hid out in a vault until it was determined we could be safely sneaked out of a rear entrance.

Henry Morgan sold out every performance at the theater; it was the most successful week of his tour. For years after, people would relay stories to me, passed on by Morgan, about that parade and the incredible, successful publicity maneuver in a little town in Maine. It reached mythical proportions in the retelling.

I had begun to make a niche for myself. When I returned to work with Bob Ullman in the fall, we represented an assortment of plays, one of which was the off-Broadway revival of George Gershwin's *Oh, Kay!* A young singer from Portland, Maine, made her debut in the chorus. I was particularly impressed by her comedic talents and became an early fan and friend of Linda Lavin, who was later to become TV's Alice.

During the winter, Mike Ellis of the Bucks County Playhouse in New Hope, Pennsylvania, contacted me. He said that he had heard of my work in Skowhegan, Maine, and would like to engage me as the summer press representative for a six-month season starting April 1. I was impressed that my efforts in faraway Maine had reached Bucks County, and it became apparent to me that in the theater what you achieve or don't achieve becomes your résumé.

I rented a small cottage in the bucolic Pennsylvania community. Unlike the Lakewood Theatre, which had touring packages with established stars, Mike Ellis tried out new plays and had a steady stream of visitors from the New York theater community checking out all aspects of a production. Bucks County was a summer hangout for the Broadway cognoscenti, only two hours from Times Square.

One of the men I befriended that summer was humorist S. J. Perelman, known as Sid, whose hilarious comedy *The Beauty Part* would be tested at the playhouse. Perelman, who had made his mark with the *New Yorker* magazine and as a screenwriter for the Marx Brothers, had a farm in Bucks County. His play starred Bert Lahr and a young actor I only knew as Mary Martin's son. Larry Hagman would later become a formidable television star as J. R. Ewing on *Dallas*.

There was a production meeting at the Perelman farmhouse. Sid's most recent success had been as lead screenwriter on Mike Todd's *Around the World in 80 Days*. Todd had been killed in a tragic plane crash; his wife, the glamorous Elizabeth Taylor, was to have been on the plane, but a last minute change of plans saved her life. During the meeting someone alluded to the Todd tragedy, and Sid commented, "Particularly for the widow Todd." I practically choked on my coffee at the playwright's sacrilegious allusion to Elizabeth Taylor. His phrase was right out of an old Western movie, hardly compatible with Elizabeth's international reputation.

Sid peeked at me over his specs as I tried to pull myself together. I realized that I was alone in responding to Perelman's deglamorized description of the screen goddess. After the meeting, Sid approached me, asking, "Who are you? What's your role with the play?" I answered his battery of questions, and then he said, "My wife and I are having a few people over for dinner on Sunday. If you are free, please join us."

The theater can be a very democratic place. I was a novice, a youth compared to most around me, but a nationally acclaimed humorist, screenwriter, and playwright invited me to join his social orbit, a guest at a Sunday night gathering of writers and humorists.

Years later, after Sid Perelman had become a widower and was living at the Gramercy Park Hotel, I would often join him for high tea. His droll stories had me in hysterics, and I always treasured the friendship.

Sid's stories were often of his Hollywood days, working with the frantic Marx Brothers. He was not enchanted with Hollywood and its social pecking order. Being with Sid, I realized that he found humor in mundane things happening before your eyes. In spite of his making me laugh, there was also a note of sadness, which I never unveiled. Perhaps wit is the salvation for sad or troubled people.

One of my attention-getting press gimmicks was to have a *Beauty Part* child contest for boys and girls under ten years of age. Bert Lahr and other actors were to serve as judges. Who knew that every parent in a hundred-mile radius would bring tots to New Hope on a Saturday morning? The judging was to start at ten a.m. and be over in sufficient time for Mr. Lahr and the others to prepare for the Saturday matinee.

Mr. Lahr was a kind, decent man, but like most clowns he was serious about his craft. It took us nearly four hours to finally get through all the kids and name a five-year-old boy and a six-year-old girl as the *Beauty Part* children. Protesting parents of also-rans nearly bombarded the theater, but pictures of Bert Lahr with adorable moppets appeared everywhere. It was a photo editor's dream—the Cowardly Lion from *The Wizard of Oz* with milk-and-honey kids.

In the early spring, a photo appeared that altered my professional life. The Bucks County Playhouse is situated on the banks of the Delaware River, and a small stream and waterfall are only a few feet from the theater's entrance. One sunny day, a goose appeared with a handful of her newborn goslings. I grabbed producer Mike Ellis, called the staff photographer, and had pictures snapped of Mike and the goose family in front of the playhouse. I told Mike it was a perfect photo and would get mileage for Mother's Day: a theater producer with a mother bird and her flock. That picture was how and why press agents lived. It made the wire services, and the Bucks County Playhouse received national attention.

Mike thought I was a publicity find. I was twenty-seven years old, two years in the business, and generally unknown to the Broadway community.

Mike's good friend was Broadway producer Alexander H. Cohen. Alex had revealed to his intimates that he was on the lookout for a young public-relations person to work exclusively on his Broadway shows. He had realized that none of the established men and women in the field would work for only one producer. He assessed that such an arrangement might appeal to a younger person, someone on their way up.

After the success of the Mother Goose photos in Bucks County, Mike Ellis suggested that Alex Cohen might want to meet me. I received a note from Cohen asking if I would come to New York City for a chat with him. A few weeks later, we met in his office and talked about the possibility of my joining his staff. He was convinced that he wanted me on his team. Brazenly, I declined his offer, telling him that I would like to work with him in the future but I needed another year working in the field as an apprentice learning the business before I took over full responsibility. I didn't want to fall on my face. There was a great deal for me to learn before forging ahead and accepting Alex Cohen's generous invitation and challenge.

Alex was apparently fascinated that I turned down his offer. He courted me during the next Broadway season. I was doing publicity in another office, working on the Richard Rodgers musical *No Strings* with Diahann Carroll and Richard Kiley; Tennessee Williams's *Night of the Iguana* with Bette Davis and Margaret Leighton; Morris West's *Daughter of Silence* with Emlyn Williams and Rip Torn; *A Shot in the Dark* with Julie Harris; *Gypsy* with Ethel Merman; and *The Sound of Music* with Mary Martin. Colleagues and friends would catch a glimpse of me at an opening-night party or lunching at Sardi's with a star who was being interviewed. It appeared as if my life were next to the spotlight, all glamorous and exciting.

In fact, most of the time, the publicity man was at the desk, on the phone, appearing as enthused as an accountant or stenographer. The job entailed assembling biographies for *Playbill*, working the phones, coordinating interviews, talking to editors and writers and selling them on the inherent dramatic aspects of the incipient production... or arranging seats for the press and demanding agents. Every show had its share of unpredictable drama, depending on the voltage of the production and the people assembled for it. I spent endless time calming irrational fears and complaints of pampered personalities. Production meetings and gatherings with ad agencies punctuated any day around a Broadway opening.

It was exciting for me to spend several days with Diahann Carroll before she went into rehearsal for her career-changing lead role in Richard Rodgers's *No Strings*. All of the entertainment media were anxious to report on and photograph this talented beauty, the first African American woman to play the lead in a Richard Rodgers musical. In 1962, this was ground-breaking.

It was more of an adventure than work for me. I'd meet Diahann at her West End Avenue apartment, and the journey would begin. *Look* magazine was following her every move. As we visited Bendel's on Fifty-Seventh Street, where designer Donald Brooks considered stylish outfits for her, cameras were clicking. My assignment was to keep the actress happy, make sure the photographers got what they needed, and make certain there was harmony between the various parties. That was a particularly pleasant task. Sometimes tempers, egos, and insecurities can intrude, and the press person must become psychologist, social worker, and diplomat.

There is a special energy with a young artist, as Ms. Carroll was then, who is about to assume her first major role. Different from that of a star like, for example, Bette Davis, who had survived years of media scrutiny. An old pro like Davis knew the drill—could, in fact, be the drill sergeant. Diahann Carroll, like me, was all wide-eyed wonderment, asking me for my opinion of hair and dress styles. I insisted that I had only a layman's perspective of such things, and she indicated that that was exactly what she wanted. It is only in hindsight that you realize your daily drill was not only guiding your future but becoming an asterisk in theatrical history.

During the Philadelphia tryout of the Broadway-bound play *Daughter of Silence*, adapted by Morris West from his best-selling novel, Mary Martin was ubiquitous, since her husband, Richard

Halliday, was the producer. The legendary Ms. Martin recognized her entitlements and asked me to arrange interviews with the Philadelphia press, using her star electricity in Philadelphia to draw attention to her husband's play. The stars of *Daughters of Silence*, Emlyn Williams, Rip Torn, and Janet Margolin, didn't have the marquee power that drew people to the theater. You work with what you've got, and we had Mary Martin.

Most Broadway shows in those days had out-of-town tryouts, usually in New Haven, Boston, and Philadelphia, with frequent trips to Toronto or Wilmington. For most of us in the 1960s, the world existed in Manhattan between Forty-Fourth Street and Fifty-Ninth Street, between Sixth and Eighth Avenues. When you are out of town with a show, you make quick friendships. Theater people tend to cling together when in unfamiliar territory. It was not unusual for me to enter the hotel coffee shop and have Mary Martin and Richard Halliday or Rip Torn signal me to join them for breakfast. Mary was an engaging woman—all surface kindness. I once asked how to contact her when we returned to New York, and she purred, "I'm in the phone book." It never occurred to me that Broadway's leading musical star would be listed in the phone book.

That was enough of a dose of Broadway to convince me I was ready for the big time as the man in charge. In the spring of 1962, I told Alex Cohen I was prepared for the next chapter in my life. I joined his office that June.

Incidentally, years later he told me that it was one thing I said that had made him gamble on a comparative novice. I, of course, didn't recall it, because I had been so intimidated by the theatrical trappings in his office. He had said to me, "You are very young and have only been in the theater for two seasons. How can you do the work for me? Do you know all the newspaper and TV people well enough?"

I had apparently responded, "If I don't know a person, a good idea will serve as an introduction." Alex liked that response.

FOUR

Broadway

I savored the months I worked with Bette Davis, who was starring in Tennessee Williams's *Night of the Iguana*. My boss at the time, Ben Washer, had a long relationship with the Hollywood star. During previews he brought me backstage to meet her. We immediately entered into a long and enjoyable chat about the theater, movies, living in New York, and the newly arrived Kennedy administration. Ben was so relieved by Bette's fancy for me that he assigned me as her press contact during the run of *Iguana*.

Before I met her, veteran wags in the theater had alerted me about Ms. Davis, describing her as opinionated and demanding. One old-timer had warned me, "She gets a hold of a kid like you, she'll chew you up like bad meat and spit you out." I found her to be something quite different.

My first event with her was to arrange and accompany her to a radio interview on WOR with Martha Deane. Back in those days, a radio interview was a press coup. We arrived early, and the three of us talked in the studio before airtime. Bette removed one of her famous cigarettes, took out a kitchen match, and stroked it across the table as if she were a firefighter. I let out a laugh. She was playing Bette Davis to an audience of two.

Martha Deane mentioned to Bette that she had been in Hollywood the previous year but that the studio had denied her an interview with the legendary Ms. Davis. Bette let out a *humph*, a comment she made frequently when studio procedure was introduced as a topic.

"But," Ms. Deane added, "I did have an opportunity to interview Gary Merrill," an actor who had been married to Bette, but whom she had since discarded. "What is Mr. Merrill dong now?" asked Ms. Deane. "Drinking," Bette snapped back, and I let out a howl, after which I was confined to the sponsors' booth. Bette made me laugh and seemed to enjoy that I was so comfortable responding to her Davis-like intonations.

When the interview concluded, we entered the elevator at WOR. Three businessmen were openmouthed, immediately recognizing one of the world's most famous actresses. Bette, seeing she had a new audience, turned to me, and in the quickly recognized staccato Davis voice said, "David, take a lesson. Don't be like the studio idiots; always let a star make her own decisions." When we entered her car, she laid out the rules. I was to come to her about any interview possibilities. She would agree if it worked around her schedule, if it would sell tickets, and if the interviewer wouldn't insult her intelligence. We continued that way for a few weeks, and one day she said to me, "David, you decide. I don't have to be bothered."

I realized she was saying to me: "I consider you a professional, a colleague, and I don't have to be burdened with details; you can handle that."

Demanding? Yes. What stars like Ms. Davis demand is professional competence that allows them to do their job. Years later, when I would hear Bette Davis stories, I would merely ask the tale-teller if they had ever worked with or met her. Usually they were passing on second- and thirdhand fables.

What I learned from Bette Davis permitted me to work successfully during my show-business days with an array of divas, most of whom were described as "difficult" but in most instances were either insecure or surrounded by inadequacy.

My life in the theater was dramatically altered when I began working with Alexander H. Cohen, one of the most colorful and prolific producers in the golden age of American theater, in the early sixties. I was indeed privileged. With Alex Cohen, I entered the pantheon of American theater. Suddenly my colleagues, people with whom I interacted daily, included Sir John Gielgud, Richard Burton, Elizabeth Taylor, Alfred Drake, Charles Boyer, Sir Ralph Richardson—not just the kids down the block.

I was never in awe of the company I was keeping. It was all about the work. Over the years, it became pro forma to socialize, mix and mingle, attend the endless social events and parties that are part of the routine—certainly the most celebrated and publicized aspect of show business. The public rarely sees the work. Television exposes the glamour and the various red carpets.

Alex Cohen was my boss, but our working relationship evolved into a friendship that would last for the remainder of his life.

He was an old-school, hands-on producer, familiar with every aspect of getting a play on the boards. He had started as a boy wunderkind, a coproducer of a 1941 play, *Angel Street,* that ran for three years. He was a clever and inventive promoter. He made things happen.

By the time I met him, he had suffered a series of interesting but financially unsuccessful productions. His luck changed with the creation of the Nine O'Clock Theatre—inexpensively produced, topical reviews.

The first thing I learned working with Alex was that my life would not be boring. His workplace, a neatly appointed office on East Forty-Sixth Street, was saturated with bright, ambitious young men and women, all reflecting Alex's tireless energy. There was enough socializing inherent with any production, no need for me to go running after it. I loved the work and I was good at it.

My life took a new shape. We were traveling to Toronto often, producing shows at the O'Keefe Centre in that Canadian city. One morning, Alex called me at home at seven a.m. "Hildy's not feeling well"—Alex was married to Hildy Parks, a dynamo actress-writer—"and we are set to fly to Rome. Do you have a passport?"

Of course I did, because of my frequent trips to Canada.

"Good," he responded, "meet me at Idlewild. We're going to Italy—Rome, Milan, Turino. There's an Italian musical called *Rugantino*. I need your opinion."

That was my first visit to Europe. What a way to go: a colleague of a celebrated New York producer, meeting Pietro Garinei and Alessandro Giovannini, who were the major Italian theatrical impresarios as well as composer-lyricists. They were the producers of Rome's Teatro Sistina and were internationally successful with their song "Arrivederci Roma."

They were two of the most charming men I ever met, and they were our hosts. Pietro became a lifelong friend. Years later, when I visited Rome, he and his wife introduced me to an Italy that you see only in Technicolor movies with people who look like Cary Grant or Grace Kelly. Pietro and his missus drove me to a *canta-giro* (songfest) in the mountains. Everyone hailed the famed Pietro, and I was the recipient of the plush dining and wining that was extended to theatrical royalty. The Garineis had me join them for a weekend in Spoleto, where we saw a young Russian dancer, Rudolf Nureyev, and where we were guests of Gian Carlo Menotti, the composer and impresario. On another occasion, Pietro and I visited the film studios of Dino De Laurentiis, where a job was offered to me if I would remain in Rome.

On that initial visit in 1963, Alex negotiated to produce *Rugantino* on Broadway and along with it introduced the notion of using *sottotitoli* (subtitles), a simultaneous translation of the Italian into English as done in foreign films. The titles, however, were above the actors, not below them. Nino Manfredi played the title role in the Italian musical, and that fine actor—and charming man—later became an international film star. The entire cast was a joy to work with, and I became a devoted Italophile, which prompted my later visit and reunion with Pietro, Alessandro, and many of the cast members.

The first Broadway production I represented under Alex Cohen's banner emerged as one of the biggest hits of the decade. Four young Englishmen, none professional actors, had scored a comedic triumph at the Edinburgh Festival in 1960. They had not been invited to participate in officially sanctioned activities and were one of the many ragtag groups on the fringe of the prestigious festival. London and New York producers became excited by this quartet of college students, two from Cambridge and two from Oxford. Their topical humor was biting and brilliant. They were on the cutting edge of a new wave of comedic social commentary. They titled their show *Beyond the Fringe.*

The quartet was quickly contracted to play in London, and Alex, alerted about their potential, arranged for them to appear as part of his Nine O'Clock Theatre following the London success. Alan Bennett, Peter Cook, Jonathan Miller, and Dudley Moore came to America by boat, and I joined Alex and Hildy to greet them at the pier for their arrival.

They played in Washington, D.C. and Boston before opening at the Golden Theatre on Forty-Fifth Street. Their pungent political satire was a triumph, and because of their rousing reception out of town, we had great hopes for a Broadway hit.

The first preview at the Golden was on the evening that the world paid notice to the Cuban Missile Crisis. Americans had just learned that Soviet missiles had been identified in Cuba, ninety miles from Florida's coastline. President John F. Kennedy had delivered an ominous and threatening speech that afternoon. Political commentaries on the network news were suggesting that we were on the verge of World War III with the Soviets. They had nuclear missiles pointing at us.

The political satire of four young Englishmen with sketches about Armageddon fell painfully flat that night in New York City. People were walking around in a mummified state. Few were in the mood for sardonic commentary about the state of the world.

We were scheduled to open on Saturday night, but theater and political comedy seemed insignificant in a city, a nation, awaiting its fate.

On Saturday, the Russians announced they would dismantle their missiles, averting a possible conflict with the United States. The world let out a collective sigh.

The opening-night audience of *Beyond the Fringe* roared: it was the laughter that explodes after unbearable tension. The play was the perfect tonic for a public that had viewed itself on the brink of destruction.

Dudley, Peter, Alan, and Jonathan were all in their late twenties when they hit the theatrical jackpot, about the same age as I. Representing them was a different experience than with established stars, people accustomed to being pampered, with a sense of entitlement. The *Fringe* guys were bright, fun to be with, and appreciative of New York City's generous reception.

Beyond the Fringe ran for three years and toured around the country with replacement actors. The gifted quartet all moved on to enjoy distinguished careers. The play was no accident. Peter, Jonathan, Alan, and Dudley were very special, creative artists.

Alan Bennett is one of England's finest playwrights. Dr. Jonathan Miller's direction of several operas has won international acclaim, as have his published books. Dudley Moore went on to surprise us all as a movie star in films like *Arthur* and *10*, before his early death. Peter Cook published a satirical political magazine and opened nightclubs in New York and London. Peter and Dudley also costarred on Broadway in a comedy revue, *Good Evening*, which Alex produced ten years later. Like *Beyond the Fringe*, it was an enormous success with the critics and the public. I had already founded the Fortune Society by then, and at the height of their triumph they came and entertained at a benefit we held at the Harvard Club.

Alex Cohen presented several Nine O'Clock shows in addition to *Beyond the Fringe*, including evenings with Yves Montand, Victor Borge, Maurice Chevalier, Marlene Dietrich, Flanders and Swann, and Mike Nichols and Elaine May—all successful. He once whispered to me, "All I'm doing is raising the curtain twenty minutes late and defining that as sophisticated. It sells. Go figure."

At Alexander H. Cohen's memorial service in 2000, *New York Times* critic Frank Rich, appraising Alex's theatrical daring, stated: "Even with such failures as *Rugantino* . . . he was always impressive." I followed Frank to the podium as one of the eulogists at the service, which was held onstage at the Eugene O'Neill Theatre, where Alex's final production, *Waiting in the Wings,* was playing. I recalled the adventure it had been for me working with Alexander H. Cohen. "But," I noted, "I never considered *Rugantino* a failure of Alex's. Perhaps from a critic's perspective. However, there was an ad in *Variety* from Pietro Garinei that simply stated, 'Ciao, Alex.' Forty years after *Rugantino,* our Italian friends still cherish the opportunity to have played on Broadway. I don't consider that a failure." It was an example of international goodwill created by a theatrical innovator. Success has many definitions.

With Alex, I had entered the theater world, where producers would fly to Europe as frequently as I rode the IRT to Columbus Circle. A hint of a play with promise, trying out in London, Toronto, Rome, or Des Moines, would send Alex booking plane passage to consider the work.

My initial journey to London was with Alex to attend the opening of Flanders and Swann's *At the Drop of Another Hat.* Alex had produced their first show, a massive and surprise Broadway hit. Two men sitting around a piano, singing and bantering, Flanders and Swan were sophisticated and ebullient.

Binkie Beaumont, the prolific English producer (his firm was known as H. M. Tennent), invited Alex and me for after-theater dinner at his town house. The small party included Ingrid Bergman, her daughter Pia Lindström, Sir John Gielgud, and the actress Joyce Carey. I sat through dinner listening to Ingrid Bergman, feeling like Rick in *Casablanca*, absorbing this beautiful and gracious woman.

Sir John was by then an old friend and colleague. Alex had presented him on Broadway in a stunning production of Sheridan's *The School for Scandal*, which Sir John directed and costarred in with Sir Ralph Richardson and a cast that included a young Richard Easton and a Broadway debut for the glorious Geraldine McEwan. We also worked with Sir John in a revival of his acclaimed one-man show *Ages of Man*, which I would watch every night, prompting him to invite me one evening to view the show from the wings. He had a stool placed there for me so I could gain a unique perspective of this stunning evening of theater. By the time we supped at Binkie Beaumont's gorgeous abode, this kid from New Jersey was greeted by Sir John with "Dear David, how nice to see you again. We welcome you to England."

We would meet again soon when Alex engaged him to direct *Hamlet* on Broadway and also to be the voice of the ghost of Hamlet's father. Richard Burton had agreed to play the tortured Dane. That would prove to be an experience, almost unparalleled in theater lore. It would also determine how and why I would reshape my life. I knew none of that when the hullabaloo began over Burton's return to Broadway in *Hamlet*.

It all started in Rome. I was not the only English-speaking person to have an eventful visit to that golden city in the early sixties. Film director and screenwriter Joseph Mankiewicz was creating an expensive remake of *Cleopatra* with the stunning Elizabeth Taylor in the title role. Stephen Boyd and Rex Harrison were her initial costars.

For reasons unknown to me, Boyd departed, and show-business history was rewritten. Richard Burton was selected to replace him.

The charismatic Burton had appeared in several films, but he was more celebrated for his stage work, particularly in Lerner and Loewe's musical *Camelot*, in which he had costarred with Julie Andrews. He was a charming Welshman, married for many years to Sybil Burton, whose energy and effusive manner had helped her survive Richard's notorious womanizing with his leading ladies. I had met Richard briefly during the Broadway tryout of *Camelot*, when I saw it at Boston's Shubert Theatre. A client of mine, M'el Dowd, was playing Morgan Le Fey, and she introduced me to some of the cast members, including Richard.

All eyes were focused on Rome when Burton joined the cast of *Cleopatra*. Both he and Elizabeth were known as bawdy, no-nonsense actors—as determined to have as good a time as they were dedicated to their craft.

There was no E! channel or *Entertainment Tonight* in those days, so overseas show-business rumors trickled back to the States rather than exploding in your face as they do in our sophisticated, technological twenty-first century. But once the tabloids began picking up the Roman whispers, it was a front-page story. The press became obsessed. Elizabeth was at that time the reigning queen of Hollywood, the great beauty who had grown up with the world's eyes watching. When filming began, she was married to the singer Eddie Fisher, who had been a consoling friend after Elizabeth's third husband, film producer Mike Todd, had been killed in a plane crash. Eddie had divorced Debbie Reynolds to marry Elizabeth. And Richard was, of course, married to Sybil. The script was already played out for the gossip columns and the paparazzi.

Apparently, the couple did little to conceal the passion. Filmdom's most glamorous and beautiful woman, several times married and once widowed, was clearly responding to the obvious macho charms of the playful Richard Burton. It became a worldwide scandal when they left their respective mates and began living together. In 1963, this was breaking new ground. No one admitted to living with a person to whom they were not wed, particularly when both were married to other people.

It was during this time that Alex Cohen sat me down and said, "We're doing *Hamlet*. Sir John will direct. Richard Burton will star. And you have to deal with the press."

After *Cleopatra* concluded filming, Richard and Elizabeth flew to Mexico, where he was starring in *Night of the Iguana*, his final stop before *Hamlet*. From New York, we paid close attention to the obsessive media coverage in faraway, obscure Puerto Vallarta. Photographers and reporters from around the world managed to earn assignments for this out-of-the-way film site, where every move of Richard's and Elizabeth's was recorded and reported.

Alex determined that we would rehearse in Toronto at the O'Keefe Centre, where the play was to open prior to Boston and Broadway. The wisdom was that the paparazzi would be less intrusive in Toronto than New York City.

We were wrong.

I arrived in Toronto on a cold December day and headed for the King Edward Hotel, where I and most of the cast would be staying. Richard, Elizabeth, and their entourage were booked in an entire floor of the hotel. By taking the whole floor, they assured themselves of some privacy. Bodyguards and private detectives were in evidence.

When I arrived at the hotel, I discovered it was being picketed by the Canadian Legion of Decency protesting an unmarried couple cohabiting openly. The sidewalk and hotel lobby were filled with reporters, photographers, and the curious public. It was bedlam.

Alex greeted me with an announcement that we were having lunch with Sir John, Richard, and Elizabeth to discuss the production and the press. We were to meet in the dining room.

That took some engineering. Hotel officials had to empty the area of reporters and photographers. After the last diners had finished, the eating area was ours. Everyone in the hotel lobby was straining their neck to gain a glimpse of Richard and especially Elizabeth, a scene I was to witness over and over.

So there I was, in an empty restaurant in a hotel, at lunch with the world's greatest living English-speaking actor, Sir John; one of the theater's most successful producers, Alex Cohen; and a man and a woman who were the epitome of Hollywood glamour and international scandal.

I later described it to friends as "a business lunch."

The first order of business, Alex declared, was publicity. I had a list of about fifty people who had requested interviews with Richard. I explained that I had talked with Tom Prideaux of *Life* magazine and had noted that we would be opening on Broadway in April, the month of worldwide celebrations of Shakespeare's four hundredth birthday party. It would be appropriate, I thought, that Richard as Hamlet be the *Life* cover to celebrate that auspicious anniversary. Prideaux had agreed, so I said to Richard, "We could have a photographer up here in Toronto for that session." Richard had his own personal press agent, the legendary John Springer, and I suggested that John and I could make a priority list for other interviews.

That was agreed, so Sir John said, "Let's talk about our production schedule," and Richard asked, "What about the cast?" The distinguished players included Hume Cronyn, who would win a Tony for his performance as Polonius, and Alfred Drake, Eileen Herlie, George Rose, and John Cullum. (One of the smaller roles was played by Gerome Ragni, who had already informed us that with his partner, James Rado, he was coauthoring a play called *Hair*.) At which point Elizabeth turned to me and said, "They don't need us for this talk. Let's sit over there." She rose from her seat and took my arm, and we settled at a table a few feet away from the others. I was to have lunch with the most beautiful woman in the world.

Like almost everyone who ever worked with her, I fell in love with Elizabeth Taylor. Her much-described purple(ish) eyes were like nothing I had ever seen. It wasn't just her beauty and glamour. She wanted to know all about me: Where was I from? How had I gotten into the theater and publicity, and to work on such a production when I was so young? I was twenty-nine at the time but still needed an ID in an establishment that served booze. My youthful appearance was a disadvantage at first, but I made it work for me. People under-estimate the young, just as—I have recently learned—the elderly are invisible.

We became fast friends. She told me that, unlike Richard, she had never been able to hang out. All this paparazzi business was relatively new for him: when he starred on Broadway, he would barhop at Downey's, Sardi's, and other public venues. Elizabeth, she informed me, had been under the spotlight from childhood, and her friends always came from the people with whom she worked. I was working with her, so she had a new friend. So did I.

I was Elizabeth's date at the opening night of *Hamlet* at the O'Keefe Centre. By then, both she and Richard had divorced their mates, and they had eloped over a weekend in Montreal. We had a celebratory wedding party for them in the greenroom. I once told Henry Morgan that I should appear on *I've Got a Secret*, my secret being that I had dated Elizabeth Taylor but didn't marry her.

Opening night was an eye-opener for me. We were seated on a wide aisle, which enabled us to escape at intermission to a protected area backstage. However, the second-act curtain rise was delayed about twenty minutes, as the entire audience paraded themselves past our seats to gain a glimpse, a close-up of the fabled Elizabeth. People were uttering comments right into her face as if she were an inanimate creature. One woman was critical of her hairstyle, another uncomplimentary about her dress. I turned to her and asked if she was okay. Her hand dug into my arm, and I watched her—in her mind—go away. She had developed the capacity to withdraw into her own head, to turn off the world's judgments, an extraordinary maneuver of survival.

I told her I couldn't imagine a lifetime of having to withstand a stranger's sense of entitlement about assessing your person.

I was with the world's most glamorous woman in the most celebrated theatrical production of its time, and I was starting to feel that this was not the world I wanted to be in. I loved the work, but the offstage drama was beginning to take its toll.

In the next few weeks, I was to witness this repeatedly.

Boston was the next stop for *Hamlet*. A chartered plane was to arrive at Logan Airport on a Sunday afternoon, the play having concluded a sold out, three-week run in Toronto on Saturday night. I traveled ahead of the company, an advance man arranging not only press interviews but hotel accommodations and transportation from the airport to the various hotels. My assignment that Sunday was to be at the airport with instructions. What I didn't predict or realize was that the Boston radio stations were announcing the arrival of Richard Burton and Elizabeth Taylor at two p.m. When I reached Logan, thousands of fans, photographers, and reporters had gathered. Boston's finest were also in evidence, a sea of blue officers holding back the crowd from the reception area of the airport.

I arrived with my briefcase, ready to tell each cast member how they were traveling to their hotel. We had chartered vans and limos. I asked permission of a police officer to get through the blockade of blue uniforms. Before I had a chance to explain that I was the advance man (granted, I looked like a post-teenager), he ordered me to get back. I insisted it was important for me to get through, and when I made a side-step move, I was introduced to Boston's finest with a rabbit punch in my gut that put me to the floor.

When I awoke a few minutes later, I was in a room for ailing or injured passengers. I had the packet of instructions with me and insisted to an airport employee that I was the advance man. Apparently, the plane had landed and had been put into a hangar because there were no instructions for the people on board. The cast of *Hamlet*, including Richard and Elizabeth, was being held hostage because their advance man was in absentia.

The woman looked at my folders and yelled, "He is the advance man!" And I was suddenly put on a motor scooter and raced to the hangar. When I arrived, the cast began screaming at me, until I told them what had happened. Suddenly, I became the purple-heart hero in a company that had endured continued intrusions since the first day of rehearsal.

I rode with the Burtons in their limo to the Plaza, where they were staying. Word was out about that location, resulting in a new crowd of hysterics as we reached the hotel. It was vile and violent, with Elizabeth being pinned against the car door upon her exit and her hair being pulled from her head. I think she sustained a back injury from the jostling before she and Richard were able to successfully enter the hotel.

Boston's welcome was less than civilized; the show, however, was a triumph.

After Beantown came the New York opening: a couple of days of previews and then the gala. Alex had taken over the entire top floor of the RCA Building at Rockefeller Center so hundreds of the company's most intimate friends could gather.

On the afternoon of the opening, in addition to coordinating the usual press demands, threats, and insinuations from people who couldn't attend, I met with a bomb squad at the Rainbow Room. They wanted to review the press and the guest lists, as they were responding to threats of violence that were pouring in. This was not to be like other opening-night parties. Security resembled a bad spy movie.

I had the most unlikely date for the opening. Suddenly I was the best friend of Hollywood columnist (and fabled mistress of F. Scott Fitzgerald) Sheilah Graham, who had insisted she be my guest so she could get close to everyone involved in the production.

I recall a businessman at the Rainbow Room greeting me after I met with the bomb squad. "Kid, you look glum. You aren't even thirty years old, and you're at the top of the heap in this business."

I looked at him and said, "If this is the top, I want off." It was no longer theater.

Hamlet, of course, was a box-office smash and a critical success.

Every night at the Lunt-Fontanne Theatre, thousands of people would be outside at the play's conclusion, hoping to gain a glimpse of the Burtons, since Elizabeth came to the theater almost nightly. The police had blocked off West Forty-Sixth Street, and it became an event, unprecedented in theater history. Mounted police officers on horseback patrolled the street to handle the throngs. If I had business at the theater, I had to arrange to get backstage through the front of the house, avoiding the stage door at all costs. I introduced myself to some of the regular policemen on horseback so I wouldn't have a repeat of the Boston mauling. That enabled me to get in and out of the Lunt-Fontanne with police protection.

I was no longer working on a show. I was maneuvering crowd control. It was no one's fault in the company. They were a nice group of actors, and Elizabeth couldn't have been more gracious. She was often apologetic, as if she were responsible for the behavior of the paparazzi and hysterical fans.

A few days after the opening, I told Alex that I would remain with him to the conclusion of *Hamlet*, but that after that, I wanted out. I had decided I had to evaluate my professional status. I had no personal life. The theater was everything to me...but what appeared to be glamour on the outside seemed irrelevant and superficial to me.

As with many of my generation, the sixties were the defining decade for me. The world was going through abrupt changes, matching my social passions. The social and political protests in which I had participated as a college student were deeply ingrained in me, even as I pursued my professional career far from the maelstrom brewing across the country.

The theater was an exciting life for me, and I was succeeding far beyond my expectations. But I began to explore unlikely theatrical venues, experimental plays with challenging themes. I saw hints that theater could be reflective of the social unrest that was unraveling around me.

There was an increasing awareness of the United States's misguided policies in Vietnam. Martin Luther King was gaining attention as civil-rights protests forced America to consider the prevailing duplicity in our nation, how we boasted of our democracy while many citizens were marginalized because of color or gender or religion or sexual orientation. In the first half of the decade there was a distant rumble, but if you listened closely, you could predict the outbursts that would define the last part of the sixties.

My life was on the red carpet, and that was not a preferred location for me. The decade was exploding with possibility, and at some level I didn't want it to pass me by. The very success I was enjoying in the theater seemed to be in conflict with the world evolving around me. It wasn't so much that I was leaving the theater...I was being pulled toward something else. I wanted to be a participant, not an observer. I wondered if the theater could be part of this accelerating turmoil.

After *Hamlet* closed—the longest-running presentation of the bard's classic in history—I booked a freighter that took me to Genoa, Italy. I hitchhiked to Rome and spent several months there visiting with my friends from *Rugantino*.

I had to determine what success was and what I wanted to do with my life. I thought the theater was where I wanted to be...but the theater had to be of substance. I didn't want to work crowd control and fan hysteria. There had to be something else.

These days, when I watch the red-carpet ritual before the award shows, I always focus on the people at the stars' elbows. I shudder when I see the bulbs flashing and hear the screaming.

In the autumn of 1964, I returned to New York from Rome. I opened a small office at 1545 Broadway, a six-story building that housed many theater producers, agents, and entities—including producers Kermit Bloomgarden and Bob Whitehead, director Elia Kazan, the American National Theatre and Academy (ANTA), and *Theatre Arts* magazine—and had an entrance hidden behind the Victoria movie-theater box office. Rent was seventy-five dollars a month for my small room. I had acquired a reputation working with Alex and had no trouble attracting clients, producers who wanted me to represent their plays. My living style was modest. I wanted to see where all of this was going to lead me.

FIVE

Fortune and Men's Eyes

It never occurred to me that a play would reroute my life. *Fortune and Men's Eyes* was the second play I produced. In 1966 my friends Jordan Charney and Nancy Cooperstein invited me to a workshop of Joe Chaikin's Open Theatre, where we viewed Megan Terry's *Viet Rock*, a ferocious antiwar play. This appealed to me as theater but more importantly as the theater's first clear dramatic statement against the ugly Vietnam War.

I had participated in early demonstrations opposing our folly and lies in Southeast Asia. *Viet Rock* afforded me an opportunity to be part of the escalating antiwar protests. I never considered this to be un-American, as many charged, but rather an act of patriotism, exercising the right to speak out when our government is in the wrong. The war, as history has recorded, was my country at its lowest ebb.

There is an interesting sidebar to the play's arrival off-Broadway. In the spring of 1966, Robert Brustein, a critic and distinguished scholar, had been tapped to be dean of the new Yale School of Drama. Bob and I had become friends, having had many discussions about what theater could be. He invited me to spend a day in New Haven, and as we walked around the campus, he shared his vision of what the school would be under his leadership starting the next fall.

Bluntly, I asked him, "Why am I here?" He responded that he was looking for a number-two man, an assistant to the dean. That was what I was looking for in the theater, and I envisioned myself spending a life in the groves of academe.

There are mysterious twists in life, as I was to find out.

Brustein told me to go back to New York and think over his offer. I was already packing my toothbrush, ready to move to New Haven for the next school semester. I told him there was nothing to think over. I left New Haven under the impression that the job was mine and my future was locked in.

A week later, Dean Bob called and informed me that his only hired staff person, a former theatrical boy wunderkind of Broadway named Bobby Weiner, had suggested that I didn't have enough production experience to be of help to him. Weiner insisted that I was a press agent and that Brustein needed a more experienced production person from the theater world.

It was true that my work in the theater had been as a press representative, but I told Brustein that when working with Alex Cohen, I had been involved in all production meetings and decisions— *Hamlet* alone had been a doctoral thesis in production, press, and endurance—and I had a clear handle on the complexities of putting a show together. That, along with a modicum of common sense, should be sufficient. Brustein, apparently anxious about his first year as dean, asked if I would wait six months until he was comfortably entrenched in his post. I had already opened my own theater office in New York and was doing quite well. I told him my life would go on and he should call me when he thought he was ready.

I was representing plays by Pulitzer Prize winning playwrights Edward Albee and Tennessee Williams, as well as England's Harold Pinter. My office was also handling the publicity for several off-Broadway shows. In a word, I was "hot."

Then along came *Viet Rock*, which I was producing with Jordan and Nancy. We organized the traditional backers' auditions, performing scenes from the play for would-be angels, folks who would invest money to see the play come to fruition. In that summer of '66, we rented the Sheridan Square Playhouse for the event, and I invited my old pal, now dean, Bob Brustein to come to New York to see it. I suspected he would approve of this kind of theater, not traditional in form and certainly making a statement about contemporary politics.

He attended that backers' audition and was excited enough to determine that he would like to open his year as dean of the Yale School of Drama with our production of *Viet Rock*. He was ready to postpone his planned opening play if he could present our production. He wanted it at Yale before it came to New York for an off-Broadway presentation at the Martinique Theater.

This, of course, proved to be a great irony. Brustein, who had been convinced not to hire me at the outset of his tenure because I lacked production experience, now had to enter negotiations with me in order for Yale to present *Viet Rock*.

The show did open the Yale School of Drama under Brustein's deanship. Bob Weiner, who had expressed opposition to my being at Yale, had already been disposed of, apparently lacking the people skills Brustein demanded under his leadership.

By the time *Viet Rock* opened in New York, I had decided to produce *Fortune and Men's Eyes*. My life was on a different route, and Yale would have to plug along without me.

Viet Rock had a modest run, and in retrospect, I realize that an antiwar play in 1966 was two years too early for mainstream press consumption. Walter Kerr, reviewing the play in the *New York Times*, reflected the prevailing establishment sentiments of that time. He opined that it was fine for these young people to exercise their right to protest against the war, but must they be so "strident"? *Viet Rock* made a strong statement but couldn't survive the critics at a time when the war was still popular. The reviews were more disapproving of the politics than of the dramatic ingredients of Megan Terry's opus.

I turned my attention to *Fortune and Men's Eyes*.

During my many forays to Toronto working with Alex Cohen, I had become friends with the drama critic of the *Toronto Star*. Nathan Cohen was from the old school, feared by the theater community in Canada for his stern inspection of their works—a throwback to an era of fabled theater critics like George Jean Nathan and Alexander Wolcott. In addition to his acerbic criticism, Nathan Cohen was an erudite scholar of theater and literature, a man of wit and intellect. I savored the many meals we shared, arguing about theater and politics.

Like many Canadian intellectuals I would meet, Nathan Cohen enjoyed dissecting U.S. politics. He frequently alluded to our history of imperialism and sense of entitlement. I was severely critical at that time of our policy in Vietnam and our disgraceful history of racism. Yet it was ironic: I became proudly defensive, arguing the virtues of the USA. Our verbal exchanges were heated but filled with laughter, passion, and frequent allusions to theatrical characters of the past.

Nathan was adamant and critical of the mediocrity he witnessed in the theater, and we often examined the current season, play by play. I was stimulated by his insistence on high standards and attentively absorbed his critical insight. These days I frequently see a play and wonder what the late Nathan Cohen would have written of it and how he would have orated to me about it.

He was a man confident of his tastes and perspectives and smart enough to make his case effectively. His *Toronto Star* theater column was for years essential reading among enlightened Canadians.

Nathan often called from Toronto, announcing a visit to New York to see Broadway's latest offerings. We would meet for breakfast at the Plaza, where he stayed in the city, and banter about theater, films, politics, and social trends. We talked incessantly about the Vietnam War.

At one such tête-à-tête, he informed me of a play that was creating some interest in Toronto's theater world. A prison drama called *Fortune and Men's Eyes* had been given a reading at the Stratford

(Ontario) Shakespeare Festival, where on dark nights at the theater new works were revealed. The gifted Canadian actor Bruno Gerussi was the driving force behind the initial reading of the play. Nathan had been sent a script by Gerussi, who was having difficulty luring producers for a Canadian production. Cohen informed me, in the ostentatious Plaza ambience, that such a gritty play would never see the light of day in Toronto without the imprimatur of a New York success—a stamp of dramatic approval, if you will.

This was not a man who often expressed such enthusiasm. He told me the play needed careful handling. He warned me it was a drama that would offend and confuse people. Intrigued, I asked if I could read it. He sent me a copy within a week.

In bed for the evening, I picked up John Herbert's script and never halted for a moment. I was up all night, reading and rereading *Fortune and Men's Eyes*. I was devastated by what I read. I drafted a letter to the playwright, stating, "I felt that I was locked in a room with four cobras." John Herbert had clearly been in prison, because this story was so vivid, unlike anything I had ever read or seen.

In the play, Smitty, a juvenile and a first offender, is dumped into a dormitory with three other inmates. Later, John Herbert told me that the dorm he'd been placed in had had many more teenagers in it, but for theatrical purposes he had created prototypes of the prison population.

Smitty is immediately taken over by the keen-eyed veteran jail recidivist and tough named Rocky, who begins to show Smitty the ropes. He offers the "new fish" cigarettes and protection, convincing the green newcomer that everyone needs an "old man" to protect him from gang splashes. Smitty is naïve and frightened, and cautiously agrees to be Rocky's pal. He begins to sense Rocky's intentions but is overcome by the power and rage of Rocky, who drags him into the shower and rapes him (offstage). As prison doors clamor, the first act concludes.

The second act is the evolvement of Smitty from frightened victim to jail-wise predator. He is no longer the innocent kid. By the play's ending, six months after Smitty has hit the joint, he has become the Rocky of his cellblock. Alone onstage, smoking a cigarette, he looks at the audience and declares, "I'll get back at them. I'll get back at you all." Door clangs shut. Curtain.

On paper and onstage that last scene always gives me chills.

Fortune and Men's Eyes is a clear exposure of how the prison experience destroys the spirit, molds a new kid, and increases the odds of recidivism. Alienation is nurtured in that atmosphere. In ensuing years, I found that Herbert's play was painfully accurate. I also discovered that many people don't want to hear this story. Prison is where we send the bad guys, and there has always been little interest in cause and effect—even if this moral indifference has a boomerang result, contributing to an increase in street crime.

It was not a simple task raising money for a play that takes place in a prison cell. Dorothy Olim, our general manager, presented a budget of $15,000 to get the play presented off-Broadway. (A similar production today would need about $600,000 to $700,000.) Friends and relatives of mine and of the playwright's were the hardcore investors, to the tune of $8,000. We had hit a stone wall. People would read the script and look at me as if I were mad. "Interesting," they would say, "but hardly commercial." I committed the cardinal sin of producing: I took out a bank loan of $7,500 to get the play on the boards. We finally had the money necessary for an opening in February 1967 at the Actors' Playhouse in Greenwich Village.

Four fine young actors—Terry Kiser, Vic Arnold, Bob Christian, and Bill Moor—were hired, and we were ready—almost ready. The fifth character was Holy Face, a prototype of one thousand corrections officers.

Before we went into rehearsal, the actors insisted they wanted to visit a prison, a necessary ingredient for preparing to create stage characters who were incarcerated. We arranged a visit to Rikers Island, New York City's penal colony, where thousands of men are locked up. It was my first trip to such an institution.

It was a shocker. All we were witness to was young men being herded about or sitting morosely in dayrooms or dormitories. JoAnne Page, who would become CEO of the Fortune Society decades later, accurately describes it as "death by boredom." It was clear to me, immediately and instinctively, that no matter what in these men's lives had brought them to jail, nothing would improve as a result of this experience. Later I told a reporter that I found it to be "an exercise in institutional futility," a viewpoint that only cemented in my mind as the years passed.

On that trip to Rikers, when all the inmates were in a dayroom, each of us was placed in a cell and locked in for a few minutes. I couldn't imagine being confined like that. On the locker next to the bed where I was sitting was a photo of a young woman holding a baby. The man who lived in this cage was "an offender," defined as such by society, but also quite possibly a husband and a father. It is more complicated to look at the totality of a person than a dismissive label. I was becoming an advocate in my head before I ever found a podium from which to express my outrage at society's failure in criminal justice.

The entire rehearsal period and the preview dates of *Fortune* were an emotional roller coaster for me. In early February, on the Monday following the first weekend of previews, my father, Leon Rothenberg, died of a heart attack. My last day with him had concluded with a drive out to New Jersey, where my parents lived. He was still smoking, even though he had experienced two heart attacks. I took his cigarettes off the dashboard and threw them out the window. He told me that he had to do it his way, and I had to get the cigarettes back. I couldn't bear watching him do this to himself. During his last stay in a hospital, he had been in an oxygen tent, but he still would not surrender the cigarettes. He was only fifty-eight years old but told me that he was exhausted from it all and was ready to go. We embraced in the car, and I told him we weren't ready for him to leave and he should try to chuck the cigarettes. But he did it his way, and one day slumped over his desk at work. I received a call from my brother-in-law, rented a car, and joined my mother, sister Carla, and all the relatives at my mother's apartment in Hackensack.

My father would have loved *Fortune and Men's Eyes*, the excitement of the production and the subsequent activities that emanated from the play. He was a humanist and a dreamer. I regret that he was not able to share what was ahead for me.

Three weeks later, the play opened. My mother attended the performance. Her appearance there on her first night out after my father's death, together with his absence, created a maelstrom of emotions for me.

The modest opening-night party was across the street from the theater, at the Limelight, which had become the cast's hangout. The reviews were all over the place, and we didn't know what to make of them. The first reports came from the television critics, who in those days still reported and reviewed New York theater. The NBC and ABC commentators called the play "powerful" and "brilliantly acted and produced." We had a positive start. But we had to await the all-important early edition of the *New York Times*, whose review could make or break a play, no matter what everyone else expressed. The *Times* had sent a second-stringer, Dan Sullivan. His review came in, and I read it aloud. He was dismissive and unmoved by John Herbert's explicit play. We thought we were dead in the water.

Cruel irony of the theater: Clive Barnes, who at the time was the dance critic of the *Times*, came to the play and told me it was the most exciting theater in New York. Later, Barnes would become the *Times*'s first-string theater reviewer. A few years later, when Sal Mineo directed a revival of the play and brought his West Coast production to New York, Barnes, reviewing it in the *Times*, suggested that the revival lacked the incendiary power of the original production. We finally got a rave review in the *Times*, three years too late.

After reading Sullivan's review, I trudged home, convinced the play wouldn't run, no matter how excited the preview audiences had been. I went to my Times Square office the next day. The box office was to open at one p.m. With dread I called the theater's treasurer to find out if there had been any nibbles as a result of the TV reviews. The line was busy for twenty minutes. When I finally got through, the man in the box office hollered he didn't have time to talk. He was too busy taking ticket orders.

I raced down to the theater. On the way I picked up two afternoon papers. Norman Nadel in the *New York World-Telegram and the Sun* was more brutal than the *Times*. He called the play disgusting, and, referring to Rocky's rape of Smitty, said that unless you were obsessed by seeing sodomy, there was no reason to see this play. Jerry Tallmer in the *New York Post* had the opposite reaction, comparing *Fortune and Men's Eyes* to the great Italian film classic *The Bicycle Thief* and saying that the theatrical emotions could be compared to *Marat/Sade*, a Broadway triumph transported from London. He described the play as "shattering and brilliant."

The play would last longer than Norman Nadel's tenure as a drama critic. The next week, a full-page rave by Michael Smith in the influential *Village Voice* was another hopeful sign. Smith suggested that critics offended by the play should save their outrage for the reality it reflected.

The play was not to be a runaway sellout. With these diverse reviews, it was clear that we had a fight on our hands. Many traditional theatergoers did not want to spend an evening in the company of four young men in a prison cell, witnessing their power plays and sexual violence. Many didn't want to feel like they were locked up in a room with four cobras. But people came, enough for us to continue for more than thirteen months.

Shortly after opening night, a sociology professor contacted us, saying he was bringing a group of about thirty students and asking if they could remain afterward for a discussion about the play. That was right up my alley. We placed a note in the program inviting the entire audience to remain for the discussion, and most stayed. It was a play that prompted discussion and involvement for those who attended.

Three of us came out onto the stage after the curtain call. Vic Arnold, who played Rocky, had become infatuated with penology. He was greatly moved by the entire experience of this play. Vic went on to have a fine career in films and television, but he always insisted that Rocky and *Fortune* were the brightest time for him as an actor. David Hannigan, our stage manager and understudy, also wanted to participate in the discussion. David had revealed to us that he had served time in a juvenile institution in Iowa when he was a teenager. The play hit home for him. I was the third member of that first discussion group, serving as the moderator and introducing the actors, calling for questions and comments from the audience.

The crowd was filled with praise and concern about what the play revealed. Then, after a few minutes of plaudits, a man shouted out, "This is a lot of crap. These characters are all stereotypes, and I don't buy any of it." The room froze.

After a stunned silence in reaction to his refreshing candor, a man in the back of the house stood up and responded, "This play is so real that I thought I was back in my cell. When the lights went up at intermission, I had to remember I was out here. If my twenty years in these joints count for anything, this play is so real you people couldn't stand watching what happens offstage."

We urged him to come down and join the panel. Pat McGarry hit the boards and mesmerized the audience for nearly an hour, relating stories of time he had done at Rikers Island, in Dannemora State Prison in upstate New York, at San Quentin in California, and on a Florida chain gang. That night, *Fortune and Men's Eyes* had an epilogue that was deeply profound. Pat McGarry convinced us all that John Herbert's play was more than good theater. It was a mirror for the lives of men whose stories had never been told. *Fortune* was about the system's destruction of the spirit and how society would pick up the bill at a later date. No, it wasn't easy to watch, but it was theater as it could be.

Among the many people who consciously stayed away from it was my friend Dean Bob Brustein. I implored him on several occasions to see it, and in a burst of candor he sent me a note that stated, "Something in my subconscious keeps me away from this play."

John Herbert (born Jack Brundage) and his play had a great impact on my life. Six feet four inches tall, slightly epicene, but with a determination of steel, John was one of the most complex individuals I ever met, certainly one of the most unique. We once appeared on a panel together, and one of the other panelists, a police officer, defended police abuse. He stated, "Sometimes after an eight-hour shift, a nasty young kid is more than a tired cop can withstand, and a few slaps might be understandable." John quickly responded, pointing out that when he worked as a waiter, he was often exhausted after an eight-hour shift. He asked the cop to grant permission to "piss in the officer's soup—understandable after such an exhausting day." The stunned audience applauded once they got their bearings.

John's stories about his past never failed to galvanize his listeners. After spending six months in Guelph Reformatory as a teenager, he traveled around Canada and the United States. He played the piano in a Chicago whorehouse, was a barker at more than a few carnivals, and waited on tables for survival money. John was bitterly critical of Canada's criminal-justice system and social hypocrisy. He reserved his most acidic comments for his country's theatrical establishment, which was mired in British-influenced tradition. John was a self-described outcast.

His prison stint should never have happened. An altercation with some thugs caused a police roundup of the rowdy crowd. Because of John's less-than-masculine posture, an offended judge summarily sentenced him to jail, making unprofessional comments about the juvenile's assumed sexual orientation.

In *Fortune and Men's Eyes*, the passive inmate, Jan, describes his court experience: "No real defense. A deal. Magistrate's court is like a trial in a police station—all pals, lawyers and cops together! Threw me on the mercy of the court. Oh, Christ—that judge with his hurry-up face, heard the neat police evidence and my lawyer's silly, sugar-sweet plea. So half-hearted—I wanted to shout, 'Let me speak; leave me some damn dignity!' The fat, white-haired frown looked down on me—'Go to jail for six months!'—like I'd dirtied his hands, and that would wipe them clean. Six months! Six thousand would have sounded the same."

After the yearlong success of *Fortune and Men's Eyes* in New York City, we brought the original cast to John's hometown of Toronto. The play was scheduled for four weeks in a four-hundred-seat theater, but it received such critical acclaim and public response that it remained for four months of sold-out performances.

Opening night in Toronto was an emotional event. Disgraced in his youth by imprisonment, John had taken the worst experience in his life and channeled it in play form, becoming Canada's most successful playwright. By the time the play premiered in Canada, the Fortune Society had been created, and the implications of his work extended far beyond the proscenium arch.

At the Toronto opening were John's mother and sister, Nana, who had been his strength, always supportive of him in his darkest moments. In the play, Jan tells Smitty about the courtroom scene, stating, "Only voice for me—my poor, shocked mother, and sitting out there trying to smile at me—eyes dark, afraid—God help her—my younger sister!"

John's mother, Mrs. Brundage, was a remarkable woman. I was immediately drawn to her quiet wisdom and kindness. In my many visits to Toronto, hectic with theater planning, I always made sure that I treated myself to a visit to the Brundage home, simple and comfortable. It was not difficult to determine the origin of John's sense of fairness and will of steel. It must have been in the DNA.

John's mentions of his late father were dismissive and unflattering. But Mrs. Brundage, with her radiance and intelligence, allowed her children to know real love, and she created an atmosphere that encouraged intellectual curiosity and pride. She was also a quietly religious woman, and I often attempted to shock her with my agnosticism. She always listened respectfully, allowing me room to express my youthful heresies. Once, I recall challenging her during one of her delicious dinners: "Who is this God of whom you speak?" She whispered, "Oh, the autumn leaves." It is incredible how one person can deliver such a simple statement of belief, and it has stayed with me forever. I never fail to marvel as I witness the mystery of the changing seasons, and particularly the autumn leaves, and that thought is always in concert with my memories of a truly decent woman. Her love for her son was unconditional—a quality I witnessed in short supply in the family stories of men and women I would later meet at the Fortune Society.

John's sister, Nana, was his close confidant. He told me that after endless cross-country trips, hitchhiking and living like a hobo, he had one of his frequent stopovers in Toronto. Nana took him to a rehearsal of a community-theater troupe with which she was involved. John was immediately attracted to the ambience and the creative people, who were not judgmental about his past but curious about his present. He began helping out, painting sets and sewing costumes, absorbing the mystical qualities that often seep through a play being brought to life.

After working backstage on several productions, he realized there was a play in his head. He wrote ferociously for two weeks, and the result was one of the most successful dramas in Canadian history.

After our production played in Canada, the sun never set on *Fortune and Men's Eyes*. It played around the world for the next two decades, including a production in Turkey, directed by author James Baldwin. A few times each year, I receive correspondence from Canadian students preparing a thesis or school report on John Herbert and his play.

In later years, John and I would often visit in Toronto, and until his death in 2001 at the age of seventy-four, he would often call me late at night with tales of current plays and productions. He started his own theater company, offering plays that consistently challenged the mores and respectability of his home country. He was never less than a maverick. His success as a playwright never diminished his vehement criticism of the criminal-justice system.

John Herbert was not around when the *Fortune* after-theater discussions began. He would have loved them. But a few nights after the opening in New York, he and I were standing outside during the intermission. A nicely dressed gentleman approached us. "Are you the playwright?" he asked John. When John confirmed that he was, the man continued, "Congratulations, this is a powerful play." And then he reached into his vest pocket, pulled out a paper, and introduced himself as an investigator from immigration. He told John, "You are an alien ex-convict. You are not permitted in the United States. You have two weeks to remain here, and after that you cannot return without our government's permission."

We stood there stunned. John packed and left within a week, and he never legally entered the United States again. He did once slip across the border and visit the Fortune Society. He told me that the only reason he wanted to enter the States was because he was so proud and honored that his play had instigated a movement for social change in criminal justice.

SIX

The Fortune Society

That after-theater forum marked a new chapter in my life.

After the audience left, Vic Arnold, Pat McGarry, and I went across the street to the Limelight, continuing the talk. We asked Pat if he would return the next week. He said that he'd done "white time." He told us about segregation in the prisons and said that if we wanted the whole story, we needed someone who could talk about "black time." I indicated that he was the only American ex-con I knew and that I wouldn't know where to begin finding someone. "Look," he said, "there's a guy who comes into the shop where I work. I'm sure he did a bid."

Pat arrived the next Tuesday with Clarence Cooper. Later I learned that Clarence had written a novel, *The Farm*, reflective of his harrowing years as an inmate in a federal institution in Michigan. Where Pat was flamboyant and outrageous, Clarence had a commanding presence and a quiet intelligence. Beneath the surface there was a powerful and angry man. I was immediately impressed by him.

The theater was electric that night. The audience remained glued to their seats when the play ended, having been alerted to Pat's and Clarence's participation. As the moderator, I had found a perfect role for myself. I asked all of the naïve questions that reflected the audience's lack of information and insight about crime and prison in our country.

That was the start of a career shift, and I wasn't even aware of it. I was acquiring a graduate student's education in crime, penology, and the invisibility of a large population in America.

Tuesday nights became discussion night at the Actors' Playhouse. Parole officers, elected officials, and judges revealed themselves in the audience and frequently joined us onstage. The *New York Times* sent a reporter and photographer. The headline noted: "The Drama Continues After the Curtain Falls." That feature story in the *Times* served as a balance to the paper's critic's uninformed, unfavorable review.

It became apparent that many people were returning to the theater every Tuesday. Some were relatives of inmates; others were men (and later a few women) who had been incarcerated. Even some corrections officials made an appearance.

The play was crying for something. Teachers and ministers had begun contacting me at my office, hoping I could arrange for "live ex-convicts" to speak to their schools and church groups. Alienation was omnipresent in the late sixties, and these formerly incarcerated men were the epitome of Americans in shift.

We were on the circuit. I called for a meeting with Pat and Clarence and the other men who had started hanging out with us at the theater. We had the nucleus of an organization, I stated. If we continued to speak out, we could influence change in the prison system and the way the entire criminal-justice system was counter-productive. Who said I wasn't a dreamer?

We agreed after much discussion to call the group the Fortune Society, from the play's title, which had itself been taken from a Shakespearian sonnet that begins, "When in disgrace with fortune and men's eyes, I all alone beweep my outcast state." Our roots were Shakespearian.

My theater office on West Forty-Sixth Street would be headquarters. Sixteen people at a Tuesday night discussion, hearing our announcement of a new organization, donated two dollars each, and we opened a Fortune Society bank account with thirty-two dollars. I promised to send a mimeographed report of progress to all who signed up.

The Fortune Society was in business. My theater work continued, but speaking engagements and radio interviews with the guys were filling up a great deal of my time. In early 1968, I suggested to TV producer Jean Kennedy that she consider featuring us on her program, *The David Susskind Show*. She had presented panels with compulsive gamblers, recovering addicts, and alcoholics, but she informed me they had never been able to find people willing to talk about their incarcerations publicly. Usually ex-cons would appear on TV with paper bags over their heads. Anonymity was almost a necessity if you were job hunting or looking for a place to live. The stereotypes dictated public policy.

That all changed on a March night when the nationally syndicated program featured four men from the Fortune Society. Clarence Cooper, Frank Sandiford, Eddie Morris, and Rob Freeley were the panelists. The Sunday night program was not only historic; it was TV drama at its best. The air was electric at the studio taping. At the program's conclusion, Susskind informed the audience that the men were all part of a new organization, and to contact them at the Fortune Society, 1545 Broadway in New York City.

We suspected the public would respond en masse, and we would be sending teams of speakers all over the map. Before that happened, however, something different and unexpected occurred. When I arrived the next morning at my small theater office, located on the sixth floor, I discovered that the stairwell was filled with guys lined up waiting to talk to someone. Nearly two hundred fifty men surfaced that morning. They anticipated a thriving organization that could help them with employment, housing, or any of the other desperate needs people face when they are released from jail or prison. They wanted anything but what life was offering them. What they got was . . . me, sitting in my office with a large poster of *Hair* behind me and a wall cluttered with theater pictures and posters.

I wasn't what they needed. Actually, I didn't have a clue. I kept explaining that we were advocates for change but couldn't help their immediate needs. A tall white guy with a toothpick in his mouth stood there watching me. He walked over and said, "You don't know what the fuck you're doing, do you?"

That's how Kenny Jackson introduced himself to me. He told me to move over. He grabbed a chair and started talking to one guy. Kenny told me that he was in AA and that they stay sober by talking about things. He kept rapping to various guys, urging them to hang around. A few of them did.

Kenny Jackson, on the spot, became the first counselor at the Fortune Society.

One of the men who showed up that week was Mel Rivers—out of Bedford-Stuyvesant, out of prison, and out of work. I told him we didn't have jobs. He responded that he was checking us out to see what we were doing. Kenny and Mel hit it off, and along with Pat McGarry and Clarence Cooper they became the core of those early days of the Fortune Society, hanging out in my office and driving to a multitude of schools and churches.

I continued working in the theater. The shows I represented were underwriting the costs of the Fortune Society. We were receiving honorariums at some of the speaking engagements, which paid for gas and office expenses, but rent and phones were my fiscal responsibility.

During that period, I was doing the publicity for *Hair*, Harold Pinter's *The Birthday Party*, Edward Albee's *Everything in the Garden*, Mart Crowley's *The Boys in the Band*, *Alvin Ailey on Broadway*, and of course *Fortune and Men's Eyes*. Many of the young performers from *Hair* were also frequent visitors to my office, so on any given day you might find Melba Moore, Paul Jabara, or Mary Davis hanging out with Kenny Jackson and Mel Rivers. It was an unlikely, stimulating, and exciting period.

I arranged for groups of guys from Fortune to attend Broadway plays, an experience totally alien to them. We began changing the demographic of the New York theatergoer. Socializing with mainstream people was part of a new life that these men were considering. I realized it wasn't just about going to see a play; it was about being part of society—a dramatic new experience.

My old friend Alvin Ailey joined Fortune's newly formed advisory council. He offered fifteen tickets to see the Ailey company on any night they were not sold out. Hundreds of formerly incarcerated men and women were introduced to the Alvin Ailey American Dance Theater. Kenny Jackson once quipped that when you get out of a prison in New York, "you get forty dollars, a baloney sandwich, and two tickets to Alvin Ailey."

While I was bringing ex-cons to the theater, I was also introducing theater people to the subculture of the released prisoner. We began having fundraising events, mixing stars and former inmates. My good friend Jean Bach, who was producing the Arlene Francis radio show on WOR, had joined our board, and she opened her Greenwich Village town house to us. She invited Bobby Short and Blossom Dearie to perform. Many other theater friends hosted events, including Melba Moore, Zoe Caldwell, and Christopher Reeve.

Our one-room office was bursting when Attica happened in September of 1971. Every day, for weeks afterward, newspapermen and television cameras were at Fortune. We were the only game in town to offer an inmate's perspective. Al Cruz, who had been released from Attica ten days prior to the riot, told us that he couldn't go to the bathroom without a microphone in his face.

Those first days home from prison are crucial. Reentry is a minefield. Decision making has been eliminated from incarcerated men and women. They have to learn how to navigate in a fast-moving society diametrically opposed to the traditional prison experience.

Al Cruz, as an Attica spokesman, made for good television. We were concerned that all the attention could derail his determination for a new life. TV producers have little idea how destructive the spotlight can be for someone just out of lockup. Many people without the burden of incarceration are flattered and distracted by the attention, but the newly released parolee rarely sees the traps.

Everyone has to make their own choices. What I discovered was that we were road signs, alerting someone of a curve in the terrain. Sometimes, if you don't follow the instructions, you can go over the cliff. Al Cruz stayed with us, surrounded by caring people who protected him from distractions. Eventually, as we gained funding, he became a staff member.

Many volunteers came to us in those days after Attica. One woman, Melanie Johnson, arrived with her newborn strapped to her back. She offered to help in any way possible, answering phones, stuffing envelopes. She stayed around long enough—about thirty years—to start a tutoring program. Danny Keane, a personable guy with an Archie Bunker personality, said he couldn't go on speaking engagements because those college kids were too smart and he didn't have the vocabulary. Melanie started tutoring Danny with a book, *How to Build Your Vocabulary in Thirty Days*, and it worked.

Danny began bringing other men to Melanie, those who had shortcomings in English grammar or math. By the time she had four students, she told me we needed other tutors, and the call went out. A young woman named Lynn Ornstein was among the respondents, and she and Melanie created a model tutoring program, one that thrives to this day, offering classes for the illiterate, GED preparation, and college prep, as well as English as a second language. Computer classes have been added to the mix in the current century. It's a small school that began with grit and determination and now has more than two hundred students all year-round.

I was still being offered new shows—but opening a Broadway show was more time-consuming than keeping a hit show running. I was running on a full tank with two full-time careers. I had to make a choice, because I couldn't continue to do both. After Attica, we were testifying before Senate and House committees in Washington, D.C., as well as commissions and committees in Albany and other state capitals around the country. Fortune was calling me.

Two phone calls made the decision for me.

I was on the wire with a woman who had heard the Fortune Society speakers on a radio program. She needed help. Her husband was in prison; she couldn't work because she had two small children, plus, she had a physical disability. Her welfare check hadn't arrived, and she had no food for the kids.

A second phone rang, and I asked the needy woman if I could put her on hold. On the second line an agent was telling me she had a Hollywood star coming in and she must have four tickets on Saturday night for *Hair*.

I returned to the first caller and said I would call her back because I had "an emergency" on the other phone.

After I hung up, I looked at the phone and said out loud, "What did you just say to that woman? Are you out of your mind?"

I was able to get the *Hair* tickets for the agent, and then I called back the woman whose husband was in prison and directed her to immediate help. Right then the choice had been made for me. I had to devote full time to the Fortune Society. My love for the theater would have to be confined to being a member of the audience...at least for the time being.

After Attica and the national publicity that ensued, the Fortune Society grew in quick spurts. Our small one-room office was clearly not sufficient. Producer Robert Whitehead, our neighbor down the hall, was moving out of his three-room suite, and we claimed it. By 1973, even that space was not ample for the overflow of people entering our doors each day.

We had begun as advocates for the formerly incarcerated, but we were being redefined by the men coming out of prison. Not that we were letting go of our public advocacy. Our frequent radio and television appearances attracted hundreds of people, men and women, living marginal lives because of their prison past. They were insisting we respond to their real and immediate needs. There is a thin line between trying something new and going back to old habits and putting yourself in position of returning to prison. Helping the formerly incarcerated stay on the right side of that line is at the heart of crime prevention in any town or city.

The first stop for any man or woman arriving at Fortune was to talk with a counselor, Kenny Jackson or Mel Rivers. We had limited resources in those early days, but Kenny and Mel would provide a reality check and point out pitfalls and barriers for anyone wearing the label "ex-con." They weren't spouting theory; rather, they were sharing personal experiences.

We sent teams of speakers to high schools, colleges, civic organizations, and church groups, often as many as fifteen or twenty a week. We started by speaking in the New York metropolitan area, but the idea spread like wildfire. Suddenly we were being invited to Harvard, the University of Chicago, Indiana University, and state legislatures in Oklahoma, Arkansas, and Massachusetts.

If we were heading for a school in Long Island or Brooklyn, Kenny would grab a couple of the new guys and say "stick with us," and they would attend the speaking engagements. For many of those men, it was the first time in their lives they were part of anything positive. They also saw that people were responsive to their plight.

My role, once again, was as moderator—introducing the speakers, giving the background of the Fortune Society, and fielding questions at the conclusion. I gained my real education in the car, listening to my companions' reflections of the prison experience. With no civilian audience, the uncensored tales would emerge—the fears, rage, absurdities, and irrelevance of lockup. Kenny and Mel would always direct the discussion to alternatives, everything from drug programs and AA to educational opportunities. While the talk was serious, the mood was supportive and always accompanied with lots of laughter. The Fortune Society, by the sheer dint of the personalities involved, created a comfort zone for an ostracized population.

We were naïve about an administrative structure. We realized that we couldn't continue as a volunteer organization. We all had other jobs and yet were devoting all of our energy and most of our time to this new entity. Kenny, Mel, and I knew that we were part of something bigger that any one of us. You could feel it happen every day. I continued representing Broadway and off-Broadway shows, with two long running hits, *Hair* and *The Boys in the Band*. Two staff members were able to handle the routine aspects of those shows. I began declining representation of new plays because my time was consumed with Fortune business.

A small family foundation (which chose to remain anonymous) offered Fortune $5,000 of seed money to professionalize us. That amount of money was a windfall for our meager bank account. Their attorney discovered we lacked nonprofit status and guided us through a government maze, enabling us to have a 501(c) label, which permitted foundations and individuals to support us and receive a tax benefit. Fortune was three years old, and we were babes in the nonprofit woods. When the paperwork was concluded, Kenny, Mel, and I went on salary at a hundred dollars a week.

We met Dr. Karl Menninger at a speaking engagement in Chicago. Menninger, founder of the famed Wichita, Kansas, psychiatric clinic bearing his name, was a critic of the criminal-justice system. Dr. Karl was excited by the Fortune men he met, and he championed us for the remainder of his life, often guiding us to foundations and individuals who would support our efforts. When in New York City, he always visited our offices.

We needed larger space outside of 1545 Broadway. Real-estate brokers recoiled when they heard of our mission and our target population. We found a loft in a triangle building on Sixth Avenue in Greenwich Village, but when tenants learned of their prospective new neighbor, they rose up in protest, and we were denied a lease. It was ironic. Our friends at 1545 were imploring us to stay. They realized we were good to have in the building. They loved the men and women they were meeting from Fortune. They also knew that 1545 Broadway was the safest and most protected building in the crime-filled Times Square area. Word was out on the street: "Don't mess with 1545." Many street guys came to us for direct services, sometimes just to rest and cop a free cup of coffee, and if any negative-thinking hood approached 1545, two or three of our guys made it clear that they should move on. One would always say, "When you're ready to get your life together, come back."

Finally, we located a loft on Twenty-Second Street, an entire floor-through partitioned into offices and meeting rooms. With the new space, we established an organizational chart. We would offer one-stop shopping for men and women returning to New York City from jail or prison. After seeing a counselor, a new arrival would be told of daily group raps reminding them of pitfalls on the street. Many who arrived were reading at a low grade level, which made the prospect of meaningful employment rather slim; volunteer tutors were on hand for one-to-one teaching. Finally, we had a job unit, preparing people for interviews with prospective employers. Before going on an interview, they would have to prepare a résumé and know how to fill out an application form. Role-playing sessions also revealed that most guys who'd done time did not know how to conduct themselves in a job interview. It was a tough situation. So many of the men and women had limited education and few skills to offer. Little of this was ever discussed or confronted while they were doing time.

Years later, when AIDS was in its infancy, we received letters from inmates with tales of men dying and little information being provided about the epidemic. Rumors abounded, and panic was evident. I called Deputy Commissioner Marty Horn in Albany. Marty had first contacted the Fortune Society when he was a parole officer in New York City. He thought Fortune was an appropriate place to refer parolees. Clearly, he was a man with a different vision from any of his colleagues. (Later Marty became commissioner of correction and probation.) I alerted Marty about the fears being expressed, and said that trouble could be averted if inmates received whatever information was available.

The only game in town at the time was the Gay Men's Health Crisis, and I sent their literature to Marty so he could pass it on to the various prisons. I was under the impression that we had made a start in alleviating inmate fears. But never underestimate the deadly thinking of traditional people in the Department of Corrections. Marty called, somewhat embarrassed, to inform me that wardens would not allow literature that had the word *gay* in it. Ignorance triumphs over reason in the northern plains of New York.

Clearly, that was a wake-up call for me. I was startled at such narrow thinking. How do you get around the irrational? I met with some leaders of Gay Men's Health Crisis and discussed the problem with them, and they designed literature that merely used their initials: *GMHC*. The word *gay* was never spelled out. The wardens permitted the brochures to enter, and the Department of Corrections took its first step in recognizing an epidemic that was having a profound effect on the inmate population.

In the years to come, we discovered that nearly one out of three former prisoners was HIV positive.

In 2012, the Fortune Society celebrated its forty-fourth anniversary. Our original one room has become a two-floor, enormous 65,000 square feet of office space and meeting rooms, with a staff of 150. I am in contact with hundreds of the men and women who have passed through our doors in the intervening years. Many have reclaimed their lives and are doing wonderful things, vocationally and in their personal lives. I wanted to gain their insight on how and what the Fortune Society played in their lives.

I talked with Rod Taylor, who came to Fortune after completing six years in the New York State prison system. That had just been his most recent experience in lockup: Rod was a product of the system, having been incarcerated on the installment plan since he was nine years old. His street time was at a minimum. We first met in 1972, when he began attending the Saturday afternoon group raps. Rod had been holding down a weekday job, pushing clothes racks in the Garment District, a low-paying gig that guys like him could get off the books. It was one of those "I'll take anything" jobs that guys grab while they are deciding if the world will let them back in.

Rod recalled those days for me: "I was twenty-nine years old when I hit Fortune. I was ready for something else in my life. Prison was no longer a deterrent, because I learned how to live there. It was out here that I didn't know how to live. Looking back, I remember arriving at Fortune and meeting people who were like me, except they had done a U-turn in their lives—guys like Kenny Jackson, Mel Rivers, Eddie Rabsatt, Vinnie DeFrancesco, and Charlie Jackson. I think the most important thing they taught me was how to like myself. That was a big hurdle for me and a new start." I mentioned to Rod that he must have met men like himself while he was in prison.

"Yes," he responded, "but in prison, nothing fosters good thoughts. At Fortune, it was a garden of positive thinking. There was hope." Rod was clear that the education and job-finding programs were important...but more important were those first few weeks when he found himself with other men who had done time.

Rod's observations intrigued me. There are few real studies about men who have done a lot of time and then changed their lives. What was the motivation? Some social scientists argue that people mature out of antisocial actions; they burn out. That hardly explains the high recidivist rate around the country. It also doesn't take into account the fact that many men who are burned out and stay in the community often lead desolate lives, homeless and a burden to the taxpayer.

Motivated by Rod's comments, I talked with others.

Sam Rivera arrived at Fortune in 1990. He was twenty-seven years old and had recently finished five years behind the walls. Sam, self described, was "a very angry young man. Fortune was my last resort. I had been turned down for jobs everywhere I went. A parole officer instructed me to try Fortune. I said to myself, If this doesn't work, I'll go back to the streets, doing what I have to do to get by. I walked in and found a community of people who had been where I had been. They accepted me. More than that. They welcomed me. It was crowded that Monday morning, and I didn't know if I would wait around. Nancy Lopez came over to me and said, 'Don't leave; give it a chance. I promise you that we'll help you to change your life if you just give it a shot.'

"Then I saw a counselor, Charlie Alicea. He saved my life. It's that simple. I marched into his room and spit out a lot of bullshit, feeling very sorry for myself. He just sat and listened until I got it all out. Then he told me that he grew up in my neighborhood, the Lower East Side, and it turned out that we knew a lot of the same people. Then he said to me—I'll never forget it—'Just sit still and drop the bullshit. Try something different if you aren't afraid to.' I kept coming back, mainly to talk to Charlie. Nobody ever understood me like he did. Then I told myself, 'This is too good to be true,' and I stayed away for a couple of days. Charlie called me at home. I couldn't believe it. He told me to get back in. I did, and I stayed for a decade, ending up as a staff member." After ten years, Sam was hired by another program, Exponents, as their chief operating officer, working with recovering addicts and formerly incarcerated persons.

That story was played over and over. One person understanding another and making him feel welcomed, opening a door and challenging him, daring him to confront his fears, his demons. Everyone I spoke to recognized the importance of Fortune's education and job units, but it was the atmosphere of acceptance that resonated. Fortune calls it counseling. The organization is much more. It is a life-saving bureau, saving the lives of men and women who have been in prison and lessening the possibility of an unknown person being a victim.

That is the real fight against crime, unrecognized politically and by the media. When a man coming out of prison says, "I'll do what I have to do, what it takes to survive out here," it is clear what he is saying. Or, as one man said to me, "When I put a gun in his face, he isn't going to ask for references." Fortune is often the determining factor in that type of situation not taking place. When you read about the fight against crime, the press and politicians always allude to the number of cops on the street. No matter how many cops are out there, a man determined to go back in the life will not be stopped. Fortune deals with that man each and every day.

Victor Rojas is a deeply sensitive man. He arrived at Fortune in 2009, having done jail and prison time for thirteen of his 46 years. His childhood was one of foster homes, shelters, and a dysfunctional family enmeshed in alcohol and drugs. Victor moved in to the Fortune

Academy—the Castle—the residence we created in 2002 as a safe haven for formerly incarcerated men and women. He told me, "At night, I could rest my head with a certain clarity. There was a sense of respect and freedom. You have to do the right thing. That all that's asked of you. Freedom comes with responsibility. I watched how the staff was living, and that was the kind of life I wanted. They had all been where I had been. They understood my feelings and my fears. That makes a difference." After moving out of the academy, Victor became a staff member at Fortune, working as a family-services counselor.

I ran into Bruce Jones on the subway and asked him to recall coming to Fortune after serving a quarter of a century in New York state prisons. He admitted that he had had great doubts about making it "out here." All he'd known was prison life. Six years had passed since that first day.

Bruce used that word again: he said that what mattered when he arrived at Fortune was that he felt *welcomed*. That had made it possible for him to consider a new and different type of life. He and I had some laughs recounting a group in which he participated. It was for long-timers, and it was focused on adjusting to civilian life—"squaring up." The discussions were about the little things that get people hung up, like dealing with crowds on the subway, or shopping for items when you have had all decisions made for you for twenty-five years. They were about feeling inadequate in restaurants, overwhelmed by the multiple choices after having had food placed on your tray for endless years.

Making choices was intimidating.

One meeting was memorable. The guys began talking about how difficult it was to meet women who were not "in the life." Most only knew women they met in bars or places where drugs were plentiful.

My friend Janice K. Bryant, then an editor at *Essence* magazine, accepted my invitation to meet with the group. With her were three young, attractive staff writers at *Essence*. The men and women talked about subjects of shared interest. The men admitted that they didn't know how to approach women. We created some role-playing scenes. Bruce was particularly uncomfortable, until one of the women in the session suggested that he invite her to share a cup of coffee. The following week Bruce told the group he hadn't consumed so much coffee in his life. In a supportive environment, the participants were confronting a situation that was significant in their lives.

Bruce now has his own apartment and is holding down a full-time job. Five years after doing twenty-five years, he describes himself as a full-time civilian—and he is dating. It all began because he felt welcomed when he arrived.

And the women. I asked Vilma Ortiz Donovan to record her arrival at Fortune in 2006. She lived at the Fortune Academy.

> The Fortune Society has made a difference in my life by helping me find myself. For years, I didn't know who I was or where I belonged. I was in and out of rehabs and prison. I always felt like I was being judged. I knew I was a better person, but I didn't think I deserved a better life than the one I had made for myself.
>
> I wanted to change my life but I didn't know how. I needed guidance and support from people who understood where I was coming from and had to feel safe while doing it. When I walked into the doors of the Castle, I knew in my heart and soul that I had found where I belonged. I remember saying to myself, "I made it." I remember having an overwhelming feeling when I was told "Welcome home," and that's when I knew I was in a safe place and change was going to happen.
>
> I met all of the staff and learned that here were people who had gone through what I had and now they were directors, case managers, and even cooks. I admired them and wanted to be just like them. No one cared what I had done, just wanted to

know how they could help me. They became my role models. I had a great case manager who I shared my deepest, darkest secrets to. Things I never told anyone. She listened, didn't judge, cried and even laughed with me. To find a person who is committed and dedicated to helping me made an extraordinary impact on my life. I made sure that I met with her on a regular basis. All of the staff always knew what was going on with me. They met every Thursday to review all of us who lived in the house. It didn't matter what day or time it was, there was always someone to talk to.

I was guided in all aspects of my life from doing relapse, outpatient, and women's groups, computer classes and career development, which by the way I didn't want to do because I thought I knew it all. You see, I learned that trusting, listening, and wanting to change was the key. I lived and learned with people who wanted to see me succeed and were willing to help me in any way. Nothing was given to me and I worked hard for what I have. I learned how to love myself for who I had become and forgive myself for the person I once was.

We had morning focus and I made sure I was there every morning to start my day on a good note. I kept a positive attitude because nothing on the outside was worse than being in prison. We had evening focus at night, where we were able to share about our day. Granted, we were not all on the same page, but I found people who were just as determined to change as I was. I had a cleaning assignment which I gladly did because this was my house and I had to keep it clean. I was told by staff and others to believe in myself and yes, I did deserve better. I even had a wonderful parole officer.

Living in a safe environment, surrounded by caring, positive people who are nonjudgmental and who want to help you in changing your life, made the difference for me. Some may call it luck, but I call it wanting to change with people who have changed. I have a lot of respect, gratitude, and love for Fortune and for what it has helped me achieve. I always say, "I GREW UP IN THIS PLACE."

Years ago, I was a panelist at a criminal-justice conference. One of the other participants was James Q. Wilson, a former Harvard professor who had authored a best-selling book, *Thinking About Crime*. His criminal-justice expertise had been achieved by riding around in the back of a police car in Cambridge, Massachusetts, for a couple of months.

Professor Wilson and I didn't agree on many issues. He was not pleased with my published review of his book, which began, "The main problem with James Q. Wilson's book *Thinking About Crime* is that it appears he didn't give it much thought." Wilson claimed he was tough on crime. I argued that tough was a posture, not a solution.

At the conference, I related stories of the men and women who came through Fortune, how they had been institutionalized but had dramatically altered their lives. Wilson's predictable response was, "You only have anecdotes; I have the statistics." I responded, "Your statistics are only a compilation of mine and others' stories about real people, not statistics. The people I know can tell you more about crime, punishment, and reclaiming their lives than all the statistics you can gather."

Wilson went on to become an advisor on criminal-justice affairs in the Nixon White House, before the president and his team were shamed out of office for their criminal activities.

The recollections of Rod Taylor, Sam Rivera, Bruce Jones, Victor Rojas, Vilma Ortiz Donovan, and hundreds of other men and women who walked through the doors at Fortune Society are evidence that lives can be reclaimed. The journey is difficult, but possible. The main barriers facing formerly incarcerated people are the damage done by a prison system that destroys the spirit, and the obstacles and prejudices upon release that create new problems. And still they triumph.

It has always been clear to me that prisoners, who have often had a lifetime of crime and punishment, don't find the severity of prison to be difficult. What is tough for them is to come to terms with the inner demons that remain dormant.

Caz Torres, a resident of the Fortune Academy, remarked, "I was never afraid of the dark. It was daylight that scared me."

SEVEN

Early Years

As a kid, my dream was to be a sportswriter. The reasons were obvious. All the ball games would be free and I'd be paid for going. By my sophomore year in high school, in addition to being sports editor of the high school paper, I was a stringer for the *Sunday Sun* and the *Bergen Evening Record*, two newspapers in north New Jersey, one a weekly and the other a daily. I began living my dream, being paid to cover sporting events.

My passion for baseball, basketball, and football never waned, but my vocational pursuits were reshaped. After college and two years in the U.S. Army, my thoughts turned to the American theater, and I successfully pursued that dream.

It is fascinating how events unfold. There was nothing in my childhood aspirations or my foray into the theater that would have predicted my being an advocate for prison reform or a voice for men and women who were incarcerated or out of prison. Who we become is a culmination of a multitude of experiences, and it is only in hindsight that you can detect the path that led you to your destination.

I often asked my mother if we were poor when I was a child. Her feathers ruffled, she would respond, "You never went to bed hungry," which was her prideful assessment. In fact, I was a Depression baby, and my earliest memories of family life, of my mother, father, and older sister, Carla, were of our moving with my aunt Lil and uncle Lou into a two-family house in Ridgefield Park.

That's how families coped with the Depression—doubling up and sharing rent and food costs. Everyone was reduced to finding creative ways of survival. Our family would never have labeled itself as *poor*. "Rough times to get past" was my mother's explanation. It was the Depression, and everyone—well, almost everyone—had money problems.

Ridgefield Park had a handful of Jews, but Carla and I were the only Jewish kids in our grammar school. We had plenty of friends, but we did not escape anti-Semitism. I was about ten years old when my uncle Danny was shot down over Germany during World War II. A schoolyard argument erupted amidst a softball game, and my antagonist shouted, "I'm glad your uncle's dead. That's one less Jew." It wounded me deeply. I'm not sure if it was the Jew part as much as his being glad that Danny was dead. Danny was one of my childhood heroes and best friends. My father's younger sibling, he was only a decade older than I. He treated me like a kid brother and would carry me on his shoulders to the playground or to football games. I refused to go back to school after that kid yelled at me. I acquired a defensive shell, thawed only by using humor to deflect ignorance.

My dad had a series of jobs, and by the end of the war, things were on the upswing, good enough for us to move to Teaneck and buy a house. Teaneck was an upwardly mobile community, and my parents gradually adjusted to financial advantages. They took up golf and were firmly established as upper middle class by the time I entered high school. They were people of good heart but not particularly political. Their spare time was filled with social activities around their golf interests, a world that bored me.

My father, Leon, was the oldest of seven children. His parents, Elliott and Adelaide Rothenberg, moved to Teaneck in 1920, the first Jewish family in that northern New Jersey town. My grandmother became a devout Christian Scientist. My father's siblings—Marion, Murray, Hilda, Uncle Danny, and Ruth, all except June, who had died at the age of eight from spinal meningitis—were a part of my life. Holidays, weekends, and summer nights were all about aunts and uncles and cousins.

It was a volatile group—interested, energetic, and involved in a multitude of activities. My uncle Murray had been the star quarterback at Teaneck High School during the early 1930s, and he was named first team all-state. That honor was diluted by the fact that he never started a game. The coach, I learned, hadn't wanted a Jewish name in the starting lineup, even if the student was the best player in the county and the state.

My aunt Hilda had a great impact on my life. I always teased her, saying that she discovered me between husbands. After she divorced her first, she would take me to the movies on school nights, and we would have deli or ice cream before the pictures. She told me I was special and infused me with a confidence that gave me strength when facing adversities. She was my Auntie Mame—promising me that life would present barriers but I would be able to overcome them. More than anything else, her rich humor made me laugh.

I've often met men and women at the Fortune Society who can't identify a single adult person from their childhood who nourished their spirit. Every child should have an Aunt Hilda. She was the best part of my childhood.

My aunt Marian met my mother at a summer-camp program and later introduced her brother Leon to the woman who would become his wife and my mother. Leonore Weinberg grew up in Ridgefield Park. Her father died when she was twelve, and after that she and her sister, my aunt Lil, were raised by their mother, Molly Stern, and their stepfather. It was a household with tension; my mother and Lil never totally adjusted to the man I viewed as my grandfather, Sid Stern. He was nearly fifteen years younger than my grandmother and only a dozen years older than my mother. His stepdaughters never viewed him as an acceptable replacement.

My parents married on New Year's Eve, 1929, and my sister was born ten months later, squeaking in just under the gun. Three years later I entered their world. It was the height of the Depression, and my mother always let me know that I hadn't been planned.

My mother and I were always in a state of near battle. I loved her more than anyone in the world, but we argued continuously, probably because we were so similar. We could make each other laugh, confide in each other, but we fought furiously. As I grew older, I always blamed her for any limitations or self-doubt I had, but I suspect she is responsible for the best things about me, also. I always wanted her in my corner yet never felt secure that she was.

My father's love was unconditional. There was never any doubt about it. Who knows what the ingredients are of good parenthood? Grown men and women, dealing with their own life struggles, are suddenly interrupted by a baby, who is demanding. Sometimes they are not ready for full-time parenthood. My father was; I'm not sure if my mother was. I think if she had been born a generation or two later, she would have had a career before becoming the wife at home and the mother of two.

It is difficult to assess parents. I recall a friend commenting that my mother was pretty. I thought, "Really?" Years later, when my niece Judy located some home movies from the forties, I was astonished to see that my mother was so attractive. They're Mom and Dad—who knows from pretty?

The bottom line about Leon and Leonore Rothenberg is quite simply this: if they weren't my parents and I met them socially, I would have wanted to develop a friendship with them. They were really decent people with great humor.

My mother had no shortage of homilies, shortcuts for good living. I find myself repeating them frequently. My sister and I can spend an evening putting together her prescriptions for life, starting with "I don't care if Arnie isn't wearing galoshes. If Arnie jumped off of the George Washington Bridge, would you follow him?"

Somewhere there is a mother school where they teach bromides and torture. My friend Bernard White, who grew up in Harlem, agreed with me that we had the same mother, because the maternal clichés were identical.

When I started hearing stories from men and women at Fortune, many of whom had been abandoned and abused as children, I had to take a long, hard look at my own childhood. I was blessed. My mother and father were good people with clear and decent values. My childhood wasn't perfect, but it gave me the foundation for the decades that would follow.

My first political hero was Jackie Robinson. I celebrated his groundbreaking entry into organized baseball, even though the Brooklyn Dodgers were not my team of choice. For multiple reasons that I only later came to understand, I identified with his symbol as an outsider.

All of the kids in junior high school read the reports of Jackie's ostracism by players, and that prompted me, in a virtually all-white school, to explore civil-rights issues. I had little encouragement while in Teaneck High School, but at the University of Denver the history of slavery and segregation were mapped out. The cloak of ignorance was being lifted.

I wasn't much of a student and was not impressed by the teachers at Teaneck High School. They seemed to stifle curiosity. Average grades limited my collegiate aspirations, but a high SAT score brought me provisional acceptance at a few universities.

Whatever was cooking in my teenage mind, I knew I wanted to travel far from New Jersey, and I accepted an offer to attend the University of Denver—on probation because of my grades. None of my friends ventured more than two hundred miles to college. They were attending Rutgers, Colgate, Yale, and Columbia. Denver, in 1951, was looked upon as a trip to the moon.

College and Denver were a new adventure for me. From the outset, my scholastic achievements were good enough for me to be invited to the Freshman Honor Society. I also became political. Nurtured by wonderful professors, my political instincts found an activist direction. Dr. Charles Merrifield, a social scientist, opened doors and windows, challenging and encouraging me. John Greenway, an English professor, brought authors to life and reinforced my joy in reading.

When I was a freshman at DU, a representative of Students for Democratic Action spoke on campus in an effort to establish a campus branch of the liberals in the Democratic Party. He tossed out names like Hubert Humphrey, Walter Reuther, and Mrs. Roosevelt. I was enthused and became the campus contact and organizer. Later I was elected campus president of Students for Democratic Action. In the summer of 1952, I attended the national SDA conference at Brandeis and was elected to the national board of directors. I suspected that I was elevated to this group because they were anxious to have representation from the Rocky Mountains, and I was the only student between the University of Chicago and Berkeley.

Several events took place during my college years that cemented my political and social outlook. During the summer of 1952, Harry Truman was president, and the party conventions named Dwight David Eisenhower and Adlai Stevenson to compete to be his successor. I participated in an SDA-sponsored summer program in Washington, D.C. Two dozen undergraduates from around the country gathered at the Barksdale Rooming House near Dupont Circle, where we lived and congregated each night for political seminars and activist training. We were an integrated group, so we resided in the black section of D.C., which in 1952 was a segregated city. I came to realize our nation's capital was a southern city. Apartheid best describes it.

At the Barksdale, I was living, sharing and eating with young men and women of color. They weren't symbols or causes. They had become my friends. I couldn't grasp why anyone would deny any of them a cup of coffee, sitting alongside me.

My first instincts were to shield them from pain. I understood that wasn't enough—nor could I protect them from reality. I had to fight ignorance. I was determined and angry—but with a team of equally concerned, young, passionate college students. That can fuel you. It wasn't sufficient to voice rage at ignorance. I had to act on it.

In addition to the speakers, we had weekend activist programs. We joined with the American Friends Service Committee on Saturdays, entering communities that sought help in upkeep. We assisted families by painting rooms and babysitting while mothers took care of outside tasks. On Sunday, we joined with students from CORE (Congress of Racial Equality) to participate in sit-ins at the segregated People's Drug Store at Dupont Circle. Blacks could enter and purchase goods but could not sit at the counter. Thus, sit-ins.

We had training sessions guiding us in passive resistance—how to *not* respond to comments, threats, or physical violence. We would venture into a store on Sunday morning, in time for the arrival of the pious churchgoers, and place ourselves black-kid-white-kid-black-kid, filling up all the counter stools. The waitress would approach a white kid for an order, and he or she would respond, "I would like coffee and toast," and, nodding to the youngster alongside, "and my friend would like the same." Naturally, we were refused, because it was Washington, D.C., in 1952, nearly a decade before the modern civil rights movement ignited.

It was mostly peaceful. We could hear people's groans and gripes but not much more. One Sunday, I felt a tap on my shoulder and turned around to see an older white woman, probably the age I am now, who was nicely dressed but with the most hostile look, one you could not ignore. A half century later, I can still see her pinched-up face as she hissed at me, "Nigger lover," and feel her spit, which landed on my cheek. The young man next to me took my arm and said, "That is your medal." I let the spit slide down my face, refusing to give her the satisfaction of my wiping it off.

I have always had difficulty hearing today's young black kids call each other "nigga," because I was branded with the hatred that the old woman in the People's Drug Store revealed on that Sunday after-church morning. I know the youngsters today feel they have neutralized the word as they use it . . . but I still see and hear hate.

My best friend that summer was Nancy Koehler, who had just graduated from the University of Nebraska. Nancy was from a small farming town in western Nebraska and had a populist political perspective. She had come to D.C. with classmate Ruth Sorenson, whose brother Ted was an aide to a young Massachusetts congressman named John F. Kennedy. Ted Sorenson spent many evenings with us at the Barksdale and had us all enthused about the ambitious congressman from New England.

Nancy returned with me to Denver in the fall. She lived with her aunt and found work there. We joined the city's Young Democrats Club and became active in the political scene there, an interesting pastime for me, while I wrote for the undergraduate newspaper and was able to maintain my grades at an A and B level.

At one of the political meetings, we met a woman who worked for the Anti-Defamation League. She invited us to be spies, to visit churches outside of Denver that had ministers preaching hate, racism, and anti-Semitism. We were trained and given fictional biographies: we were to be a young couple angry at the Socialists who were taking over our country. If asked, we had appropriate answers about blacks and Jews.

Compared to today's evangelical ministers of hate on television, Harvey Springer and Kenneth Goff seem small-time. They didn't have TV channels, but their rap was the same I hear today. Springer, the more successful of the two, had a tabernacle in Englewood, Colorado. On our first night there, he announced he had to raise $10,000 for the cause. He asked if there was anyone who thought that he would not raise that much money. A few hands were raised, and the reverend said, "I'd like to welcome the newcomers." Beefy men in the back of the building bolted the doors, and Springer went into his act, threatening the audience with what Jews would do to them and pleading for money to fight the invasion of *those* people, who were going to open the doors of society, culminating in a black invasion.

Both Springer and Goff would always say to the congregation that there were probably spies in the house from the Jew-run Anti-Defamation League. Nancy and I would look around, angrily searching the crowd for the invading Hebrews. It was fascinating and frightening.

We couldn't spy for more than a few months, because it was suspected that ADL and Young Democrat meetings had Springer spies and we would be identified.

I became the editorial-page columnist for the *Clarion*, the school's undergraduate newspaper. Eisenhower had become president, but the most dominant political figure in the country during the first half of that decade was Joe McCarthy. The junior senator from Wisconsin was on a witch hunt, accusing almost everyone in the Democratic Party of having Communist sympathies. He altered the political terrain of the nation. I took the opportunity in print to be a serious critic of Senator Joe. This would prove to become the basis of a serious battle.

The *Clarion* was a weekly college paper, and during the McCarthy era it seemed most concerned with sorority and fraternity social events, save for my column. Greek organizations controlled most campus activities, including student government and the student papers. They were politically indifferent, which was the prevailing student sentiment of the fifties. How that would change in the sixties when fraternity men feared being sent to Vietnam.

In the late spring of my junior year, I decided to enter the competition to be editor in chief, the most influential campus post for an undergraduate. I was vying with two other student journalists, both affiliated with fraternities, and it was generally assumed that one or the other would be the next editor, continuing the fraternity domination on campus

We had to appear, one at a time, before the Board of Publications, a body of about sixteen people—faculty members, administration, and student representatives. Clearly the underdog, I went before the board and quietly gave them my philosophy of what an undergraduate newspaper should be. I also informed them how to financially restructure it, through advertising and cutting frivolous costs, to be published twice a week—a great departure from its history as a weekly. I was prepared and efficient in my presentation.

To everyone's surprise, they named me the editor in chief of the '54–'55 *Clarion*. The celebration lasted less than twenty-four hours. I learned that a petition was circulating through the fraternity and sorority houses calling for the student senate to override the decision by the Board of Publications. Word was being spread that I was a member of a Communist cell, and that I planned to make the campus paper a voice for anti-American sentiments. There was also a stated fear that as editor I would challenge the fraternity and sorority discrimination clause, an issue that had remained unchallenged on campus. In the McCarthy era, red-baiting was in high gear, and any ambitious combatant could undertake a red smear campaign for their own self interest.

I was living on campus. At DU, we had apartment dormitories, and mine was a two-bedroom apartment with six guys living there. My roommates weren't particularly political. They were more involved with their studies than campus activities and were amused but supportive of my activism. John Carr, a business major from South Jersey, was particularly concerned about my safety when I started to receive physical threats and anonymous phone calls. I was twenty years old and not prepared to be the subject of such fury. It seemed incomprehensible to me that my advocacy for Adlai Stevenson would result in accusations that I was a Communist. I don't think I had ever knowingly met a Communist. John Carr's combined maturity and strength enabled me to have the courage to fight the absurd charges.

The university chaplain, Glen Olds, who was later to serve as an advisor in the Nixon White House, gave a Sunday sermon lamenting that McCarthyism had invaded our campus and put a blot on a great university's reputation.

The circulating petitions succeeded in the convening of a special student-senate meeting. Hundreds arrived at the usual meeting room, and to accommodate the crowd they had to transfer to a larger hall in the library. I thought the campus Greeks had successfully mobilized and I would be mauled. It dawned on me that the accusations could stain my future professional life, whatever vocation I would pursue. McCarthyism was destroying lives out in the bigger world, and my life was just beginning. My dorm mates surrounded me for protection and assurance. I was practically numb.

The meeting was called to order by the newly elected student president, an active fraternity man. To my surprise, Byron Johnson, who had been my economics professor, asked for the floor. (He was later elected to Congress from Colorado's second district, the home of hate preacher Harvey Springer.) Johnson asserted that he was in the company of the dean of the law school, and that if statements were made, written or vocal, about David Rothenberg, the accusers would face charges of slander or libel if their allegations could not be substantiated.

The chair then asked for other comments. One student after another, and faculty members too, stood up and said they were in attendance because they were ashamed that DU had joined the parade of character assassination. Apparently, the fraternity and sorority people were not as organized as I had thought. The smear campaign proved to be mostly the work of the two men I had defeated for the editorship. The chair noted that no objections had been put forth concerning my incipient assignment as editor of the *Clarion*. He asked for an adjournment, and the nightmare was abruptly concluded.

I proved to be a good editor, conscientious and innovative. The paper was published twice a week. On the first day, I entered the editor's office; scribbled on the wall was a painted sign proclaiming, *TOUR OF RUSSIA BEGINS HERE. 15 RUBLES TO GET ON.*

The subject of fraternity and sorority discrimination was an issue to be confronted. But I didn't open the topic. I approached the president of the Interfraternity Council to write a guest column explaining the Greek position. That done, I invited Asa Hilliard to pen a response. Asa was the university's first black student to be elected president of the Arts and Science College. Not only was he a close friend, but I had served as his campaign manager in his run for student government. With Asa on the student senate and me as editor of the *Clarion*, the independents (those not in a fraternity) suddenly had unprecedented visibility.

Asa went on to have a distinguished career as an academic and author on black history, and died from malaria while leading a student tour in Africa in 2008. He was an outstanding leader when we were at Denver University, and his special skills continued for decades.

His essay in the *Clarion* prompted a host of letters to the editor and also an editorial. The world didn't come to an end, and some of the students most concerned about my being named editor would later tell me we had published a fine campus paper. They would also state that a good campus paper was important and that forcing discussions on vital issues, airing student concerns, was great for all of us.

I came to realize that the McCarthy tactics imposed on me by the men I had defeated for the job had been an appeal to fear and insecurities about the unknown. Later, many realized they had been pulled into a conflict not of their choosing. It was an important lesson, and I recognized such maneuvers in political battle years later. McCarthy didn't invent it. Nor did Goebbels. They just improved the deceit. They were cleverer than Machiavelli ever intended.

Another memorable event evolved when I was a student editor. One Monday morning when I entered the *Clarion* office, there was a call informing me that a coed had been raped at a fraternity-house party on the previous Saturday night. I immediately began making phone calls to get a lead on the story. Within minutes I heard from the president of the university's alumni association, who was one of the most influential and successful businessmen in Denver. He invited me to his office and sent a car for me. It indeed was a business that had all the trappings of success. I was ushered into the VIP's plush, carpeted office. He literally offered me a Cuban cigar. This was going to be a man-to-man talk, I sensed.

He immediately told me he was an alumnus of the fraternity in question, which was famous on campus because most of its members were varsity athletes. He told me that the accused young men were honorable, and that the comments and accusations of a "slut" should not be dignified by a story in the paper. He assured me that the best route for everyone would be silence, and that nothing should appear in print. He indicated that he had assurances from the two dailies, the *Denver Post* and the *Rocky Mountain News,* that the students' privacy would be protected.

I left making no promises. I also had a bad taste in my mouth. In 1955, young men like me were not acquainted with feminist literature;

it was almost nonexistent. But I had a sister and aunts who had sensitized me to the extent that I knew that a raped coed's claim should not be summarily dismissed by a fraternity's alumni champion.

No one at the university would speak to me for attribution. I wrote an editorial, which in retrospect was mild and timid. But it created havoc on campus. I called for an investigation of allegations about an assault at the fraternity party. I mentioned no names, but the story was out there. The university, under alumni pressure, responded by firing the fraternity-house mother. The unnamed coed left school, and the accused boys were untouched.

I was a naïve twenty-one-year-old. This was a rude awakening. I was seeing a political power play up close for the first time. Growing up, being wiser, is not an enjoyable transition. Disillusionment is painful.

At my graduation, the diplomas were handed out by the alumni president, the gentleman who had unsuccessfully attempted to influence me into a state of editorial silence. When I reached for my diploma, he dropped it on the floor—his public statement of disapproval.

That chapter should have concluded with that petty and hostile act, but decades later, when I was at the Fortune Society, I read that a former Miss America had made public statements that she had been sexually abused throughout her childhood. This saga became a *People* magazine cover story and a tearful presentation on *Oprah*. Asked why she was exposing her father's sexual abuse, she proclaimed it was a warning for young girls facing abuse to seek help and refuge. Her father, long since dead, was posthumously exposed.

Marilyn Van Derbur, a former University of Colorado coed, had been chosen as Miss Colorado before she was anointed as Miss America. I recalled the photos of her proud father standing with her when she was crowned the reigning beauty. Of course I recognized Francis Van Derbur as the man who had summoned me to his office in hopes that I would shield the sexual assaults of a handful of fraternity boys.

A proud boast: The annual yearbook published by students at Denver University named ten outstanding graduating seniors. Two of these were Asa Hilliard and David Rothenberg.

EIGHT

Stories

I remained at the Fortune Society for eighteen years. The criminal-justice system angered me, but the men and women I met inspired me.

Lessons concerning the underbelly of American life were delivered, often with wit and wisdom. Many of the men and women I met at the Fortune Society became a part of me—the candle to light rather than cursing the darkness.

Harry LaCroix was a fifteen-year-old Haitian kid who arrived at the Fortune Society in the late sixties. He just sauntered through our door one morning. He was homeless, having fled from a taunting aunt. There was no evidence of parents in the picture, and his aunt apparently couldn't handle him. Part of his teenage protest included using weed and sniffing glue.

Harry was drifting. He had been arrested and had a case pending in juvenile court. There were no adults prepared to accompany him to court. He was charged with a misdemeanor, so if he were an adult, he would face a fine and perhaps probation and a scolding. Because Harry was fifteen, the judge could send him to Spofford, a juvenile nightmare in the Bronx. Kenny, Mel, and I had paid frequent visits to Spofford and were horrified watching the young kids there, especially when we learned that most of them had been incarcerated merely because an adult was not available to assume responsibility. There were a handful who had been accused of violent crimes, and they tended to be at the top of the inmate pecking order. Spofford was a breeding ground for alienation. Most of the boys were throwaway kids—groomed for our prison system.

We determined that I should accompany Harry to court. Since the other guys had prison records, we assumed the judge would have less resistance to my presence. On the other hand, Kenny and Mel were better acquainted with the maneuvers of juvenile court, both having experienced it firsthand.

Harry and I entered the judge's offices. It was a first-time experience for me. In attendance were the judge and a social worker who knew Harry only from the paperwork. The judge seemed impressed that the Fortune Society was there on behalf of Harry. He stated clearly that for Harry to walk from his court, he must be entered into a street program, specifically one that would confront his use of drugs. But, he added—and it was an enormous *but*—he would need a legal guardian to assume responsibility for him receiving the appropriate treatment.

I looked at Harry, then turned to the judge and said I would be his legal guardian. I signed the papers and left the juvenile court with Harry, for whom I was now legally responsible.

When I returned to Fortune and told Kenny and Mel what had gone down, they asked me what I was planning to do. "He'll stay with me until we find a program for him," I answered. Kenny looked at me, and in his usual understated way, asked, "Are you out of your fucking mind? You have a fifteen-year-old kid on drugs." Using AA language with which Kenny was familiar, I merely responded, "One day at a time."

I was living on Sheridan Square in a one-bedroom apartment, but the couch in the living room opened to a bed. I showed Harry the apartment, gave him a key, and laid down the rules of the house. He would have a curfew and would have to assume some tasks in the apartment, such as making up his bed each morning and helping with the dishes. I realized I hardly knew this homeless fifteen-year-old boy, and he would be living in my home. I outlined a schedule for him to follow. He would come to work with me each morning until we could find an appropriate program or schooling for him. He would have his afternoon free if he told us where he was going, and he had to meet me for dinner.

Harry followed my instructions and guidelines without a peep or disagreement. Part of me was listening to the warnings of my friends and colleagues; another part of me recognized that Harry longed for this order and structure in his life.

A week after he began living with me, I came home and found him on the floor, scrubbing away. "What's up?" I asked him. He looked up at me and simply explained, "We have to keep our house clean. The floor looked dirty." I was moved by his initiative and his decision to extend helping out beyond my original instructions. He became so industrious in the house that I told him to slow down or people would think I was running a slave shop. I told him it would look like I had a sleep-in maid. I suggested that he cool it, and he said I should relax. Harry was staking a claim. This was his home. I had to keep reminding him that it was only temporary.

When we went to the store, shopping for food or anything for the apartment, he would demonstrate how store clerks would respond to him when he entered alone, a dark-skinned teenage boy. Then their behavior would change when I came in and indicated that Harry was with me. He instructed me that black kids learn early in life that they are walking on eggshells when they go "downtown"—when they enter the white world. When you witness this duplicity through the eyes of a kid who has become a friend and a responsibility, it is an experience of growth and insight. I began having a protective feeling for Harry.

After a few weeks, I no longer viewed Harry as a challenge. I cared about him, his future, his problems. It suddenly dawned on me that I was experiencing the feelings of a father, and that was appealing. It was also to be viewed with caution. I talked with Kenny and Mel, seeking guidance, putting borders on what I was experiencing.

Of course, it was still our mission to have Harry enter into a structured program. Though the judge insisted it be a drug program, Harry vowed that he would not use drugs while living with me, and he stayed true to that pledge. Drugs had been his escape from reality. He was enjoying this reality and didn't need to run from it.

After living with me for several months, Harry LaCroix was admitted to a residence program, which provided him with schooling as well as a well-structured, drug-free environment. He had maintained his pledge to me and been clean for the six months he lived with me.

After a few months in the program, Harry was granted weekend passes, and he would call me or stop by. He always kept the key to the apartment but would call before coming over. When he was eighteen, he moved out of the program and hooked up with a brother to share an apartment. Harry and his brother George were both working, and they would visit the Fortune Society when they were in midtown. George called me one day to tell me Harry had had an epileptic seizure and had died before anyone could attend to him. He was nineteen years old.

Harry would have been surprised to learn that he was one of my life's teachers. Who would have figured that? It breaks my heart when I think of his life, aborted just at a time when he was discovering it.

Eddie Morris was a gangster—like DeNiro in *Goodfellas*.

Born in the South Bronx, Eddie started stealing to survive as a kid. Abusive foster homes were a poor substitute for an abusive home. Poverty surrounded him, and he was the runaway kid who landed in a youth house, then graduated to adult prisons. On the streets he teamed up with the men he had met in upstate prisons.

Guns, booze, and beautiful women were how he went through his first thirty-five years, before the next crime put him back in a cage.

He was out of Clinton Prison and ran into Izzy Zimmerman. They had been on the same "court" in that bastille near the Canadian border. Courts are the jailhouse equivalent of college fraternities, where men of similar backgrounds hang together. Izzy's group was New York Jewish wise guys. His court was merely a plot of land in the yard, but it was the center of their universe.

Izzy won national attention when he was released from prison, having been found innocent after serving twenty-four years for a homicide he hadn't committed. He had come within hours of being electrocuted—had been served his last meal and had his head shaved—before a call from the governor's office called a halt to it. Vic Arnold, the actor who played Rocky in *Fortune and Men's Eyes*, had met Izzy during the run of the play and brought him to the theater. Izzy in turn introduced me to Eddie Morris.

In those early days of Fortune, Kenny, Mel, and I were always putting guys up for a couple of days before welfare came through with an SRO (single room occupancy) bed. It always amazed me that the press and politicians lamented about the recidivist rate. Men were coming to us right out of prison, with no families, no money, no housing, no food, no prospects for jobs. Parole merely issued them a set of rules and provided no guidance. The failures of the system determined how crucial Fortune Society was. It would often take days, sometimes weeks, before welfare provided a survival check and emergency housing. The system, then and now, seems geared to create crisis conditions, which send people just out of prison back to crime.

When I heard Eddie's plight, I told him he could stay with me until welfare came through. He looked stunned. "What's the angle?" He was from a world where kindness was weakness—or there was a game being played.

Because of those few days in my apartment, Eddie and I were solid. I listened to endless horror stories of his past life. He was an accident waiting to happen. On that first night, he talked until the early hours of the morning about his childhood, gangs, crime, jails, prisons, fights...just about everything negative that someone could experience. He wanted something else in life but didn't have a clue where to find it.

A few weeks later, after he had moved into an SRO hotel, I received a call in the middle of the night from a hospital in Westchester informing me that Eddie was there. He had been shot—circumstances unknown. He gave the authorities no information, just my phone number.

When he was released from the hospital, we hooked up. He acted as if bullet wounds were an inevitable part of the human experience. No complaints and no talking about who had shot him.

That's the tough-guy side of Eddie. It's the other side that stays with me. Along the way, he told me his name was Emmanuel Morris but "nobody calls me that." He was very clear that Emmanuel was not to be used. I let him know that Eddie was okay with me, but that if I ever decided to call him Emmanuel, he would know that I was pissed.

Once when he was busted on some petty charge, I went to the Tombs to meet him when he was bailed out. I greeted him with "Hello, Emmanuel." He lowered his head. He got the message.

Eddie was in the car with a group of us from the Fortune Society, traveling to a speaking engagement somewhere north of the city. I absorbed the wondrous beauty—the woods, the sunset—and suggested, "Look at that...nature at its most beautiful." Eddie turned and peered out the window for a moment. Then, with his tough-guy, corner-of-the-mouth, Bronx- and prison-influenced accent, he began reciting a beautiful passage of poetry. He had a look of serenity that was a contradiction to his usual pose of suspicion, fear, machismo, and contained rage. He was at peace.

"What is that?" I asked.

His surprising answer was "Lord Byron."

Here was a man who had grown up on the streets and in kid joints, never with a formal education—and he was at one with Lord Byron.

Having opened the floodgates, he began reciting passage after passage, all from the eighteenth-century English romantic poet. I made inquiry if he recited Keats or Shelley. "Only Byron," he whispered, almost reverentially. He told me this story.

"I was in Coxsackie. Seventeen years old. A wild kid. The hacks [prison guards] hated me. Called me all sort of Jew names. I got thrown into the hole... it was me and four walls, a cot, and a toilet for six months. Can you imagine putting a boy in there, no matter what he did? For some reason, there was one book there. How and why someone left it, I don't know. It was *The Complete Works of Lord Byron*. I began reading them to myself, then out loud. He brought beauty into that dungeon. I memorized all of them. He saved my sanity. I would later read anything by and about Lord Byron."

So, in this car filled with ex-cons, driving somewhere in New York State, Eddie shared with us the poetry of Byron. The other guys found nothing unusual about it. Everyone clung to something that brought them civility or sanity. You took what you could get wherever you found it.

I began to wonder what Eddie could have achieved, what he might have been, had he not started out in life with three strikes against him in the South Bronx.

He stuck around Fortune for a few years. He was burned out. No more crime. No more prison. Growing old, he became one of those haunted, sad faces you notice in big cities in bus and train stations or cafeterias, going nowhere.

A few years ago, I received a call from Eddie. He was a patient at St. Vincent's Hospital. I figured he was somewhere in his mid-seventies by then. When I entered the ward and looked around, I couldn't figure out which old man was Eddie. I asked a nurse to point him out. She walked me over to a man who looked comatose. I sat by his bed until his eyes opened and introduced myself to him. He asked if I could get him cigarettes.

It was a sad reunion, and it was evident I was talking to a man in his last days. I called the hospital a few times, but no information was forthcoming.

I have been left with the memory of a man who found poetry and beauty in isolated prison cells. His life otherwise tortured, he found a refuge with a poet who had preceded him by two centuries. When Emmanuel "Eddie" Morris recited Lord Byron to me—which he did often—he was totally at peace with himself.

Charlie McGregor and Chuck Bergansky had two things in common: each had spent more than twenty-five years in prison, and each had his speaking engagements with the Fortune Society serve as a springboard for a career in the movies and television. The second halves of their lives were a dramatic departure from childhoods of neglect and encagement.

Charlie McGregor was a crowd-pleasing storyteller. High school and college students would surround him after we concluded an assembly program. He was the students' favorite. It was Eddie Morris who introduced him to Fortune. They had been in Clinton Prison together, and Eddie had read an interview about Charlie in the *Daily News* and raced uptown to tell Charlie about Fortune. Eddie told him his talking skills could be put to good use with us.

Born and raised in Harlem, Charlie "Peewee" McGregor was in his late forties when we met him, but he had the energy and enthusiasm of a teenager. I don't recall who surfaced as his movie godfather, but after he'd been with Fortune for about four years, he was being offered film roles. Charlie was Fat Freddie in *Super Fly*, appeared in *Across 110th Street*, and had a memorable role in Mel Brooks's *Blazing Saddles*. He moved to California in the late 1970s and appeared in various films and television shows. Often, I would receive a phone call from a Fortune friend shouting, "Put on Channel Four, Charlie is on!"

We took great pride in his success. Charlie was always looking for acclamation and attention. As a kid, he thought he had few options; in his later years, he found a spot on the sunny side of the street. With his shaved head and expressive round face, he tried to convey a militant look, but there was always something impish in his eyes, a contradiction to the tough pose. Fellini would have been fascinated with Charlie's many facial expressions.

We witnessed some tough situations, and he was always the mood breaker, enabling us to find some levity. When Kenny Jackson, Mel Rivers, Charlie, and I visited the Delaware state legislature, we asked if we could visit their soon to be demolished bastille. To our surprise, permission was arranged. After being led through the scrubbed part of the prison, we made inquiry of solitary confinement, usually the most accurate barometer of treatment in an institution. It is where they house those being punished within the house of punishment.

The deputy warden escorted us to the basement. Among the men we saw there was a teenager named David, who looked like a skeleton in those post World War II photos released from concentration camps. His deeply set eyes showed only fear, and his large Afro was a dramatic contrast to the absence of flesh on his exposed bones. He told us that he was in isolation because he refused to cut his Afro haircut. He was also on a hunger strike in protest against racism in the institution.

David was a man-child issuing a protest in the only way he knew how. In the few minutes we had, we implored him to eat some food and get his hair cut if it got him out of isolation. We told him he could use his defiance and opposition to oppression in a creative manner that would enable him to live. We were pushed along before we could determine if our pleas, our words, reached the young man. Ours was a desperate attempt to reveal concern and provide guidance.

When we boarded the train from Wilmington to New York City, the four of us were enveloped with sadness. Young David's haunting look and the smell of solitary confinement stained our clothes.

Charlie snapped us out of it. He recognized that we had had a constructive day, talking with state legislators and also allowing prisoners to see that there were former prisoners speaking on their behalf. He wanted to break us out of the gloom.

He announced to all around us that black folks had always been abused in various and creative ways. Did we know about the giggle barrels in Skipadeedoville, Georgia? "No," we all responded, which was Charlie's performance cue. He regaled us with talks about people in that fictional southern town, where there was a giggle barrel on Main Street. You see, black folks were not permitted to laugh on Main Street. When something struck them as funny, they had to race to the giggle barrel, hop in, and let the laughter loose. In great pantomime, he demonstrated how those folks contained and released their giggles.

He related incident after incident, joke after joke that had prompted colored folks to rush to the giggle barrel in Skipadeedoville, Georgia.

Charlie had the entire train car roaring with laughter, but Kenny, Mel, and I were on the floor. He was a triumphant performer. It was what could be described as relief laughter, the letting loose that is the antithesis of great sadness. Families, after a funeral, frequently experience such an episode.

Charlie broke the mood for us with his wit. More importantly, he recognized that a long and productive day meeting with legislators had been fractured after we witnessed a young lad who was halfway to death, making a futile protest. He allowed us to reach New York in a clear state of mind. He knew that seeing a young man like David would make us more determined to challenge the archaic prison system. He instinctively realized that depression was not a good weapon and enabled us to find equilibrium. I've tried to tell the story of the giggle barrels, but I've never been able to evoke the unrestrained joy that Charlie gave us on a train ride from Wilmington to New York.

In the early years of the twenty-first century, I received a call from Charlie. We had been out of touch, our lives going in different directions. Through the Internet, he located the Fortune Society, asked if I was still around, and then put in a call to me. We talked and laughed on the phone for nearly an hour, reminiscing, catching up on our friends, and recalling the visit to Wilmington. He kept telling me how wonderful those days with Fortune had been, a crossroad that had allowed him to fulfill dreams he'd never anticipated would come true. It had allowed him to have a second half of his life with some serenity and memories. Who would have thought Hollywood for Peewee out of Clinton Prison?

His lady friend called me about six months later and informed me that a sudden heart attack had felled Charlie, and that he died peacefully and without pain. He was in his late seventies. She said, "Charlie always talked about you and Fortune. Those were good days for him."

Chuck Bergansky faced the death penalty in New Jersey. He had kidnapped a cop during a robbery and had held him hostage. In New Jersey, the Lindbergh Law dictates that kidnapping can mean curtains if you're convicted. The cop's testimony saved him. At the trial, the police officer stated that Chuck had been gentle and caring, and that he'd never felt he was in danger. The death penalty was averted. I used to call Chuck "Billy Budd," a true innocent in a garden of weeds. Chuck had seen Charlie McGregor on a TV talk show, which prompted him to visit the Fortune Society. He had little faith in organizations but had known Peewee from time spent together in New York State prisons.

From the moment he visited Fortune, I recognized that Chuck Bergansky was a very special man. His horrendous background—years of child neglect and abuse—was not unusual for us to hear. That he survived it was the miracle. He was born out of wedlock and abandoned at birth, then raised in orphanages, youth houses, and foster homes. Later he learned that his birth mother was a young girl who had had an affair with a prominent New York City judge.

When he was about seven years of age, he was sent to an upstate facility, the New York State Training School for Boys. The kids lived in cottages with supervising parents in a cottage next door. Chuck's house parents were a black couple, Mary and William Niles, who were kind and caring. He was the only white kid in his cottage and did everything to endear himself to the surrogate parents. As other kids came and went, Chuck remained at the training school and always maneuvered to be in the cottage with Mr. and Ms. Niles doing house chores—anything to please them. He described himself at that time in his life as a male Cinderella. He longed for their nurturing.

The love was reciprocated, and the Nileses filed papers to adopt him. This was in the early 1940s, and state officials were not thrilled with the notion of a black couple adopting a white child. One day, a pair of suits arrived to remove Chuck and take him away from Mr. and Mrs. Niles. He hid under the bed as the state officers tried to capture him. This was a seven-year-old boy, blond and blue-eyed, clutching the bedpost, hollering, "I'm colored; I'm colored!"

Years later, driving with Ossie Davis and Ruby Dee to an auditorium where they were performing a benefit for Fortune Society, I said to them, "Do you want to hear a story that would be a terrific movie for you two to make?" When I got to the part with Chuck hollering, "I'm colored; I'm colored!" Ruby Dee, in tears, said, "Stop. Stop." Ossie laughed at her tearful reaction, but I could see he was clearly moved.

Chuck recently reminded me that his first movie, *Gordon's War*, was directed by Ossie Davis.

The film business began at the Fortune office. A fine character actor, Mike Kellin, was hanging out with us, impressed by our goals, and he talked to Chuck about acting classes. Chuck has a real New York accent, and some theater folks suggested he take speech lessons. I balked at that, telling him he would never sound like Laurence Olivier, and that if he was serious about acting, he was a great type— don't mess with it.

Later he became friendly with actors Joe Bologna and Renée Taylor, a successful, married acting and playwriting team. They were very supportive of Chuck, whose first play in New York was Ronald Ribman's *The Poison Tree*. After that, he auditioned for and won a role in Miguel Piñero's riveting prison drama *Short Eyes,* which was being presented at the Vivian Beaumont Theater in Lincoln Center. Ironically, he was cast as a prison guard. His new career was underway.

He did some work with an acting troupe, Theater for the Forgotten, which went into jails and prisons. The film and TV roles were coming in, and when Joe Bologna and Renée Taylor moved to California, Chuck went with them. For many years he lived in their beautiful Beverly Hills home, which had once been the residence of Shirley Temple.

I stayed at the house for a week when I came to the West Coast to appear on *The Mike Douglas Show*. Mike Farrell of *M*A*S*H* was cohosting for a week; he was told that he could have one guest of his choice, and he selected me. Farrell had visited Fortune on a trip to New York and has been a staunch supporter and friend ever since.

When I called Chuck and told him I was coming to LA, he said that Joe and Renée insisted I stay with them. Mike Farrell did a *M*A*S*H* fundraising party for Fortune while I was out there, and

Chuck resumed his role as a Fortune speaker at the event. When I told Linda Lavin that I would be visiting LA and invited her to the *M*A*S*H* party, she said, "Well, we'll have an *Alice* party." Linda was then at the top of her game, starring for nine years on the popular TV show in which she had the leading role. Indeed, on the evening after *M*A*S*H* celebrated the Fortune Society, the cast of *Alice* were our hosts.

Chuck never stopped trying to find his roots. Through the Internet, he discovered he had a half brother. His birth mother had married and had a son, Ben, who now lived in Connecticut. He told me he was coming east to meet his brother, but he had fears of meeting family and asked if I would be around if he needed a shoulder to lean on.

I didn't hear from him for days. Finally, an excited call came. He was ecstatic. He had been with his brother's family for a week and felt reborn. His brother had arranged for Chuck to visit his birth mother, now an older woman living in Westchester County. That had been an emotional reunion, with his mother begging forgiveness. Chuck was generous and told her she could do only what she was capable of at the time when he was born.

He was anxious for me to meet his brother, Ben, and they drove down to New York City, where we had a memorable afternoon visit. The following year, Chuck's mother was dying, and he flew back east and stayed with her as her caretaker during her final days. This was an enormous irony, the abandoned child at the bedside of the adult, the lost and dying birth mother.

Chuck still lives in Los Angeles, and we talk on the phone a few times a year. I'm always urging him to come back for a visit. He has told me that he has a comfortable, older man's existence. He watches old movies and is very involved with his church. He assured me he has a strong support system of friends.

He was always Billy Budd to me, a genuine innocent at heart, whose painful childhood and history of imprisonment couldn't undo his continued searching for something better in his life. After two dozen years in prison, he emerged devoid of guile. I am happy his older years are serene in contrast to his Oliver Twist like childhood. He has found self-acceptance. And I have been blessed with a friend for a lifetime.

Fran O'Leary was petite, a little over five feet tall, fiery and vulnerable at once. When the movie *Klute* was released in 1971, with an Oscar-winning performance by Jane Fonda, everyone who saw it said that she was portraying Fran, who had that look—defiant, yet with the need to be accepted at the same time. She looked like the girl next door but at times had a mouth. I once asked her if she was auditioning for a role in *On the Waterfront*.

She learned of the Fortune Society from an article in the *Daily News*. As she later told us, "I was looking for a crime partner. What better place to find one. I was working on some scheme, and when I read the article, I thought, 'Here's a bunch of ex-cons pulling a fast one on the squares.' Call them and see who bites. When I called, David answered the phone. When I told him I was living in Ridgefield Park [New Jersey], he told me they were speaking the next night in nearby Ridgewood at a church, and I should meet them there. So I showed up early and met Kenny, Mel, and David, but when the church folks started pouring in, I went for the exit. Mel Rivers came after me and asked, 'What's wrong?' I told him that I hated those people, and he said, 'Maybe you're just afraid of them.' So I stayed around for the program and liked what they were saying and afterwards went out for coffee with the guys. They were serious about what they were doing, so I thought that I'd stick around and see what they were really about."

Fran became our first female to speak in public. We learned she had had a suburban upbringing, eleven years of Catholic school, before she ran away and came to Manhattan. With four years of Latin and lots of church indoctrination, she didn't have much of a résumé. She was quickly hired by a dance hall. She had the requirements: she was cute and young. Fran had arrived in time for the final days of an institution that is only remembered by Rodgers and Hart's song "Ten Cents a Dance."

After a few weeks as a dance-hall girl, Fran learned there was another way to make money, much more money, and she became a call girl. The roller coaster life had begun, and she was still a teenager. A few arrests and time on Rikers Island were the result. There she learned more tricks of the trade and was promised fewer risks. She never asked why, if it was so easy, were her teachers in jail with her? She became more sophisticated, learning how to move paper—credit cards and forgery. She left New York for California, and her new trade landed her in California State Prison for Women. When she was released, she returned to New Jersey, and that was when she hooked up with the Fortune Society. She was still deciding which way her life was to go. She still distrusted the "square" world but was starting to listen.

My aunt Ruth and uncle Harold—the Ebys of Haworth, New Jersey—were early and avid supporters of the Fortune Society. On holidays, their home was open to men and women who had no families with whom to share Thanksgiving or Christmas or Easter or Arbor Day. Those holiday feasts often found at least a dozen guys having potluck with the Ebys and their four children (Laura, Jeff, Jennifer, and Rob). The Eby kids grew up with ex-cons as friends and teachers.

In Ruth Eby, Fran found a "civilian" she could befriend. Her fear and suspicion were starting to thaw.

As the first woman to join our speaking team, Fran was a natural—funny, quick, and cleverly channeling her anger. Fran was also candid about her experiences as a prostitute, and for many students and churchgoers, she was the first woman they had ever met or heard talking about that overglamorized profession. She quickly took the glamour out of the life. Of course, there were always the lascivious or embarrassing questions, which she learned to handle with finesse. I liked it when she or Mel Rivers would say, "Would you mind repeating that loaded question?"

Before she went to jail, Fran had given birth to two girls from different fathers. Kathy and Patti had been raised by Fran's grandmother, but when she became involved with Fortune, she reclaimed them. She became a working mother. Her job was as a counselor for teenagers at the Fortune Society, mostly gang kids who arrived with weapons and hostility. She was terrific and tough with them, and they learned to love and respect Fran. She was particularly effective with the teenage girls, most of whom were still working on the streets.

When we were asked to testify before Congressional committees or state legislatures, Fran had a great impact. We both loved the political world, and she taught me a great deal. Once, after we made a presentation before the Democratic National Committee in Washington, D.C., we attended a reception. Fran pulled me aside and said that one of the guys was hitting on her. I told her she must be mistaken. He was the attorney general for a large midwestern state. She pulled me over to him, and he whispered, "For someone who has been through so much, you have come out so charming and beautiful." I nearly barfed. She said, "See. They never believe you have closed away your past. They're all johns."

With our encouragement, Fran returned to school, taking college courses at night. After she graduated, she went for a master's degree in human resources. She had decided it was time to move on. It was becoming tougher for her to speak before square audiences. She had become one of them. She reflected, "When the guys rap, people say, 'They had a tough time, and look how they have put themselves together.' But with a woman, it is once a tramp, always a tramp." I told her that she was only hearing a handful of negatives, which would always be there, and that in fact she was a role model and inspiration for many young women.

Her great insights on youthful alienation prompted an invitation to speak at a conference in Hawaii. The end result was that she was offered a job there at a clinic working with troubled girls. Fran ended up in paradise, twenty years after first arriving at Fortune. She married a wonderful man, and she and John adopted an infant who had been abandoned by his teenage mother. Fran, John, and young Dylan come to New York every couple of years and always visit Fortune.

Fran is a most remarkable woman: she is never dull and never forgets where she came from, but she has moved light years from her troubled past. She is one of many reminders that the system under-estimates the capacity for people to reinvent themselves.

Every September 13, Fran calls me from Hawaii to remind me it is the anniversary of the Attica slaughter, an experience we shared together, listening to the radio on that ominous day, hearing the state troops firing and the helicopters patrolling overhead. Fran was with us in all the postmortems of Attica.

Stanley Eldridge was a poet...to the depths of his soul.

He was a teenager when I first met him in the late sixties, an inmate at the Adolescent Remand Shelter on Rikers Island. Beverly Rich and Akila Couloumbis, two actors who had formed the Theater for the Forgotten, told me of this young man who was in their performance workshop. They had suggested Stanley send me examples of his poetry to be considered for publication in the *Fortune News*, our monthly paper. We began a correspondence. His poems impressed me. In his letters he wrote of the literature that had influenced him, and he made many detailed observations about prison life. It was clear this was a fertile, curious, and original mind.

I was invited by Beverly and Akila to attend the Christmas variety show on Rikers Island, in which some members of their workshop would be participating.

Prison talent shows, particularly at city jails, are depressing. Not that some outstanding talent is not revealed, but the false gaiety seems to accentuate the loneliness and despair that permeates the walls. At that first show I saw, there were sissies in full drag, teasing and undulating. The macho teen boys in the audience were howling and crotch-grabbing. The singing and dancing revealed a wide range of talents.

Suddenly a singing group moved to center stage, and a young man with a full Afro hairdo transcended the surroundings. Onstage, expressing joy through song, he conveyed the impression of pure freedom. His eyes and feet were both dancing. He alone seemed outside the barbed wire. There was a spirit onstage. That was my first view of Stanley Eldridge, for whom creativity was salvation.

After the show, we were introduced. We had become acquainted through the mail, but this was man-to-man. He was exhilarated by his performance, an opportunity to let loose, to find expression.

Beneath the momentary reflections, Stanley was intense and revealed a great sadness. Life had not been his friend. He had been a runaway child, and by the time he was ten, New York authorities were already condemning him to confinement. Before his tenth birthday they could not find a bed in a training school or foster home, so he was placed in a hospital for mentally and emotionally challenged adults in Rockland County. To escape harassment and sexual abuse, he hid out in the library. It was there that books became his refuge.

By the time we met, Stanley had been encaged in a variety of institutions for littering, vagrancy, and petty thefts (to feed himself).

After one session with the drama workshop, Stanley wrote a poem and sent it to me.

Visitors

There are people around and
they are free
          you can tell the way they
influence minutes
               and cross their legs
                    no secrets there
they seem to imply...
the birds were silent
               the walls were limp with opportunity
touch them, not cold
After the captain said they were crazy
I told him about Rockland
And he said I'd be president
               this all allowed a schedule
in which these people smiled
And gave us their first names to use

               they didn't set the schedule,
neither did I
               but looking at them I can
see for miles
               a new concept
replacing tomorrow with
               poignant freckles.

At that initial meeting on Rikers Island, we talked about books, a comfortable starting point. He informed me that the library on Rikers was pitiful. I volunteered to send him some paperbacks, and his eyes lit up. He asked, "Could I read something by Joyce Carol Oates?" That was not the usual book of choice for adolescents in jail.

At Fortune, we began to compile Stanley's poems. Some of my theater friends read them, and a few agreed to use them when they did special attractions. Eli Wallach and Anne Jackson included poems by Stanley in their two-person evenings, Ossie Davis and Ruby Dee performed an entire program of his work, and George C. Scott read a couple of Eldridge poems when he appeared on various interview shows, including *The Tonight Show*, hosted by Johnny Carson.

We decided to publish a book of Stanley's poetry. After print costs, all the money would go to Stanley when he was released from Rikers.

After some eighteen months on the Rock, Stanley came directly to the Fortune Society, and we presented him a royalty check of nearly $2,000, which permitted him to have less pressure upon reentry into society than most homeless teenagers.

Fortune had opened a store in Greenwich Village, selling goods made by inmates and the formerly incarcerated and only employing those who had spent time in prison. We were demonstrating that formerly incarcerated persons were capable salesmen. When corrections departments in several states put a nix on our selling prisoner art and pottery, the store was not able to fulfill its dream mission, but for two years we were a visible presence in the Village.

Stanley's first job was at the counter of our store. Chuck Bergansky, George Freeman, Charlie Starkins, and Mike McCaughlin were some of the other men there who greeted the public and forced them to reconsider their stereotypes.

We had a built-in security system at the store. One afternoon, I arrived there with George Freeman, and we learned that some expensive bags and other items had been shoplifted. One of the guys, furious, yelled, "Who steals from us? The outrage!"

"Not to worry," advised George, who left the store and returned a half hour later with all of the purloined booty.

"Explain it," I demanded.

George, smile on his face, said, "Quite simple, Watson. Most thefts like these are done by junkies who need fast money for a fix."

"Go on," I insisted.

The Cheshire grin even wider, he continued, "I went to the local fence and assured him it was not a good plan for his contacts to steal from the Fortune Store."

More he would not reveal, other than that he always checked an area for the fence. It was an instinct from his past life that served him well. "You never know when you might need it," he said with smug finality.

Stanley fit in well at the store. He was the youngest by decades, and everyone took a proprietary interest and concern. His charm and handsome presence meant that most of the high school and college girls who came to the store developed a crush on him. He was our Romeo.

There was one discordant note: outside of jail, Stanley stopped writing. Poetry had been his prison passion, his distraction from the oppressive walls.

Over the years, we stayed in contact, until he was missing, unseen, out of the picture. In early 2000, I heard from him again. He informed me he had been living on an island in the Caribbean for a dozen years. Now back in the metropolitan area, he was residing and working in Jersey City. He had seriously injured his back on the job. With no medical coverage, he had been unable to get the care he deserved.

We republished his book of poetry and presented some readings, giving Stanley survival money, though not nearly enough for a decent life, which he deserved.

He was in great physical pain but complained little. We saw each other infrequently because of geography, but we stayed in phone contact. I was continuously astonished by his insights, his keen intellect, and his humanity. Where had it come from? Growing up, he'd been offered nothing, had had none of the advantages that every American child should be offered. Yet, he was one of the most original and creative minds I have met.

How did Stanley transcend the thorns of modern society? I became sad and angry that this most decent of human beings had such a difficult life. It is because of Stanley and the thousands of men and women who, like him, have been denied an opportunity to vie for the American dream that my commitment to Fortune Society continues. I become more indignant each passing year as I clearly see the inequities that result in denied lives.

My cousin Jeff one day said to me, after hearing me orate about some social injustice: "Most people become more conservative as they get older; you get worse."

"Not worse, Jeff," I said. "Wiser."

Stanley Eldridge has always motivated me. His poetry moved me; his persona inspires me.

Stanley died in 2010 after a brief illness. He was fifty-eight years old.

Barbara Allen did her time on the outside.

That's what she wrote to me after seeing the first David Susskind TV show, in 1968. In that initial letter, she said that she had two little girls, Brenda and Tina, and that her husband was in a state prison. She was a schoolteacher, but her life had been turned upside down.

Barbara grew up in Long Island with a loving and supportive family. Prison was not an experience that touched their comfortable suburban existence. That all changed when Barbara Pugach met Gene Allen, a handsome midwesterner who could pour on the charm. After they were married, layers of Gene's childhood turmoil surfaced. He was the son of an abusive, alcoholic father.

When their daughters were born, there was added pressure on Gene: responsibilities as a husband and father. He began drinking, emulating his feared father, who by that time had come east, continuing the father-son conflict.

Because Gene was abusive when drunk, Barbara took the girls and moved in with her parents. One night, drunk and ranting, he called Barbara and announced that he had just shot his father. He put the phone to his father's mouth, and she listened to her father-in-law gasping. Those were his last sounds.

Gene was given a sentence of two and a half to seven years for manslaughter. Barbara then entered the world of "prison wife": meetings with lawyers and indignant and humiliating visits to the Nassau County Jail, where Gene was being held awaiting trial. She began navigating the role of a mother who was not a widow or divorcée, but married to a man who was behind prison walls.

The Fortune Society was Barbara's lifesaver. She attended a speaking engagement we scheduled in Long Island and quickly connected with us. Dinner at her house became a part of our lives. Kenny and Mel became Uncle Kenny and Uncle Mel to Barbara's two tots. She and her daughters became friendly with Kenny's wife, Lorraine. We all became involved with one another's families, and Barbara was the catalyst, bringing the notion of "family" to a group of ex-cons and a Broadway press agent.

When other wives and mothers called Fortune—and there were many—we put them in touch with Barbara. She had formed a network with family members she met at the county jails and later at Sing Sing and Green Haven while visiting her husband.

Green Haven was a maximum-security prison, two hours north of Manhattan. They limited family visits to finger touching through meshed-wire screens. Gene wanted to see his daughters grow, but Barbara didn't want her kids to see their father in such a dehumanizing setting. Her letters to elected officials and corrections authorities began. She joined us at speaking engagements and radio interviews, informing the public of indignities confronted by wives visiting their husbands in prison. She was making corrections defensive about barbaric visiting conditions.

The meshed wire came down. Barbara could bring Brenda and Tina to visit their father, and she had a sense of accomplishment. She realized that change could happen, slowly and in the face of opposition. Change sometimes needs a push.

Through her networking with mothers, wives, sisters, grandmothers, and a few—very few—fathers, Barbara formed Prison Families Anonymous. Fortune Society had given birth to an important new group. Family members would form carpools for visits to various prisons, an arrangement that cut expenses but had a more vital ingredient. Returning from a prison visit by yourself is a depressing experience. Sharing that time with others proved a relief. Barbara was also building a network of informed, involved citizens. She was making trips to Albany. Legislators had to listen when women voters talked about the fabric of family life.

When Gene was paroled after his first trip before the parole board, Kenny Jackson quipped that they let him go in hopes it would shut up Barbara.

They underestimated her.

And Barbara underestimated how complex it would be when her husband returned to his family after five years of prison. What she and her daughters endured became a new phase for Prison Families Anonymous.

In the early days of PFA, the women were providing moral support for one another and for their loved ones behind bars. One thing they noted was that visiting day at most male prisons was filled with women, mothers, wives, girlfriends, aunts, grandmothers, sisters, and a small number of male visitors—usually fathers. At women's prisons, the story was the same: all women in the visiting room. Few husbands or boyfriends remained in the lives of women behind bars.

When Gene returned to Barbara, she discovered that the punishment and the prison time had done nothing to change him. Barbara had voiced concern to the court and to elected officials that her husband would be coming back to her and her daughters. Where was the help for this troubled man?

Gene immediately alienated his daughters when he reentered the Allen home. The girls were then eight and seven years old. He assumed a macho stance in the household, proclaiming rules by which "his" house would be run. The three females had struggled for five years without him and had conquered adversity. With support from the guys at Fortune, Kenny, Mel, and me, the Allen females were quite self-contained. Gene had become an intrusion.

Reentry wasn't all it was cracked up to be. Gene resumed drinking, set fire to the house, and violated parole and returned to prison. The Allen family resumed normalcy.

Barbara used her own experience to alert other wives about the complexities of returning mates. She also pressured politicians and criminal-justice policy makers to explore the fact that men and women in prison were not being prepared to transition to a free society. Most imprisoned men and women are not aware of their social handicaps. And in frustration they often act out.

Common sense and reasonable planning could cut the recidivist rate. More than one parolee has expressed the notion that life was easier, with less pressure, behind the walls. That's difficult for most civilians to grasp, but anyone who has done time recognizes this paradox.

The prison industry is big business and has a fiscal investment in recidivism. But victims of crime on the street deserve the same consideration that is offered contractors who sell goods to prisons and fight prison closings.

The public is saturated with crime and prison tales on television. Programs like *Oz* and *Lockup* are prime examples. Violence and rage make for good dramatic television and high ratings. No one films a prisoner struggling privately with his inner demons.

Of course, the prison population contains some violent and angry men. Many are mentally disturbed and should be in other facilities. But there is another group, the majority, who want something else in their lives. They are struggling with survival in an alien environment. I still go into state and city prisons, talking with groups of men and women, who listen attentively when I tell them about Fortune Society, and they bombard me with multiple questions.

Bob Brown, who had grown up in foster homes and child institutions, once told me that when he walked the yard during his twenty-eight years in prison, he realized that most men had fantasies of the American dream: a family, a home, a job, respectability. The recidivists would tell him that no one outside had given them a chance. Bob added, "Of course, nothing inside prepares you for coming out. In prison, you are never confronted with the behavior that led you there. In fact, that negative behavior that put you behind the walls is the negative behavior needed for survival."

Bob's summation was always that prison is geared to make you return. When you get ready to hit the street, there is always a hack advising you, "See you back here in six months."

The public only sees or hears the official version. As Kenny Jackson often said, "Those walls were built not only to keep us in but also to keep you out." Fortune Society has been strong and threatening because it delves deeper into the inadequacies and failures of the expensive prison systems.

Barbara Allen started off as a woman who wrote to the Fortune Society seeking understanding about her family's dilemma. She has become a national voice and leader for families who, as Barbara put it, are doing their time on the outside. She keeps asking questions and doesn't stop until answers are provided.

Through the years, she and I have remained close. Gene was released from prison a second time with little evidence of a changed life plan. Barbara divorced Gene but remained married to PFA.

When Gene was diagnosed with cancer, Barbara, always an angel, was his caretaker in his final months.

These days, Barbara and I enjoy dinners, movies, and shared vacations. It is a comfortable and close friendship for two seniors. The heart of our relationship is an unbridled rage, which we both possess—a rage at the prison system and its monumental inadequacy. We both believe in and have been witness to people who have been written off by society and have revealed amazing talents and skills and human warmth.

NINE

Prisons

Entering jails and prisons became routine for me. *Routine* might not be the appropriate word, because it implies the absence of emotion. In fact, although I have entered penal institutions hundreds of times in every part of the country and in several foreign nations, I am always overcome with the same sense of despair. I have never altered my initial response that a prison is an exercise in institutional futility. It is a warped concept. Prisons don't work. They are counterproductive to society's best interests, but when people are constantly exposed to vivid descriptions of the most horrendous crimes and acts of violence, they view prisons—out of sight—as a justifiable solution. Kenny Jackson often suggested that if three out of four people released from hospitals returned still ill from a disease, hospitals would be put out of business. The public is rarely reminded that more than 98 percent of the people locked up will be returning to society. How prisoners endure the violent prison subculture will affect their ability to adjust when they hit the streets.

My first reaction to the play *Fortune and Men's Eyes* remains with me. Some of the drama critics only saw the story of sexual violence in prison. Like much of society, they didn't recognize that they were witness to the damage of incarceration, which smothers the spirit and sentences society to pick up the prisons' failures.

The press is greatly at fault for its endless fascination with crime and violence, often romanticizing the ingredients it claims to find objectionable, yet rarely responding to the incredible accomplishments of men and women who have survived and moved on to live inspiring lives in spite of prison and parole. No matter what former prisoners achieve, when most reporters write about them, they define them by their conviction.

My friend Sam Rivera, who has turned his back on his past street life and prison experience and is now a counselor and administrator for a self-help program, tersely and eloquently responds to such definitions, stating, "The crime is what I did. It is not who I am."

The best assessments of prison failures have often been made by people working in the system. I recall, in the early days of Fortune, meeting a visiting criminal-justice administrator from Israel, Yonah Cohen. Cohen toured our prisons and jails and then stated that if a young man is acting out in an antisocial manner, society would be better off if he were never caught, because the odds are that he will burn himself out shortly. But if we arrest, convict, and sentence him and he does even a few months in a penal institution, we might well have a problem with him for the rest of his life.

I have been in penal institutions to teach, to inspect, to visit individuals, to sponsor plays and variety shows, and to observe and negotiate during uprisings against oppressive conditions. Attica was only one story. Within a year after that historic New York riot, there was an inmate takeover at the Rahway State Prison in New Jersey, where I had been teaching. When I heard the riot report on the radio, I drove there to see if there was a role I could play, having learned much when I was part of the Attica Observers Committee.

Correction and elected officials were scurrying around outside the wall in Rahway, making predictable statements to the assembled TV crews. I ran into an old friend, Nathan "Bubby" Heard, who had grown up on the streets of Newark, done time in Rahway and Trenton, and authored an impressive novel, *Howard Street*. Nathan and I had appeared on a number of panels and radio programs together and had established a friendship. We stood there watching the unproductive officials and volunteered to enter the besieged institution to act as a go-between team for the prisoners and the officials on the outside. Nathan had great credibility since he had done time with many of the guys on the inside, and I was known for the class I had been teaching there and the variety shows I had produced for the entire population. Many of the cast members from the Broadway production of *Hair* had performed at Rahway, and those were rousing experiences.

A prison during a riot is much more complicated than press coverage implies. You don't know how much hooch and drugs may have been consumed. Many men do their time getting high; it's a way of escaping the doldrums, abuse, and indignities. It's tough to reason with people when they are stoned, and many protestors get their courage from being blotto. Nathan and I agreed that we might be able to meet the inmates halfway and help negotiate their demands. We approached an official and made our offer. State officials rushed back and forth, checking with one another about this unlikely duo going inside. Calls were reaching as high as the governor's office, but we were given our answer with two words: "No grandstanding." Nathan and I stood around for a while and realized our presence would not be utilized. The state of New Jersey didn't like the idea of a former inmate and a prisoners' rights advocate offering possible solutions.

There was also a riot at Sing Sing that year, and I received two phone calls. The first was from attorney Bill Kunstler asking if I would travel to Ossining if needed. The second was from my mother, who asked, "Can they do this one without you?" My mother was not a big fan of my participation in negotiations during a prison riot. Kunstler's offer to enter Sing Sing with an outside team was denied, not surprisingly, by Governor Rockefeller's office.

There was also a violent uprising in New Mexico, one with a brutal ending: many prisoners dead and the institution left in shambles. A few weeks after, I was brought to Santa Fe to visit the state prison where many of the surviving inmates were in solitary confinement. Most of the men there knew of the Fortune Society and my involvement at Attica.

I was ushered into solitary confinement and permitted to talk with a few men through small slits in the doors of their cells. It was a fruitless effort. I offered words of encouragement—an exercise in futility, as I was witness to their bleak surroundings. Most of the men in New Mexico had been physically battered, and I was startled to see how young they were. All I kept thinking was that most of them would return to the streets someday, and I didn't want to be around to pick up the pieces, the repayment for what was done to them in the name of justice, which was really vengeance. Prison was where they had been sent for punishment, separated from society. But the deal is soured when punishment is added each and every day. The inner demons are nestled within each prisoner; his alienation deepens while locked up, and the man is ready to explode when released.

Rahway, in New Jersey, is a maximum-security prison. Initially— long before the riot—I was invited there to appear on an inmate radio program. Having seen the Susskind TV show, the radio panel requested a spokesman from Fortune to appear as a guest. The prison authorities eliminated anyone with a record, so that left me. I was forewarned by prison officials that we could not discuss prison policy, politics, sex, religion, or any controversial social issue. That left the weather and old movies. In fact, when I got there we talked about everything that was taboo. Apparently, the prison officials didn't listen to the program, because I was invited back again and again.

It was at Rahway where I first met George Freeman and Walter Strauss, both of whom came to Fortune upon their release. George, originally from Seattle, had been caught up in some self-destructive antics. With two other guys, he robbed a motel on the Jersey side of the Holland Tunnel. They sped away in a car into the tunnel and were greeted by a galaxy of cop cars when they reached the New York side. George did four years in Rahway and, once released, never looked back. He worked at the Fortune Store, and later became a time buyer for WOR Radio, where he was an outstanding salesman. Subsequently, he opened his own discotheque, which had a run for a few years before he moved back to Seattle. George has been a successful businessman there for decades and visits New York City annually. He returns to Fortune with great pride. He called me on his sixtieth birthday and said that, looking back at his life, he realized he had met the Fortune Society when he was at a crossroads. He simply said, "Thank you."

When I initially encountered Walter Strauss, he was in the middle of his second state-prison bid. He was, understandably, an angry young man. His first term in prison had been drug-related, and he was guilty. The second trip had been a setup, an entrapment. It's an old story. A guy busted for selling drugs makes a deal with the cops and sets up other people so he can beat his rap. Walter had begun to rearrange his life, but he was asked to bring a bag of marijuana to a party as a favor for the agent provocateur. His arrest and conviction were what the cops and the prosecutor sought, and Walter was sentenced to ten years. He continued to fight the inequity of his case, and when he went to court in Bergen County, New Jersey, on an appeal, I testified on the unfairness of the sentence, and vowed that Fortune Society would guide him as he returned to society. The judge reduced his sentence, and Walter was ready to be released in a few months. He had become a self-taught jailhouse lawyer.

We greeted Walter when he hit the streets. His goal was to resume his education. He received his GED and began to attend college at night. Working part-time at Fortune, he completed college and then announced that he was applying to law school. I told him it was a long shot; because of his conviction, he might not be admitted to the bar. He said he was confident and would face that challenge when the time came. So Walter attended law school at Rutgers University, graduated, and then challenged the ethics committee of the New York State Bar Association. He became an attorney, representing tenants in the housing courts. He was our alumnus, the lawyer.

In 1994, Walter invited me to visit the courthouse. "What's up? I asked. "Just come and see," I was told. Walter was being sworn in as a judge, the first former inmate in New York State history to be so tapped. It was a historic and moving ceremony in which he told the packed auditorium that he had once been on the other side of the law. Many of his colleagues knew little of his past. He also stated that he hoped I was in the house, because I had been there for him when he was at his lowest. His wife, Luna, and beautiful baby girl were there also, along with the alerted New York press, which gave major coverage to Walter's great achievement. I was sitting in the back of the room and couldn't hold back the tears.

Walter was a New York State housing judge for over a decade before moving his family to Florida. He assumed he would practice law when he hit the Sunshine State, but he ran into some archaic laws. Even his right to vote was questioned. Walter challenged Florida's restrictive laws and is now a practicing attorney in Broward County. He and I frequently reunite in both Florida and New York.

When Walter visits the Big Apple, we invite him to talk to staff members and recently released prisoners at the Fortune Society. The impact he has is impressive. When former prisoners listen to him, the room is electric. His story is their story—until he relates his entering law school and becoming an attorney and, subsequently, a judge. Walter represents hope and possibilities. His audience at Fortune always has a multitude of questions and comments, and long applause. One woman, Martha Rivera, shouted to Walter, "I have a new hero!" I agree with her. He is one of my heroes.

My visits to the Rahway penitentiary, beginning with my appearances on the inmate radio program, evolved. The prison officials had placed a moratorium on the number of visits afforded me, so—using their prison-acquired inmate wiles—several of the men created a class, which enabled me to return weekly as a teacher. Most of the guys in the class were doing heavy time. Several had been released from Trenton State Prison's death row after the U.S. Supreme Court ruling in 1972 that declared the death penalty to be unconstitutional.

Tommy Trantino was the catalyst of the group, the man who influenced many of the students to attend the Saturday morning seminars. I had first met Tommy when he was at Trenton, a century-old fortress that was a betrayal of any thoughts of rehabilitation. Trenton was where Danny Hogan was murdered.

Tommy and I had been permitted to talk on a telephone in a visiting room, barely able to see each other through the decades-old, tobacco-stained glass—prison's traditional way of distancing prisoners from people in the free world. My correspondence with Tommy had begun while he was still on death row. Even through the glass, his energy and charisma were in evidence. There was little in his demeanor that would suggest his violent past. He was a contradiction: an artist and published author, and, a man convicted of a double homicide.

Tommy had made peace with his drug-filled, chaotic youth. In numerous speaking engagements before groups at Fortune, he would reveal that he'd had, for lack of a better word, "an epiphany" on death row. He vowed that if he were to live, his life would be without drugs, alcohol, and violence. He doesn't recall the night of the killings, having blacked out on drugs in a bar, celebrating with other members of his crime crew after a successful "score" in Manhattan.

Tommy was public enemy number one to the police and the press. The state of New Jersey refused to grant him parole, and it took a New Jersey Supreme Court ruling to release him. When Tommy was finally released after serving thirty-eight years, the *Daily News* editorialized that he should be executed on second base in Yankee Stadium before a full house. Obviously, the *News* was so opposed to violence that they campaigned to make it a Roman spectacle.

Parole placed Tommy in a community residence in Camden. Ed Martone of the New Jersey Association on Correction and I visited Tommy in that depleted town.

Long before that, back in Rahway, I would arrive on Saturday morning and read the class a page-one story from the morning edition of the *New York Times*. I would then ask for the students' reactions to the article. At first the men balked, suggesting that this was not a class. As the teacher, they argued, I should give them my interpretation of the story. I insisted that their opinion of the news event was as valid as mine.

Tommy then challenged me: "Why are you the teacher?"

My answer satisfied them: "I'm the teacher because I'm getting you to think about what is happening in the world, and your personal assessment of a story demands that you think." In fact, that was my goal. Most of the guys admitted that they were school dropouts and had hated and been intimidated by the classroom and the teachers, who tortured and embarrassed them. If I could create a classroom environment that was nurturing, they might be motivated to take advantage of some of the more traditional and formal classes being offered in the institution, and even aspire to a GED or a college course that might be available. If my class accomplished anything, it was that a few of the men, on their own, did go on to explore other educational opportunities. A few even contacted me upon their release from prison.

There was an intense man, Rubin, always sitting in the front row. Cocoa-skinned, bald, and with glasses, he listened intently but rarely spoke. In the many classes I have taught, I have always looked for that eager face, someone who is soaking up everything even if they are not asking questions. Rubin was particularly responsive when guests would join me. Judge Bruce Wright visited several times—

My parents, Leon and
Leonore Rothenberg.

When one of the residents at the Castle spotted this picture, he suggested that it
might have been taken by the first camera.

Top: Oscar winner Joan Fontaine and I spent two hectic weeks together at Lakewood Theatre in Skowhegan, Maine—but a month later, in New York City, she didn't have the vaguest idea who I was.

Right: When I went to work for Alexander H. Cohen, my first show was a smash hit. The four funny and original talents of *Beyond the Fringe*: Peter Cook, Alan Bennett, Jonathan Miller, and Dudley Moore. *(Photofest)*

During the sixties, the gifted actress Joan Hackett was my companion at many Broadway openings.

That's me peeking over Elizabeth Taylor's shoulder, as she and Richard Burton exit the theater after a performance of *Hamlet*, in which Richard starred. I was Elizabeth's date at the opening and was not the first, or last, man to be dazzled by her beauty.

John Herbert's prison drama *Fortune and Men's Eyes* reshaped my life. The brilliant original cast: Terry Kiser, Vic Arnold, Bob Christian, and Bill Moor.

Me and Eddie Morris after he was released from a New York prison in the late sixties. I learned that Eddie became a student of the poet Lord Byron while in solitary as a teenager. He told me, "Lord Byron saved my sanity and my life."

Mel Rivers and Bob Brown, two early counselors at Fortune Society, both of whom taught me more about criminology than I could have ever learned in a college class. They were my teachers and my friends.

Four guys representing Fortune Society in the early days ... outside a New Jersey town where we would be speaking at the chamber of commerce, after the criminals registered. Kenny Jackson, Charlie McGregor, Joe Senatore, and Mel Rivers.

Top: Barbara Allen wrote to the Fortune Society after her husband went to prison, proclaiming, "I'm doing my time on the outside." Barbara has become a national spokesperson for families of the incarcerated ... and our friendship has increased through the decades with a shared passion about the inanities in the criminal justice system.

Right: Teenager Harry LaCroix, for whom I became legal guardian, which kept him out of Spofford, a prison for children.

Attica prison yard during the 1971 uprising, an event that intensified my commitment to fight the archaic prison system in America *(Photofest)*

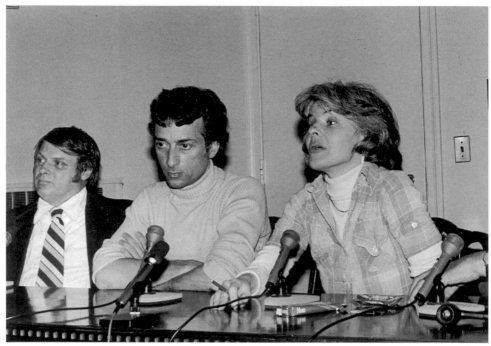

At a criminal-justice conference with a man I admired greatly, Jerry Miller, who was the innovative commissioner of the Massachusetts Department of Youth Services . . . and with Fran O'Leary, fiery speaker for the Fortune Society.

Former NFL halfback Dave Kopay, a friend for more than thirty years. We shared a love of sports and a new awareness about ourselves.

canceling his treasured Saturday morning tennis games to travel with me to Rahway—and fascinated the students with his candor about the courts and racism in our society.

One day after class, Rubin asked if I could call his agent. "Rubin, why do you have an agent?" That seemed an appropriate question to pose to a man situated in a prison. "Of course I will call your agent, but what kind of an agent is this?"

He told me he was writing a book, and I figured, why not? Everyone in here has a story to tell. I asked him to write down her name, address, and phone number, and by the way, "Rubin, what is your full name?"

He said, "Rubin Carter."

I looked at him for a long minute and asked, "Are you the Rubin Carter called Hurricane?"

"That's me."

I never asked last names in the class, nor did I take attendance. It was all voluntary. I had had no idea that the attentive young man in front of me was a former boxing champion.

In 1999, when the movie *Hurricane* was released, with Denzel Washington giving a deeply moving and memorable performance in the title role, I had heard that Rubin was going to be in New York City for some promotional interviews for the film. He had long since been cleared and released after several courtroom dramas. I called the film's publicity department and introduced myself as a host of a weekly radio program on WBAI in Manhattan. I requested an interview with Carter. "Of course," the condescending and impatient publicist said, "everyone does. We have him scheduled with PBS, *GMA*"—and some other initials were thrown in.

I listened respectfully and said, "Rubin and I go way back. Why not just ask him and let him make the decision?" The impatient rep conceded to my logic.

Ten minutes later the call came: "Rubin is anxious to appear on your radio program."

He arrived at the studio on Saturday morning looking like a million dollars, in a nifty suit with a professorial look. I told him that I appreciated his joining me, and he said, "David, you were there when no one else was. We can't forget where we came from. By the way, you were taller then."

"No, Rubin, I was standing up and you were sitting down. Now it's the reverse."

He was living in Canada, working with the Innocence Project and delivering inspiring lectures. He and Tommy Trantino had bonded in Rahway, and theirs was a dramatic demonstration that black and white guys could work together to give inmates a united voice. Because both men were charismatic and had respect from other prisoners, they were able to create some alterations in the traditional apartheid of the joint they were in.

Both Rubin and Tommy rejoined the human race in spite of prison's attempt to dehumanize them.

Edgar Smith, another student in my class, held the unenviable record of the longest duration on death row in New Jersey history. His novel, *Brief Against Death*, attracted national attention, and William Buckley, of all people, became his advocate and champion. Edgar's much-publicized release in 1971 was a page-one story. On *Firing Line* that night, Buckley spoke with confidence, but I viewed Edgar on television and said to myself, "The last thing he needs after all this prison time, including a decade and a half on death row, is to be in the public spotlight."

Buckley had brought Edgar into the city and had rented a suite at the luxurious St. Regis Hotel, where, following a celebrity-packed dinner, Edgar was put to bed. When he called me the next morning at nine a.m., I had just arrived at the Fortune Society office. There was a childlike fear in his voice. He had stayed up all night, unable to sleep, a stranger to all of the new technology that was surrounding him. "Can you come and get me?" he asked.

I told him to write down our address, go downstairs, and hail a cab, and I would wait in front of Fortune to receive him. I asked him several times if he felt comfortable doing that: could he make it with a cab? He arrived fifteen minutes later, all ticks and fears. His face showed some relief when he saw me, because I was a connection from his prison time. People coming out of prison need that. The transition is slow.

Change comes slowly, and I have always wondered why prison and parole officials have never figured that out. Edgar Smith that morning was a poster ad for reentry fears. He had been away from society for so long, he was at sea. The St. Regis was not a luxury gift; it was an alien experience for him. He stayed around me for a while, but never really adjusted. Edgar was more comfortable in prison. After he was arrested a few years later, Buckley made public statements distancing himself from Edgar. Edgar, who is now a lifer in a California prison, informed me that before Buckley died, the two men had made some adjustments in their friendship. Buckley apparently recognized his failings in responding to Edgar.

It is apparent in the letters Edgar has written me that he is at home in prison. He has rejected appearances before the California parole board, preferring life behind bars rather than learning how to function in a society in which he has never belonged. Edgar Smith was well taught how to live in prison. It was outside the walls that alienated him.

Playing witness to Edgar Smith's release, amidst television cameras and celebrity status, sensitized me to this unique situation: a celebrated prisoner who hasn't a clue of what civilian life is or could be. It was evident when some of the Attica brothers came to New York City after release, amidst some media attention. Years later, when Joel Steinberg—whose drug-induced abuse of his daughter Lisa and wife Hedda was the stuff of tabloid headlines—was released to the Fortune Academy, nearly three hundred media reps invaded the premises with television helicopters hovering overhead. That is not the essence of productive reentry.

Jack Henry Abbott's harrowing autobiography, *In the Belly of the Beast*, led to almost a duplicate of the Buckley Edgar Smith fiasco. Norman Mailer had made Abbott his pet project and mascot. After years of prisons, highlighted by violent outbursts and decades in solitary confinement, Abbott spent his first day out as a guest, with Mailer, on ABC's *Good Morning America*. The host asked Jack a question, and Mailer answered for him. Jack looked bewildered and lost. He was sweating profusely and conveyed the impression he would rather be anywhere else in the world than being scrutinized on national television.

After seeing the program, I phoned Random House, the publisher of Abbott's book, and suggested to an editor that Jack be given a chance to catch his breath before being put under the spotlight. I informed her about the Fortune Society and suggested that Abbott might best relate to men whose backgrounds were similar to his. It was an invitation. The next day, a representative of Random House reported that Abbott said he was a loner and didn't need groups. I responded, "Of course he's a loner. He was in solitary for a decade." He might not have wanted to hang out at Fortune, I knew, but loners don't need network TV interviews, either.

This prompted me to write an essay about the pitfalls facing men and women being released from prison—a subculture in which all decisions are made for them—into a fast-moving society where a thousand decisions must be confronted each day. Add to that a celebrity status, fifteen minutes of fame, and the potential for confusion multiplies.

My essay was sent to a dozen publications, none of which were interested in the subject.

A few months later, Abbott was on page one, having stabbed a young man in a Lower East Side restaurant. He was back in jail, awaiting trial for murder. On the day after the story appeared, I received several calls asking to see the essay I had written months earlier. It appeared the following week in the *Village Voice*, one of the publications that had originally passed on it. The following is the article the *Village Voice* printed.

Perhaps because I have corresponded with hundreds of convicts in the last 14 years, I did not find the existence of Jack Henry Abbott or his book *In the Belly of the Beast: Letters from Prison* to be extraordinary. And perhaps that is why I was so profoundly moved by its content, concerned deeply for the future of the author, and fascinated by the media response to Abbott and his letters to Norman Mailer.

As for the substance of Abbott's letters: it's all there. Mr. Abbott delves deep into himself, exposing the cause and effects of his life, and while it is his singular experience, it is mirrored in the lives of thousands of state-reared prisoners across the United States. I've heard it before in a thousand different ways, and it is because he is not unique that this clarion call must be heard.

Abbott's story is almost routine at the Fortune Society. He was thrown into foster homes as his family dissolved. He grew up in youth houses, reformatories and prisons. The book-jacket blurb indicated that he was soon to be paroled. In fact, the Utah prison system released him in time to promote the publication of his book. (Amazing how prison bureaucracy can accommodate the pressure of the spotlight.) By his own admission, Abbott is "institutionalized," unfamiliar with even the seemingly insignificant details of life outside, an inevitable condition of state-reared children who end up in adult prisons.

My concern for Jack Abbott does not mean that I see his future as bleak or hopeless. There are too many men and women who have come through Fortune burdened with backgrounds not unlike Abbott's.

Chuck Bergansky, now in his mid-forties, lives in L.A. He came to the Fortune Society when he was 35 years old, with 24 years of incarceration and a childhood of foster homes and orphanages and state homes. Bob Brown was past 40 when he came to Fortune, with more than 30 years in state custody. Sergio Torres was in his mid-thirties when we first met him, and his personal chronology is almost interchangeable with Jack Abbott's. Eddie Morris, now in his mid-forties, started out in foster homes before he hit the youth house and prison circuit. He did more than 24 years before he broke the cycle.

These are only four men, but each of them has been out of prison for 10 years. It wasn't easy for any of them. There was much anger and alienation for them to shed and a great deal to learn. They needed to be with caring, supportive persons. Abbott has a burden that Bergansky, Brown, Torres and Morris did not have. He now has a quasi-celebrity status, not only because of his book, but more significantly, because of his being "linked" to his "discoverer," Norman Mailer.

I have witnessed the celebrity inmates being released. They come out and become involved with the literati. It is overwhelming after a lifetime of negation and nothingness to be the focus of so much attention. It is also a trap for two reasons. The person coming out of prison doesn't have time to confront himself in a non-institutional setting. There are few opportunities to recognize the difficulty of ordering a meal from a menu, operating a TV, or riding on a public bus or subway. Most difficult perhaps is relating to persons in civilian terms (especially children and old people) and sharing your real fears in this alien world. Too much is taken for granted. If a man is a brilliant writer, it is assumed he can answer or dial a telephone or find his way around a city.

The focus of attention in the literary world is short-lived. It is like that song, "Too Long at the Fair." The new celebrity thinks that the entire world is at his feet, and suddenly he looks up one day to find out that he is alone, and his prison stories have begun to bore his listeners. They use the ex-con celebrity as a seasonal conversation piece. Ask Edgar Smith or Frank Lee Andrews about it.

I recall Edgar Smith telling me of his first days of freedom. Smith had been on death row longer than anyone in the history of the country. He had achieved national attention with the publication of his book, *Brief Against Death*. The New Jersey courts finally succumbed to pressure and made a deal, which assured the release of Smith. Quite simply, he agreed to say that he had been guilty in order to be released. If he had maintained his innocence of the original charges, it would have meant continued incarceration.

Smith's unlikely mentor for several years through the death row ordeal was William F. Buckley. Edgar's first stop, after the courts cut him loose, was to the TV studio where he did a tape for Buckley's *Firing Line*. Buckley arranged for Smith to stay at the St. Regis Hotel on his first night out of prison. After doing interviews for all of the TV networks and holding a press conference, Smith arrived, all alone, at the St. Regis. He ordered some booze and sat up all night in his luxury suite with the light on. Death row at Trenton maintained an all-night light, and Smith was unable to stay in the dark.

Edgar is a bright and rather interesting man. But he never really had a chance to make it out here. I remember attending a party with him where a newsmagazine editor complimented the hostess, "You have the literary coup of the year with Edgar Smith here." When Edgar was rearrested, neither the newsmagazine editor nor Buckley was at his side.

Edgar had a multitude of problems, none of which was insurmountable. He never had time to consider them. Initially, he was a literary curiosity, and then he attempted to live up to what he assumed were the expectations of other people.

Frank Lee Andrews was described by *People* magazine as the "convict who wrote his way out of prison." I've known Andrews in prison and out. I admire his talent and like him, and I am pained by the reality that he wasn't able to cut it out here. He adjusted to working as a writer and editor in New York City. He had been courted by other writers and editors for a spell. Andrews, like Abbott, is a product of all those kid joints. He never even began to "de-prisonize" himself, to adjust internally to the values of the outside. Andrews, for all his talent and charm, had been conditioned only to jail. His first disappointment or setback channeled him into an avenue of self-negation. He is now awaiting trial on a charge, and if he is convicted, he will be sent away for a long time.

Another man raised by the state, Stanley Eldridge, wrote an array of brilliant poems while a teenager in and out of Rikers Island. Stanley, perhaps because of his youth, was able to break the cycle of incarceration, but he stopped writing after being released.

Eddie Morris's autobiography, *Born to Lose*, is a replica of Abbott's life. Morris's tale was written with a fury, and though never properly edited, *Born to Lose* is probably the most powerful indictment of a system which nurtures alienation.

Eddie Morris with great difficulty has "squared up." His background of foster homes and reformatories is Abbott's terrain. I thought a great deal about Eddie while reading *In the Belly of the Beast*, for if Eddie Morris, an unwanted youth, tough guy, stand-up con, could put it all together sufficiently to stay out, there are paths for Jack Abbott to take.

Can Jack Abbott write about things other than prison? Who knows? He doesn't have enough street time. Claude Brown has written *Manchild in the Promised Land*, and Edward Bunker's *Little Boy Blue* is a novel of an unwanted kid in those juvenile facilities. There is little doubt that Abbott, in all those state and federal pens, met enough people who would lend themselves to interesting essays or fiction. Joseph Wambaugh has inked six books on the L.A. police force. Anyone knows that cons are more interesting than cops.

Abbott will have to slowly integrate his writing life with his resocialization. Resocialization is not an abandonment of political and social passions nor is the capacity to survive; it is merely surviving the daily indignities which are a part of life out here. Street life to most long timers is a fantasy world, and they often over personalize the initial disappointment.

It's about holding on.

John Herbert, the once-imprisoned man who wrote *Fortune and Men's Eyes*, has always stayed on the outer fringes of respectability, a choice of survival for him. Malcolm Braly, whose three books are among the finest reflections of prison life, gave all of the appearances of an adjusted writer among the social lions, but his violent death in an auto crash while driving alone has raised questions about his perception of being an outsider. Rick Cluchy, the San Quentin actor/writer who authored *The Cage*, finally moved out of the U.S.A. Miguel Piñero, the talented playwright, who won prizes for *Short Eyes*, has had a rollercoaster existence but seems to be making it. Tommy Trantino was labeled "brilliant" for *Lock the Lock*, but few of the literati seem to be aware that he is still doing time in New Jersey. There is an army of ex-prison celebrities, who have had varying degrees of street success and some failures.

There are a lot of paths to travel. Abbott can view a lot of guys who moved ahead of him, who made the right choices. Being Mailer's protégé is an entrée for a new writer, but Abbott has to decide what he wants entrée to. There are others from whom he can learn because they didn't see the traps. There are choices!

Jack Abbott was convicted and sentenced to life in a New York State prison. He was stabbed to death by another inmate in an altercation prompted by Abbott.

Riots are dramatic; TV crews and reporters are ubiquitous. Other trips to prison go unnoticed. You're flying below the radar then. All over the country, there are volunteers making a difference one person at a time, showing there are pockets of humanity. It is startling to hear how many men and women reveal that their motivation to turn their lives around was prompted by one caring person.

My friend Angel Ramos reports that a teacher he met while in the Brooklyn House of Detention was the major factor in his life. Angel served thirty years, but Mae always stayed in contact with him. She encouraged him to read and, more importantly, be attuned to his humanity. Now a civilian, Angel is a college student.

In 1982, Ramsey Clark invited me to join a team venturing to Nicaragua to inspect prisons there. Helsinki Watch was sponsoring the mission to determine how the Sandinista government was treating the imprisoned Contras, the previous ruling class in that nation, which was in social upheaval.

The Central American country was in the middle of a civil war. The Sandinistas, under Daniel Ortega's leadership, had taken over the country from Somoza. The Somozans, later called the Contras, had a long history of government complicity with large American companies, particularly United Fruit, which maintained poor working conditions and a substandard living wage. The Sandinistas were political revolutionaries who had thrown out the Somoza government and imprisoned many of its foot soldiers and political leaders.

We were to visit the prisons, interview people who had been captured by the Sandinistas, and report back to Helsinki Watch. We were a team of about eight, which included two old friends: Roger Wilkins, a columnist at the *New York Times*, and Ed Mueller, a chaplain at Green Haven Prison.

Whenever a man arrived at Fortune from Green Haven Prison and announced he was in Reverend Mueller's cadre, I knew he was among the few prisoners in that unique environment who were attempting to come to terms with the cause and effect of their imprisonment. They would always be looking for something better.

The first Mueller acolyte I met arrived at Fortune on the day after Christmas, 1969. The office was closed, and I was there to catch up on paperwork. My door burst open, and a man introduced himself as Prentice Williams. He announced that he had missed the entire decade (the 1960s) and asked what he could do in the next week to catch up. I told him to slow down, and I tried to determine if he had a place to stay or had eaten a meal. We entered into a long conversation about his future as well as his past, and he told me that Reverend Mueller had said that if he was serious about a new life, he should try a program like the Fortune Society. On his first night out of prison, I invited Prentice to join ten other Fortune people to attend a preview performance of a Broadway musical.

Prentice lamented about the drug-infested SRO where he had been placed by parole. I told him he could stay at my apartment that night. That turned into a yearlong tenancy and the start of one of the closest friendships I would have in my adult life. Prentice, out of Bedford-Stuyvesant, had been caught up in the drug subculture and street gangs, which led to his incarceration. Our pasts were dramatically different, but I had learned at Fortune that friendships are not always based on what you have in common. Curiosity about people unlike yourself makes living exciting.

During the next year, Prentice attended school for film projectionists. I also became acquainted with his teenage son, Keith, who often hung out with us. Two years later, Prentice, working and fairly productive, was married and became the stepfather of two children. We remained close during the seventies, but then his inner demons caught up with him, and he was absent. His death from a massive heart attack before he was fifty was probably prompted by drug abuse. He never returned to crime or prison, but he still clung to unresolved doubts and fears, many of the things he and I talked about when he was first released—what Bob Brown referred to as "the crocodiles of our dreams."

It was with great anticipation that I would be with Ed Mueller—Prentice's mentor—and his wife on the team that went to Central America.

We flew to Miami and boarded a special plane to Managua. When we arrived at the airport, we were immediately surrounded by little boys, some as young as six years old, asking for pennies and food, and we recognized we had arrived at a nation with great poverty. The Sandinista police escorted us to the residence where we would be housed, an impressive manor that had been the residence of a military officer before the revolution. The palatial mansions of the previous government had been turned into hotels, museums, community centers for artists, and guest homes for visitors such as ourselves.

We met with Tomás Borge, the illustrious interior minister, who was second only to the Ortegas in the Sandinista hierarchy. He instructed us about our travel plans. We would move around Nicaragua by bus, by truck, and by airplane to see how the Sandinistas were treating the Contras and also the Miskito Indians who were incarcerated. The latter was a thorny issue with outsiders sympathetic to the Sandinistas. Like Native Americans in the United States, the indigenous Miskitos were outside of mainstream Nicaragua, subjected to discrimination and abuse no matter who was in power.

Our visit to the first prison, near the town of León, was a startling revelation. There were no walls or barbed wire. The Contra prisoners were in adobe shacks, not unlike the domiciles we had seen along the roadways. Guards casually patrolled the area, and the officers in charge comfortably brought us into the rooms in which the prisoners were living. Translators accompanied us, and it was clear, almost immediately, that the Contras were comfortable, fed as well as people in the community. Most were low-level soldiers who had little commitment to the political and ideological battle between the Contras and the Sandinistas.

We went north to the Honduras-Nicaragua border and were introduced to the peasant militia, young men who had built trenches to protect their land from gunfire coming from Honduras. They told us emphatically that United States soldiers and weapons were firing on them. Continuous shots were fired at random, and at one interval we were brought into trenches to protect us from some scattered fire.

I talked at length with one man, a farmer and soldier, who spoke halting English. He expressed his love for the United States but asked me point-blank, "Why does Ronald Reagan hate us?" He held the administration in Washington, D.C., responsible for the ongoing war, an observation that seemed to be substantiated by history as it unfolded.

When we flew to the east coast to meet men and women of the Miskito tribe, we found them maintained—fed and clothed—in isolated but open spaces. There didn't seem to be blockades to prevent them from walking away, but there was nowhere for them to go. They had greater objections than the Contra prisoners, not so much about their treatment but about the continuous ostracism of their people.

Perhaps because they didn't have architects and steel and cement companies vying for contracts, Nicaraguan prisons, despite their meager resources, seemed much less damaging to the human spirit than our bastilles. In this singular instance, poverty was an advantage . . . or at least limited the exploitation of those incarcerated.

That was certainly not my experience when I visited several prisons and youth facilities in Germany. I was invited by the Goethe Society in New York to represent the United States in Berlin at a Kirchentag , a nationally sponsored student-faculty academic festival with international participation. I was presenting a paper on the philosophy and performance of prisons in the United States. The sponsors also arranged for me to visit the facilities in the Berlin area, Cologne, Munich, and Hamburg.

I arrived in Berlin after an all-night flight and was greeted with an announcement that we were to go immediately to a rehearsal of a theater troupe founded by Bertolt Brecht. I was exhausted from jet lag. There I sat for two hours viewing a theater rehearsal of *Mother Courage* in German, a language with which I was unfamiliar.

Then I went to the hotel and prepared to view the Kirchentag parade travel through the main *strassen* of Berlin. It was exciting and nerve-racking for me. My familiarity with strong German accents came from World War II movies where the "enemy" was scheming and plotting. Here I saw young men and women who looked very much like the youths I had left in the United States. Berlin, in fact, seemed to be more like New York City than any other town I would ever visit.

After the conference in Berlin, I was escorted to my first penal facility in Germany, an ominous building that housed teenage boys. It had all of the negative elements I had observed in American prisons. The lads, mostly in their teens, looked solemn and bored. That was where I first saw tattoos on the back and face, inkings that hid their faces. Several had swastikas on their necks . . . not an encouraging sight, penologically or politically. Most of the youths were lying on bunks, looking bored and uninvolved.

The trips to adult prisons were equally glum. The older men all looked like the actor Erich von Stroheim in World War II movies. My interpreter censored my more embarrassing questions, like when I asked about the number of Nazis that were in lockup.

Back in Berlin, I walked along the wall, and I was given two invitations, both of which would involve traveling on my own: one to visit Auschwitz and the other to go on the other side of the wall, which was then in Soviet hands. I have always had mixed feelings about declining both offers, but since I was alone, I felt the absence of accountability might be a factor. I didn't want to become an international incident, and so I nixed the journey to East Berlin. As for touring a concentration camp, I felt no need to view the torture chambers of a generation past. I've met with survivors and seen enough documentary films. Prisons always leave me with headaches and heartaches. I did not want to visit the remnants of a concentration camp.

Probably, the most difficult prison trip I've taken in the United States was to the Louisiana State Penitentiary in Angola. It was located near nothing. A large acreage of farms and dormitories, it was one of the most oppressive sites you could imagine. I have read the history of many jails and prisons in Louisiana, Mississippi, and Arkansas, where inmates, particularly African Americans, were subjected to plantation-type exploitation.

I wrote a letter to the warden in Angola, who allowed me to visit with Wilbert Rideau, a prisoner who had been coediting the *Angolite*, a prize-winning prison publication. Wilbert and I had entered into a lengthy correspondence. He developed into a talented journalist, winner of civilian prizes for his outstanding essays. He was in a long battle over his original case, and it would take decades before he was begrudgingly released. He was one of the many black long-termers I met in prison who, had they been white, would have served little or no time. Wilbert's prosecution and jury had been all white—not only white, but clearly storing racist sentiments.

He was permitted to show me around some of the farming areas in the prison, with sufficient correction-officer accompaniment. It was how I'd imagined plantation slaves, laboring under a hot Dixie sun. Many of the men there had lengthy sentences, much longer than the national average, and most would never see the free world again. It is all a matter of race and class and geography.

Wilbert and I continued our correspondence until his much-publicized release. His autobiography, *In the Place of Justice*, is not surprisingly the most passionate and effective prison book I've ever read.

Fortune Society's frequent visits to Colorado for speaking engagements permitted us to accept inmate invitations to visit the steel and concrete in Cañon City. That prison, nestled in the Rocky Mountains near Colorado Springs, is under beautiful skies but is also a frightening institution. On our first trip, we were permitted to sit and talk with a group of men, which led to lots of mail when we returned to New York City.

One guy, Cotton Adamson, had fifteen minutes of fame when he was released. He had a much-publicized marriage to Sue Lyon, the provocative film actress who played the title role in *Lolita*.

In our second yearly visit to Cañon City, the guards were marching us from one area to another, and suddenly I saw Cotton and a few of the other guys we had met the year before. I started to walk over to them, and Fran O'Leary cautioned me. "David, don't leave the guards here. You're not on a college campus." I shrugged my shoulders and said, "What are they going to do, arrest me?" I was painfully naïve. As I began walking toward the other men, an ominous sound echoed through the Rocky Mountain canyons. The guards on the wall had cocked their rifles, and then a voice through a bullhorn warned, "Get back to your guides immediately." Fran grabbed hold of me, and we proceeded to our destination.

A few months later, back in New York City, a young man came to the Fortune office. He asked for me and Fran, since he had met us when we visited Cañon City. During our reunion, we suggested he talk to a counselor who could provide him with guidance about housing. Fran beamed at me. "Isn't that great? The guy came to New York as a result of our just meeting him once in Cañon City." No sooner had she expressed her pride than the counselor walked into my office and said, "Did you know that this guy from Colorado escaped? He can't stay here. He's endangering everyone on parole just by his presence." I met with the man and arranged for him to meet a lawyer, someone who could negotiate his safe return to prison if that was his choice. If he wanted to stay on the run, we couldn't assist him. He chose the former and went back to Colorado.

I continue to visit prisons, mostly with the play *The Castle*, though I have spoken in recent years to people in the Rikers Island Discharge Enhancement Program (RIDE). Fortune Society has supervision over a dorm in that city jail, preparing men for their reentry, helping them to complete the paperwork that many prisoners must do when released. The Fortune counselors talk to them about the real aspects of reentry, including job finding and housing situations—all the factors that constitute a successful new life.

The United States has done it all wrong since the outset. The Quakers fought to change punishments and beatings by creating buildings of penance, thus penitentiaries. Their intentions were good, but they turned the system over to philistines, people who, historically, don't believe in the possibility of change. As a result we have an expensive, counterproductive prison system. The walls are high, and the prisons are often far from the large cities where their inmates have lived. The walls were built to keep the inmates in—and have been maintained to keep the public out.

Pat McGarry, appearing at a forum, was asked if he had received any spiritual guidance while in prison. He snapped back, "They destroyed my spirit. There was nothing to guide."

TEN

Homo

I am a homosexual...gay...queer...whatever word is being used this year. I'm it. Or as New Jersey governor Jim McGreevey bravely stated, "I am a gay American."

That declarative statement doesn't fall off my lips as casually as it might have had I been born a generation later. My sexual orientation was my deep, dark secret, my shame for the first forty years of my life. I was the classic relic from that period when everyone's secret was the cause of silence. The best way to deal with it was not to deal with it.

I am still not fully at ease putting it out there. I have always rationalized that one's sexual activity is private and is to be restricted behind closed doors. Many modern puritans would agree with me. In the best of all possible worlds, my sexual orientation or anyone else's would be nobody's business. If government bodies didn't legislate about it, if religious leaders didn't mount sermons of sin, and if schoolyard bullies didn't define their targets to express their own fears and inadequacies, it could remain a private experience.

When I was growing up, in the 1930s, '40s, and '50s, my family was silent about the subject of homosexuality. It never entered the dinner-table exchange. Nevertheless, I would hear the comments—"He's a pansy"; "He's a fairy"—or see the girl at school make the limp-wrist pantomime to describe an epicene classmate. Disapproval, judgments, and sneering laughter defined who the male homosexual was in those decades. Condescension and a sense of heterosexual superiority were part of the American fabric.

So I learned to be quiet. I dated girls through high school and college, and I had relationships with women when I worked in the theater. My furtive assignations exacerbated the guilt and shame. No matter what praise or accolades I received for my achievements, my inner voice told me: "If they really knew you, what do you think they would say?"

On a recent television show, I listened to baseball star Darryl Strawberry reflect on his self-hatred, which explained his gravitation toward and escape from drugs. The sports legend talked about his father's verbal abuse, which belittled and demeaned him. He incorporated that negative description into part of his psyche. He recalled rounding the bases after hitting a home run, with fifty thousand people cheering and yelling his name, and he thought to himself, "What do they really know about me?" He thought he was who his father said he was. In fact, Darryl was beloved by his fans, and former teammates praised his humanity, sensitivity, and kindness. He never saw what others saw.

We do quite a number on our children.

Amateur psychiatrists told me that my involvement in the civil rights movement and working with released prisoners was "transference": I was unable to deal with my own isolation, so I involved myself with others. If that's so, I ask them for an explanation of gay people who are social philistines, Republicans, neo-Nazis, or just plain indifferent. There have to be factors that define someone's social commitment other than an evasion of self and/or sexual orientation. Loneliness and isolation are hardly restricted to gay people, and those words wouldn't describe my many colleagues of the heterosexual persuasion who are my partners in the civil rights and prisoners' rights movements.

I finally determined that too often I spent my time and effort on diagnosing the motivation and not on dealing with the real social problems disenfranchised people must face in our society.

In 1969, when the modern gay rights movement began, I was living on Sheridan Square in Greenwich Village. The Stonewall Inn was around the corner. It was a scuffle in that bar that led to protests and days of marches and protests around the area where I was living.

I watched the initial protests from behind my apartment's venetian blinds. I was both exhilarated and threatened by the public display of gay people. What I didn't realize—not connecting the dots—was that this was an inevitable outgrowth of the civil rights movement. When Dr. King was defining oppression and arguing for voting rights for black Americans, other oppressed people heard his message. Self-empowerment transcended the specifics of Dr. King's oratory.

I wished the early gay activists well, but I was not a part of the movement. I was dedicating all my energy and time to the Fortune Society, and I feared that any involvement with gay rights in 1968 would discredit my work with Fortune.

Deep in the Village, an abandoned firehouse became the gathering spot for a new gay liberation organization. I went to a few meetings with a pad in hand. Should anyone ask about my presence, I would respond that I was a journalist, freelancing for the *Village Voice*. No one was particularly interested in my attendance, and my fraudulent, unused notepad was a superfluous prop. The young men and women there were discussing basic civil rights issues, such as New York City laws that discriminated against homosexuals in places of public gathering (including restaurants and bars) and in jobs and housing. These meetings were similar to all the ones I had attended concerning the rights of African Americans and, later, former inmates.

Gay rights was a basic civil rights issue. I was dealing with my own shame, my deep shame, and these young, self-accepting homosexuals were moving into the political arena. I was starting to get it: the personal is political.

By 1973, the gay rights movement was becoming more sophisticated and media savvy. Television newscasts kept looking for the stereotypes and defined almost everything gay as a drag queen paradise or continual sexual activity. Not that anyone needs to defend drag queens; they argue their position quite well. I am merely saying that of the millions of American men who are gay, only a small percentage are drag queens, so media coverage misinterpreted the wide breadth of who gay people were.

It was time for a concerted change, and the National Gay Task Force—later known as the National Gay and Lesbian Task Force—was formed. It was the first professionally run gay organization with a paid staff and efforts to link together movements in cities around the country. For its national board of directors, the leaders sought representatives from all walks of life. In the field of criminal justice, they were facing a stone wall. Gay lawyers and judges and corrections officials were not ready to get on board.

Greg Dawson, an old friend who had been head of public relations for Robert Moses's 1964 World's Fair, asked if I would consider being on the board of directors. Greg was more than acquainted with my closeted status, and he knew this would mean being public about my sexual orientation.

Perhaps it was time for me to take a step forward. At the age of thirty-nine, I had entered into my first serious adult relationship with another man—Greg Norris, a teacher whose father was an inmate in a state prison in New Jersey. Greg was teaching in a county jail. Ours was hardly the kind of courtship the media defined in their bleak reports of "the gay lifestyle." Greg and I were getting to know each other while going to prisoners' rights rallies. In the past, I had aborted anything that appeared like a reasonable relationship, because I knew that having a partner would be tantamount to coming out. I was the classic closet case, and my years of being alone had been the result.

Things were moving fast in 1973: a live-in relationship and an invitation to be on the board of directors of the NGTF.

Years of publicity work influenced my decision. If I was to become a member of the NGTF, I didn't want to discredit Fortune Society with rumors and innuendo. I would do it full throttle. Once again I called Jean Kennedy, producer of *The David Susskind Show*. They had aired programs with openly gay activists, but how about a panel of six men and women who were successfully in the mainstream, people who had been leading duplicitous lives and were now ready to chuck society's definition of respectability?

"Great," she said. "But can you recommend some people?"

"How about me?" I responded.

She paused and said, "Well, I never knew. Why not?"

Other men and women were interviewed, and the program was scheduled.

Now I was coming out to America. But I had other responsibilities first: my family—my mother, my sister Carla, my aunt Ruth—and all of my colleagues at the Fortune Society, now in its sixth year and an important part of a new movement.

I wrote my mother the following letter:

Dear Mother,

This is a belated note of thanks to you for your hosting me for four days. I am sorry that it wasn't longer or that we didn't have an opportunity to talk at any length, though our verbal communication hasn't been the strongest part of our relationship. Perhaps, it is the unstated which is the essence of my love for you.

At 40, my life, rather than having a steady pattern, continues sprinkled with crossroads, and I think I find that more satisfying and adventuresome. That is to say, I hope to continue to come to terms with myself and be more fulfilling. For the first time in my life, I am beginning to get a sense of contentment—and of self-acceptance. This is important in our relationship, son to mother, mother to son. I have held back with you, filled my being with moody silences that I now realize were underlined with fears, fears of rejection and self-negation. It is my deep hope that as I have learned to accept myself, it will fill in some of the blank spaces of our friendship and love.

This is all by way of saying to you that I have, at last, accepted a truth about myself…and in doing so, it makes my life bearable. An enormous weight has been lifted. It is that I am, and always have been, homosexual.

Growing up in Ridgefield Park and Teaneck—unknowing and affected by small-town mores, I felt cursed. In retrospect, I can understand my moods, my headaches, my boils and infections as a child. And yet, in attending some conscious-raising meetings in the last year, I have learned that I am a total human being with much to be proud of, much which I can offer, and my personal sexual orientation is a problem only if I permit it to be and if I am obsessed with the rejection of an unknowing outside world. I understand that my outrage against oppressed people was, in a sense, a transference of my own oppression, but I was not permitted to verbalize my own hurts, so unspeakable was my being. Indeed, that is the ultimate oppression.

I have talked with parents of other gay people about telling or sharing this fact with you. They have urged me to do so. I do so in hope that you will accept me as I have accepted myself—and in turn, am a happier person.

Parents, I have heard, often lament, "Where have I failed?" but since my life has been filled with purpose and meaning your question should be, rather, "How have I contributed to this success?" If there has been a failure, it is mine in not accepting myself.

Nothing about me is different as you know me. I have always been what I am, and only a changing of the times has permitted me to accept and share myself more honestly.

This letter is written to you with an enormity that I hope you understand, with tears running down my face, because at last I am asking you, who I love with every ounce of breath, to accept me as I am, not in pretense.

I am your son, with a growing sense of freedom, who loves you....

David

Years later, my friend Jean Bach told columnist Liz Smith about this letter. Liz was writing *Mother*, and she asked for a copy of my letter, which she included in her book.

In 1997, a man named Andy Carroll called and informed me he was compiling a book of letters to be published by Kodansha as *Letters of a Nation*. Someone had shown him the missive to my mother, and he asked permission to use it in his book. It appeared alongside letters by Benjamin Franklin, Thomas Jefferson, Henry David Thoreau, Harriet Beecher Stowe, Malcolm X, Rabbi Stephen Wise, Jack London, and dozens of other Americans. There was even a moving, dramatic theatrical presentation, with fine actors (I recall Austin Pendleton being one) reading the letters of William James, Thomas Merton, and Gertrude Stein, among others. I read my letter as part of the evening.

My mother wrote back after reading my letter and stated that she cried when she read it, tears for all the years she felt I could not share with her. I visited her shortly afterward, and we had the first honest exchange in my adult life. In the past, I had received all of her questions with guarded suspicion. My answers were always evasive. I kept information about my life incomplete, lest she get close to asking me about deeply personal things.

Before I mailed the letter, I had called my sister, Carla. She said I sounded so serious on the phone that she was deeply concerned and fearful. She came in from New Jersey and met me at the Fortune office, and we took a walk around the block. Later she called her daughters at home and said, "He's all right; he's gay." They were all relieved; they'd been dreading I was going to tell them I had a fatal disease. I learned over and over again that my being gay didn't matter to people who loved me. My aunt Ruth, when we walked in the woods near her town of Haworth, said, "Well, I guess that's something else we have to learn about," as she hugged me.

At Fortune, I assembled the key cadre: Kenny Jackson, Mel Rivers, Fran O'Leary, Bobby Davis, and Jeanette Spencer, all of whom were formerly incarcerated people. I announced that I had three things to tell them. "One, I am a gay man. Two, I have agreed to appear on *The David Susskind Show*, announcing that I am gay. And three, I am prepared to submit my resignation as executive director."

This was greeted with a long pause; everyone was looking at one another. Kenny Jackson broke the silence and asked, "What are you going to wear on television?"

That was the last question I had anticipated, and I looked at him, perplexed. Kenny added, "You dress like a slob. Get something nice and make us proud of you."

Mel Rivers asked, "Why would you resign?" I suggested that my "coming out" might affect support of the Fortune Society. Mel then uttered what is probably the most sophisticated political comment ever addressed to me. He said, "You've stood beside us for six years, telling us to be honest about our past lives. Why not give us the same opportunity to stand by you?"

And that was the end of the discussion. Kenny asked if we could all get back to work now.

After the Susskind program aired, my next day at work was interrupted constantly. One phone call after another from people telling me to stay strong, that they loved me, that they were proud of me. Jeanette Spencer walked by my office that afternoon and looked in. "What's the matter, baby?" she inquired. I told her of all these calls of support. She hugged me and said, "You know, baby, we spend a lot of time getting used to rejection. Sometimes it's hard when all that love comes at once. Why don't you get out of here and just take the afternoon off?" And that's exactly what I did.

I had written an essay about living a duplicitous life, and I sent it to Sheldon Zalaznick, managing editor of *New York* magazine. He called me with much excitement and said they would like to publish it as the cover story on the same week I was to appear on David Susskind. I had several meetings with Sheldon, going over nuances in the article. He stated that it was a major piece and would be viewed as an important social essay.

Two weeks before the magazine was being put together, *New York* publisher Clay Felker returned from vacationing in Europe. After reading the suggested cover story by me, he announced to his editors, "Not in my magazine." The story was killed. Ironically, less than two years later, when the gay movement had gone mainstream, *New York* magazine photographed me and a half dozen other gay activists as an example of who and what was happening in a new social-change movement.

The following is the essay that never appeared in *New York* magazine in 1973, or anywhere else for that matter.

"At War with the Dinosaurs"
by David Rothenberg
(written in 1973)

This essay is, in a sense, my coming out. "Coming out" is the homosexual's announcement to the world that he or she will no longer accept living a shadowed existence. Thousands of homosexuals seem to be coming out. The veil is lifting. It has been an event not duly recorded in the media, perhaps because of embarrassment or inadequacy. Whatever the reasons, the emergence of the homosexual as a visible factor will have vast effect on our culture and our politics.

The prospect of redefining my life at 40 years of age is at once exhilarating and terrifying. I have lived a life of fear and doubt—and now, having decided to "come out," will do it before a national television audience.

Several weeks ago, an interview with Jean Kennedy, producer of *The David Susskind Show*, concluded with the understanding that I would participate in an upcoming panel of homosexual men and women. The program's theme would be: gay men and women who were able to attain success in their vocational arenas, while maintaining a private life which was secretive and discreet.

Sitting in the comfortable office of Talent Associates, such a television appearance seemed logical, bold, sophisticated and very sensible. At the very least I would be free from the mental anguish caused by the hypocrisy which I, and most homosexuals, must embrace as we strive to exist in our heterosexual society.

Following my meeting with Ms. Kennedy, I was subjected to sleepless nights and the return of many old fears. I wasn't prepared for the personal agony and ambivalence that overtook me.

First, I knew I had to "come out" to my family and friends. I began to arrange private meetings with associates and relatives, trying to summon the strength to begin my conversation/confession/coming out. To their credit, the people closest to me responded with love and warmth. Yet their questions and fears revealed so much misinformation and ignorance in people who otherwise would be regarded as urbane and informed. Though I was personally surrounded with support, I was also cautioned against a public revelation on television. It was emphasized that my life and work would abruptly change.

One friend warned, "Our world is not ready yet for the homosexual. If you're discreet and don't put it in anyone's face, you'll get by. But go on television and you'll have doors closed to you. You've worked too hard for what you've achieved in the last few years. You are taking a gamble and may have to sacrifice it all."

The uneasiness of the last few weeks found me more determined to publically discuss homosexuality and my own personal experiences. A few months ago, I heard Dr. Howard Brown, the Health Services Administrator of the Lindsay administration, being interviewed about his "coming out." Dr. Brown had had a heart attack, and in a 48-hour period in which he didn't know whether he would live or die, he made a private vow that if he survived he would tend to matters he had omitted from his life. Among them was a public disclosure of his homosexuality.

I don't want to have any deathbed regrets.

It is now clear to me that I will endure. But I've been bothered by the prospect of personal incidents. Will someone recognize me from TV on the street and holler, "Hey, faggot"? Will my treasured lunch-hour basketball games at the YMCA be affected? These noon-hour workouts at the gym are a great personal relaxation to me. How will the businessmen-turned basketball players feel about an acknowledged and public homosexual? The macho tones of the gym have a collective tone that differs greatly from the individual tastes and prejudices. There is something specific about a locker room mentality.

The prospect of a much greater crisis concerns me as I attempt to assess my future effectiveness at work. Will my close identification with the Fortune Society affect the organization's goals and achievements?

Representing the Fortune Society, I sit in on meetings and conferences with politicians, prison, parole and probation officials, meet daily with educators, corporate executives, crime- fighters, involved citizen groups, ex-convicts, media people and students at endless speaking programs and seminars.

I also know that many persons who consider themselves sophisticated and enlightened have distorted and stereotyped views of homosexuals and homosexuality. Fortune Society and its goals and battles have been an integral part of my life, and I have to recognize that my role will possibly be reshaped. One acquaintance, when learning of my homosexuality, informed me that though our friendship was not impaired in his eyes, I would not be welcome in his home while his children were growing up.

Kenny Jackson, an ex-convict who is president of the Fortune Society, listened to all my concerns and fears of the upcoming television show. He said that the only question I must pose should be, "How do I feel about myself?" He also reminded me that five years ago I had arranged for him to appear on a network television show to surrender his anonymity about being an ex-convict.

How and why, with all of these doubts and concerns, did I reach the point to consider a public revelation of my private self?

As a 40-year old male homosexual, I have come belatedly to recognize the extent of the oppressiveness which exists for gay people. No matter what the talent, the achievement, the contribution to the larger community, the man whose sexual orientation is to someone of his own gender will be glibly dismissed with "but he's a fag."

I will no longer apologize for my life. My shadowed sexual life has provided me with a sensitivity and a human compassion which I will not surrender.

Now, in entering the spotlight and proclaiming my sexuality, I will not accept the condescension and patronization of a heterosexual world that boasts of Watergate morality as a guide-post for American male behavior.

In the last few years, my work as a prison reformist was constantly haunted by the realization that all I believed in and advocated could be subverted if my private sexuality surfaced publicly. I recognized how ideas, social change and genuine opportunity were in the clutches of a puritan morality and economic strangulation that infests our society at all levels.

It came to me as a fantastic truth that the sum and substance of my existence could be glibly dismissed because of my sexuality. I also came to realize that I was in a continual state of fear... fear of being exposed and fear that my efforts for meaningful change in the prison arena would be placed aside because of my private choice. That is indeed an oppression I no longer will accept for myself.

During the past six-year period I have worked tenaciously to restructure our faulty criminal-justice system. I have been exposed to the political and penological hierarchy, which is shamefully deceptive and irrelevant to the needs of our society. But in terms of my boldly moving forward I realized that my own sense of commitment and dedication could be mastered by a dishonest, corrupt correction official if he had a sexual disclaimer to make about me.

Recently I have talked with other gay people who have been talented contributors in a multitude of fields within their communities, and found this to be a sadly prevalent condition. Millions of American men and women have knowingly short-changed themselves because of the fear of being revealed.

It is true that people are coming out of the closet, but the movement is painfully slow, and that closet is crowded to the bursting point.

So very many men and women have grown up with fears, hates and intolerable loneliness because the world in which they live could not come to terms with homosexuality.

Parenthetically, my observations are specific about male homosexuals. That is not to say that homosexual women do not face many prejudices—in some cases, particularly legal, the hang-ups society has about homosexuals embrace both genders—but there are differences in the prejudices against homosexual men as compared to homosexual women. My frame of reference obviously is as a male.

Heterosexuals know little about what affects homosexuals the most, and that is *homophobia*, a word not recorded in my dictionary but which means an unreasonable and obsessive hatred of homosexuals.

My life, in an enlightened political and social ambience in New York City, found an approval of homosexuality that was slightly more sophisticated than Bull Connor's view of a Black Panther meeting.

I grew up in a small town in New Jersey, and the childhood realization of being homosexual drowned me in guilt. Convinced that I was a rare breed, I buried my natural instinct and prepared a life of deception and self-denial. I heard the hateful references to homosexuality at every turn. Like millions of other gay people, I gravitated to the large city to seek anonymity and survival.

As a college student in Colorado during the mid-'50s, I was actively involved in student and state politics. A state legislator pulled me aside at one meeting and questioned my future. During the discussion, he suggested I stay in Colorado, as it was his opinion that I had a political future. It intrigued me, but in a few days I went into a deep depression when I realized that there was no political future for me. Though my instincts and talents might have been apparent, I had to disqualify myself.

I recall some devastating moments of loneliness while at college. It was then that I realized that I was, irrevocably and unmistakably, homosexual. In my junior high school and high school days, it was an unpracticed inclination. In high school I submerged myself with dates and going steady, a pretense I maintained to be accepted.

By the time I was a college sophomore, I had done enough reading to have a limited knowledge of homosexuality. There was no one to whom I could talk, however. In the early 1950s, the college campus did not have Gay Activist groups. Contrarily, I knew that a fraternity member had been expelled for soliciting a freshman pledge. The upperclassman was forced out of school and the freshman transferred to a university in Texas.

There were many nights in Denver when I walked endlessly in the cool air, seeking some self-understanding. I felt so apart from everyone around me. I was in my own prison, a feeling of being rejected by society that I recognize in prisoners every time I enter a jail or prison today.

Surreptitiously, I would read all of the homosexual fiction I could find. It would usually end up with the suicide of the homosexual protagonist. Until I was in my early 20s I believed that the sole conclusion of my "situation" would be suicide.

Fortunately, in my senior year of college, I became friendly with a graduate student who was ten years older than I. He was a war veteran and world traveler. When I realized that he recognized—and did not reject—my being homosexual, I bombarded him with questions. My friend, who now lives in New Orleans, where he heads a hospital clinic, assured me that I was not alone, that there were alternative routes, and that there were people who would and could understand. My slow, evolving, 20-year liberation process began with one person who would listen.

After college I served two years in the Army before coming to New York City in 1959. Perhaps the most suffocating aspect of my self-inflicted conspiracy with illusion occurred in the 1960s. I did not travel in "gay" circles. By heterosexual standards, my homosexual life was one of quiet desperation. Not so much because it was frantic, but because I denied myself a one-to-one relationship. I would fracture any attempt anyone made to get close to me. Today, I realize that I did not want to explain a homosexual relationship.

If I ran into friends on the street, I would overexplain my companion's presence. If I was ashamed of being gay, then I would convey the same lack of respect to any prospective partner or lover.

As a result, I was, by choice, alone. Publicly, I was active and involved. But always I returned to the empty apartment, eating endless dinners by myself.

Though I had embraced the plights of all other socially oppressed and denied groups, it had never occurred to me that my own state of isolation was the result of a conspiracy carried on by me in conjunction with an unthinking world. I was restricted in my life choices and I accepted it as status quo.

In 1972, my attempt to create a special class for prisoners in a New Jersey institution met with severe opposition. My plan was to create a program for prisoners who were school dropouts and attempt to make the learning experience joyous by removing the traditional fears so many students have. I was called before an ominous gathering of prison wardens and correction leaders to defend my educational plan. It was obvious that my performance as a prison reconstructionist rather than my innovative program was the reason for this meeting. However, once before this collection of prison leaders, I found them only flirting with my educational credentials and views. They zeroed in on my social attitudes and then began a barrage of questions about my personal life. As a single male in my late 30s, I was vulnerable. They sought my Achilles' heel, and in retrospect I know that my homosexuality may have indeed been rumored. Their questions revealed stereotyped notions about homosexuality and in addition were a severe insult to my own sense of integrity.

After the confrontation, an aide to Governor Cahill, who had arranged the meeting, profusely apologized for the onslaught of questions. As a tenuous afterthought, he asked if I was homosexual. I breathed hard and lied, "No." Since I had been appointed to a special committee, created by the governor, I had become politically vulnerable. My choice to lie was one of expediency. I won the opportunity to create my special class in a state prison, and it was highly successful for two years. The students and I explored new ideas and educational concepts.

An ironic postmortem: At one point in the class we discussed social protest movements. Representatives from the outside were brought in for rap sessions with the convict students. All forms of political and social expression were sought by the students, but when the subject of gay activists visiting the class was mentioned, a few of the convicts stated that they would skip the class if some "fags" came in.

Homophobia, which is a prevailing condition in our society, has been maintained by a tacit understanding between the heterosexual world and the homosexual achievers. Frequently, we learn of posthumous revelations of homosexuality, such as in the case of E. M. Forster. The rule is that homosexuals who achieve in our society will maintain their secrecy. It is understood that a public statement of homosexuality will be the undoing of the individual. Many homosexual achievers get married to perpetuate the myth.

In this way, the homophobic heterosexual can see homosexuality only in its most apparent shades, caring not for all the variations in which it might appear.

If every homosexual in society were denied achievement by emerging from the closet, heterosexual America would be stunned by the numbers and the individuals included. Certainly, the gay psychiatrists who remained silent while the APA determined the health status of homosexuals would have provided a startling response for the jury of headshrinkers.

Today, teenage boys in the mainstream of America refer to each other as "fags" as points of derision. In enlightened suburban communities, precocious youngsters with all of the liberal beliefs, frequent civil rights champions for blacks, Puerto Ricans, ex-cons, Chavez's army of unionists, etc., will use the term "fag" as an example of the nadir of existence.

Life for a homosexual in a heterosexual world is a continual audition to prove what isn't true, merely to be tolerated. And when the Gay Activists began making their first noises, those of us who were on our way up in a larger world wished them well but prayed none of them would recognize us publicly. We did not realize our own oppression, so deep was the damage.

For most of my years, homophobia did not consciously exist. I always accepted anti-homosexuality as a justifiable and natural order of events.

About ten years ago, when I was living on West 58th Street, a murder of a homosexual male took place in my building. The victim was a dancer who lived in the apartment above me. He was not terribly discreet and often had a parade of men of assorted types marching in and out. One Saturday night when I was home alone, I heard some stomping and the sound of water running, but it all left my consciousness as quickly as it had entered.

Early the next morning, when I went downstairs, the lobby was filled with police officers, and I learned that the man over me had been brutally murdered, with parts of his anatomy gouged out and dumped in his tub. One of the uniformed officials, with book in hand, commented to no one in particular in the lobby, "It was some fag who got it bad." In retrospect, I suspect he was trying to provide comfort to the frightened residents hovering in the corridor. He rightfully had pointed out that the homosexual target of violence did not pose a threat to other residents.

There was a small note in the papers about the murder, noting that the man had been killed and making mention that he had been in rehearsal for an ABC-TV special. I never saw anything in print again, but heard from a hotel employee that a teenaged boy had eventually been apprehended. I never did learn whether the accused was found guilty or innocent or what happened to him.

I remembered that murder last year, when the Gay Activists began to protest about police and media indifference to a series of murders in which gays were the victims. I recalled that the police had never questioned me, although I was at home when the man upstairs was murdered. And it is true that even gay people learned of deaths inflicted on homosexuals mostly through rumor and the filling in of the blank spaces when a short note appeared in the press.

The brutal murder of homosexuals is the most blatant form of homophobia. Recently we read of a Bronx street gang performing a murder of a man they discovered in women's clothing. It struck me that the group of teenagers is almost performing a ritual act, performing society's deed, the ultimate dismissal of the homosexual. The small story that appeared in the *New York Times* seemed very similar to that of the young Boston woman who allegedly was murdered by a group of Roxbury black youths. Yet the symbolic murder of the Boston woman was used by the police and the press to create a near panic among the frightened Boston white community.

It would be revealing to discover or probe the attitudes, feelings and rationalizations of the Bronx teenagers whose macho act was the ultimate performance, expressed in various ways, that all homosexuals have heard throughout their lives.

Gay people can relate a million stories reflecting the absurd fears and stereotypes of our community. The New York City Council's inability to pass Intro 475, permitting fair employment opportunities for gay people, only reveals that the leadership is as backward as it is cruel.

The politics of homophobia are not nearly as explicit as the daily traumatic acts which are inflicted on the homosexual.

At a recent meeting of the West Side Discussion Group, an organization of gay men and women, adult people were exchanging stories of how their families responded when they learned of homosexuality in their family.

One man, in his mid-40s, painfully recalled that he was 16 when his father was told of his being gay. He was ordered from the house and rode the subway for a week. He then returned home, and for his entire senior year in high school his mother would not talk to him. Money was left on the table by his breakfast and he would travel to school and back. Needless to say, that was the major memory of his high school years.

More recently, a lifelong friend of mine, a successful television producer, told his parents he was bisexual. His father informed him that he was no longer welcome in the house, and for two years his meetings with his mother and sisters were furtive, outside of the home.

Of course that is not to say that all families reject their son or daughter because of their homosexuality. More accurately, most homosexuals never do tell their parents, though the younger people are advocating that they do. The secrecy has always been a part of the overbearing guilt which accumulates. The most startling comment I heard was from an actor who grew up in a small Pennsylvania town. He reflected, "I think I know my family. If I was to pick up a gun and shoot someone, my father would stand by me through the trial and face the world. But if he learned that I was a homosexual, I don't think he would be able to look me in the eye."

A few years ago, members of the Fortune Society were invited to an open house at the Phoenix House on 85th Street. One of the people who went with us was a man named Pat, who, in addition to having served 20 years in prison, was openly homosexual and made no pretense about it. After being in the lounge of this therapeutic drug community for a half hour, meeting different residents, I was called into the office of the director, who informed me that Pat would have to leave. It was explained that homosexuality had been a problem for some of the addict residents, and they couldn't have it thrown in their face. I told him that I would then have to leave with Pat. We left the drug house, which was created to deal with, honestly, the deeply felt problems of addicts.

Homosexuals who pass are like Laura Hobson's protagonist in *Gentleman's Agreement*. It is a lifetime of small deceptions, pressures and lies. But, in passing as heterosexuals, we are familiar with the small asides. We read a liberal columnist refer to "fags" or hear locker room asides when someone who is obtrusively gay walks by. Many closet homosexuals will participate in this banter of bigotry to maintain the maximum pretense.

Homophobia, like all prejudices, is based on ignorance and superstition.

Of course, the greater the personal fear, the greater the homophobia.

It has occurred to me that homophobia is not only a problem for homosexuals whose victimization is apparent, but that those who suffer from homophobia and whose fear and hate of homosexuals is severe must indeed be a tortured people. Their dissatisfaction with themselves must be painful, and since so little discussion is permitted on the subject, they must be in their own prison of the mind.

As a people we must develop the same curiosity of homophobia that we have had of homosexuality. Several million Americans are homosexuals, and they refuse to fit into a snug category.

I heard the world *liberation* applied to blacks, women, gays, etc., and viewed it only in its sociological context. Liberation, I discovered, is sociologically applied with meaning when individuals begin to come to terms with themselves.

On Christmas day last year [1973], I sat down and wrote my mother a letter. After writing it I quickly folded the paper, placed it in an envelope and went out and put it in the mailbox. When I returned to my apartment, I sat on my bed. I began to shake, and then I cried, first slowly and then cathartically.

I felt purged. It was as if a 40-year-old infection, which had begun as a small poison of little lies and had grown into a lifetime of deception, had been lanced. I was willing to be accepted for the truth of myself. No longer would I crouch behind the shield of half-truths and illusions.

I began to realize that I could not accept myself privately while maintaining a deception as a public person. Prophetically, Kenny Jackson asked me how I felt about myself. It's a question which I must ask myself each day.

When you make a dramatic public announcement, particularly on television, the future terrain is unknown. Eventually, you realize that most people are so absorbed in their own lives; your self-involved drama is merely an asterisk in their lives.

I was not sufficiently cognizant of that when I appeared on the Susskind show. I had briefed friends and family ahead of time. But what would occur on the day after the telecast when I ventured into the McBurney YMCA for my lunch-hour choose-up basketball game?

Playing ball maintained my sanity. Whether I was dealing with stars in the Rialto or men coming out from prison, I always needed the break, and basketball was all for me. As a kid, we shot hoops outdoors on the coldest days, our fingertips cracking from the frost. I was never tall enough to be a varsity player, but I killed them with my set shots in intramural games.

I was always involved with athletics. As you get older, swimming, walking, and jogging are all for the good, but the mind wanders. In the pool, I would suddenly wonder if a phone call had been made, or while jogging, I would begin accumulating must-do lists. On the basketball court, the mind is only focused on the game. You're on a team, and the mind can't travel. At the end of an hour of noontime basketball, the body is enjoyably exhausted; you steam and sauna and shower, and the mind has been put at ease. I could always go back to work with a fresh start.

So I knew this important, personal ingredient in my life might be tested. Fag jokes are notorious in locker rooms. Ass grabbing and towel snapping are part of the macho after-game rituals.

There I was on television for the entire world to see, proclaiming that my sexual orientation was inclined toward people of my own gender. The next day, I changed from my civvies into the gym costume and climbed the stairs to the basketball court. There were ten guys on the court and a dozen waiting to play "winners." I felt at least two dozen eyes staring at me.

I signed up for an upcoming game. One guy walked over and said, "Saw you on TV," and walked away. That was it. My name was called for a game. I was on a team with Chris, a six-foot-five basketball whiz from Brazil who was arguably the most impressive player in lunchtime basketball at the Y. We won a couple of games, and Chris came over, put his arm around me, and announced, "Thanks, you spoke for a lot of us." I looked up in amazement. I wasn't the only homo on the court. He made his statement to me so that everyone else heard it. Chris was letting them know that I had made room for him. He was coming out right there on the basketball court.

My basketball career, restricted as it was to lunchtime pickup games at a Chelsea gym, was not curtailed or even slowed down. I suspect that my jump shot improved with the new confidence and self-acceptance.

In 1975, I met David Kopay, a professional football player, when I interviewed him for a newspaper feature after he appeared on a national TV show. He was a ten-year-veteran halfback, recently retired from the National Football League. I was a long-ago sportswriter, so interviewing a "jock" was old stuff for me, but an openly gay pro athlete was a different kind of story. He was delighted to meet a gay man who was conversant with pro sports, as he had taken some flack from gay groups who discredited his athletic prowess. (There is historic reason for this. Many—not all, but many—gay men were not sports-minded as young boys, and they often faced abuse and ridicule, being labeled as "sissies," because sports was the dividing line between a masculine surface and social acceptability.) As a kid, I was a good baseball and basketball player, not big enough for varsity teams but respected in phys-ed classes and after-school games. I was witness to the nonathletes being physically abused and the subject of scorn. I always recognized that my love for sports and my athletic ability were my protection, the moat that saved me from being an outcast.

Athletes who are gay are in great conflict. Being part of an obtrusively macho subculture, they are often terrified of revealing their sexual orientation. Kopay's mailbox became a confession barrel of letters. Dave discovered that his coming out was more than a personal experience. He became the focal point for hundreds of frightened athletes, several of whom were married. I was to learn that many of the most homophobic-sounding jocks were men who later revealed their sexual orientation. This is a story the media have avoided. I am not suggesting all jocks are closeted homosexuals—probably no more or less than the general population. It is much more difficult for them to come out. A pro basketball player made headlines by announcing he was gay after retirement. The same was true for a major league baseball player.

The pressure must be unbearable.

Kopay lives on the West Coast, but we have maintained a phone friendship over the years. He has frequently stayed with me while visiting New York, and I have been his California guest on several occasions.

The sports world had difficulties with David's candor but couldn't ignore his story, reflective of so many other men who have remained in shadows.

ELEVEN

Social Change

It was as if my body and soul had entered a different world. Following my appearance on the Susskind show, a lifetime of lying was aborted. I moved with caution, but with a great sense of liberation.

Change comes slowly. I was invited to be a guest speaker at universities, political groups, and, of course, gay organizations. My television appearance gave my sexual orientation the stamp of acceptability. Quentin Crisp, the colorful journalist and raconteur, once remarked that in America it is acceptable to kill both parents, as long as you discuss it on TV. I had achieved a transient but very minor celebrity status in a small circle.

My candor on that dramatic television show prompted hundreds of letters from around the country. Apparently my personal recollections of a duplicitous life mirrored the experiences of many men and women unknown to me.

My dedication to the work at the Fortune Society didn't diminish, but it was accompanied by the realization of another social inequity being aired openly. Formerly incarcerated men and women continued to be ostracized by law and by policy...and being gay had many legal and social disadvantages, not the least being the punch line of too many obvious jokes.

I realized that the latter, the condescending view of gays, had directed me in my teen years to internalize all those judgments of superiority and inferiority based on sexual orientation. It is a slow process, particularly for people of my generation, to work past those self-imposed blocks. Perhaps, the most devious part is that you are not aware of the internalization until others draw a blueprint. I had been witness to that in the lives of formerly incarcerated people I met at Fortune: how they blindly accepted society's labels, which had little to do with who they really were.

There is a great advantage to going public. I began meeting people who were creative and original; my coming out was a starting point for the personal life that had never really existed for me. Perhaps that was because I was confronting people on my own terms, no veiled pretenses or lies.

Richard Feldman became more than my lawyer. He is a trusted friend, a politically sharp, compassionate man, who understood my commitment to and involvement with the Fortune Society. He too was going through a life transition when I appeared on *The David Susskind Show*. When I met him, Richard informed me that as a gay man he had watched the program with his wife and had realized that he identified with my self-realization and determination to live a less deceptive life. That friendship was one of many that evolved as a result of that first of many television appearances.

My activism and public visibility continued, first on crime- and prison-related issues and later on matters gay, such as the city council's gay rights bill, which languished for fifteen years before being passed in 1985. Church leaders argued that protecting gays from discrimination in jobs, housing, and public accommodations might convert New York City into Sodom and Gomorrah. When the bill eventually became law, the fabric of life in New York wasn't altered an iota... and hundreds of thousands of tax-paying citizens were appropriately protected. The nouns were different, but the battlefield was the same for gay rights as it was for ex-offender rights. The enemies were always fear and ignorance.

When a gay man was battered by the cops, a frequent event historically, the changing tide demanded a response. I was often called
upon to be a marshal as marchers protested against police brutality.
One such incident occurred at a West Forty-Third Street honky-tonk
bar, when a transvestite took it on the chin from an out-of-control
cop who found it necessary to define his heterosexual credentials by
clubbing someone he identified as weak and vulnerable. A protest was
organized, and I was chosen by community leaders to be one of the
marshals and spokesperson of the demonstration in Times Square.

As the marchers gathered under the neon sign of the *New York
Times*, we spotted a lineup of cops, armed and ready for action. I
looked across the street and told the striking contingent not to
worry. Then I walked with confidence across Seventh Avenue to the
police brigade and pulled aside the officer in charge. My simple
words were, "Charlie . . . we're not going to have any trouble, are we?"

Sergeant Charlie Cochrane responded, "You keep your troops
under control. I'll take care of mine."

Charlie Cochrane: one of my heroes.

I had first met Charlie at Julius', a Village hangout on West Tenth
Street. Ironically, Julius', which had been a watering hole for gay men
for many years, was the bar that was elevated to the state supreme
Court in a case that argued that taverns had the right to deny service
based on sexual orientation. Julius' was around the block from my
apartment. They made delicious hamburgers at a time when I was
still eating red meat. It was also a convenient, low-pressure, and
comfortable hangout. You could watch ball games on a TV and
always find interesting small talk. I once spotted Vladimir Horowitz,
of all people, languishing in Julius'. It has a scruffy ambience, sawdust
on the floor, and it satisfied my proletariat instincts.

Charlie was at the bar many nights following a day's work. He
seemed alert about the world, and we struck up a casual neighborhood

friendship. His quick humor and contagious laugh were appealing characteristics.

One night following a political demonstration, a group of placard-holding noisemakers rushed into Julius', followed by a handful of cops challenging them and aggressively pulling them outside. I started to rise to confront the cops. Charlie grabbed my shoulder and said, "Sit down." He then trailed the cops outside. We could see him talking to the men in blue. They listened attentively and slowly gathered themselves and walked away. The protestors went in the opposite direction. Everything was serene.

When Charlie reentered the bar, I commented, "Well, Clark Kent, that was quite a performance. You're a cop, aren't you?" Charlie's professional identity was exposed. That night we entered into a long, intense conversation. Charlie, who had seen me on the Susskind show, whispered to me that he too was tired of the duplicitous life. He loved being a cop, and he was proud of his fourteen years in service. He insisted on feedback from me—guidance, if you will. I merely suggested, "Don't let rumors leak out." I noted from my own experience that if you come out, you should do it as a positive act. That provides a cushion from the inevitable opposition.

It was 1981, and the annual hearings on the gay rights bill were on the horizon. They always attracted citywide attention. Charlie listened intently to my strategy. I informed him that the hearings at City Hall always had a full house, with half the room filled with noisy gay activists and the other side consumed by church people, ragtag conservatives, and representatives from the PBA (the police union). It was street theater indoors.

The schedule was always the same. Each speaker got five minutes. First they would hear a speaker in favor of the bill, then one who was opposed. Year after year, the council members listened and voted the bill down, responding to church and PBA pressure. The threats of Sodom and Gomorrah always trumped the Bill of Rights. The bill wasn't very complicated. It merely added the words *regardless of sexual orientation* to protect citizens from discrimination in jobs, housing, and public accommodations such as restaurants and bars.

Each year, political organizers selected speakers on behalf of the gay rights bill. Many were heterosexuals, actors, parents of gays, and a few members of the cloth in an attempt to offset the evangelical fervor from the other half of the room. I suggested to Charlie that he testify, making a public announcement of his sexual orientation following the usual testimony from the PBA president. Before he agreed, I invited him to my apartment for a meeting with a half dozen men and women, all of whom had come out publicly. They shared the positive and negative aspects of their experiences with Charlie, to give him an understanding of what he might be facing. He listened intently to the various autobiographical tales and simply said, "I'm ready."

Charlie's appearance was to be the big surprise, the one the press hoped for each year.

Following the PBA's predictable opposition, Sergeant Charlie Cochran of the NYPD was introduced to city council members. Murmurs of protest rang out from the gay side of the hall. One man shouted, "They got two in a row!" We shushed the gay contingent into silence.

I was standing in the back of the hall with Ginny Apuzzo, a former Catholic nun who had become the executive director of the National Gay Task Force. We watched and listened as Charlie, with incredible dignity, introduced himself. "I'm Sergeant Charlie Cochran." He listed all of his police credentials, honors, medals, and awards and stated, "I'm proud of being a member of the New York Police Department." This was followed with a Pinter pause, as we had rehearsed. Quite audibly, he uttered the words that would make the front page of the New York dailies the next day: "And I am equally proud of being a gay man."

His statement was greeted with a momentary silence, but after about ten endless seconds, a roar arouse from the gay contingent that sounded as if the winning touchdown had been scored at Giants Stadium.

Cameras began clicking. The antigay half of the room sat in stone silence. They knew they had the votes that year, but Charlie's testimony was a warning that the tide was turning. The opposition's strong points were being chipped away.

Charlie was also the lead story on the local television news. That night, TV crews rushed to his precinct seeking comment from his fellow cops. Those interviewed all said pretty much the same thing, which was that Charlie was a stand-up guy, a good cop, and this was his personal business.

He was changing the culture of the police department, which was one of the most vociferous opponents of the gay rights bill. Other gay cops came out to him. Charlie started a new organization, the Gay Officers Action League (GOAL), comprised of police and correction officers and later joined by parole and probation representatives. A couple of years later, when he led the group in the gay pride parade down Fifth Avenue, they were two hundred strong and received great applause all over town.

Charlie and I shared the historical reality of what was happening in the seventies and eighties. As people came out, we were putting a face on the issue. Fear and ignorance were being confronted with reality. We were two of many who no longer lived behind closed doors, afraid to share our totality with family, coworkers, and friends.

In 1985 the gay rights bill was passed, and life in New York City went on with no evidence of Sodom and Gomorrah. The gay marriage bill thirty years later brought out the same crew of opposites, one side arguing that the institution of marriage would be threatened if two people living together had a ceremony cementing their relationship.

Fearmongers rarely change their tone. Reason and humanity are the most effective responses.

Charlie was president of GOAL until, after twenty years serving the people of the city, he retired to lead a comfortable life in Florida. We frequently saw each other when I vacationed in the Sunshine State. He was too active to only lie in the sun. He volunteered with an AIDS hospice in southern Florida and did part-time work with the probation department.

In 2007, Charlie was diagnosed with cancer. He fought it with a great spirit. After months of radiation and other medical interventions, his body finally surrendered. In his last months, he was walking with a cane and lost a great deal of weight. But his eyes always had sparks. He was going to fight to the end. Charlie died in 2008.

I always called him Charlie: my friend the cop.

In the early eighties, I received a phone call from a man who identified himself as a health official. He invited me to a meeting with a group of about a dozen doctors, nurses, and other health officials, plus a few community and political activists. We gathered at six a.m. at Eleventh Street and University Place, where a new clinic had opened. There we learned that eighteen men, all homosexual, all currently patients at NYU Medical Center, had an unidentified life-threatening illness. They suffered from extreme loss of weight and severe body swellings. The condition had a name: Gay-Related Immune Deficiency, or GRID.

The medical people were perplexed and deeply concerned about the medical implications, but they also assumed, wisely, that there could be serious political and social consequences because the patients had one similarity: they were all gay men. The doctors were contacting other hospitals to determine if similar diagnoses were surfacing elsewhere. They suggested this might be the start of a dangerous epidemic. They asked if we would meet with them weekly to help develop a strategy.

This was to evolve into the major health story of the second half of the century, not only in the United States, but worldwide. GRID was later renamed AIDS. In fact, it was at one of the early meetings that Ginny Apuzzo protested the name GRID. She argued effectively that dubbing a disease for a group of people was dangerous and would probably prove to be inaccurate. Her wisdom was heeded when the CDC (Centers for Disease Control) convened an emergency conference in Washington, D.C. Apuzzo's political foresight was acknowledged, and GRID was discarded and replaced with a new nomenclature: Acquired Immune Deficiency Syndrome, or AIDS.

It was later realized that before homosexual men had been diagnosed with GRID/AIDS, many homeless IV-drug users had been identified with similar ailments. Mostly, they had died and been buried in a potter's field, unclaimed and unmourned. The addicts uptown were mostly individuals isolated from mainstream America—a segment of the population viewed as disposable. That reminded me of a prevailing attitude I had discovered at the Fortune Society, an undercurrent that sent chills through me. Throughout history, wars have been fought over such attitudes.

In contrast, the gay men initially identified with the disease were all middle class, mostly white, and had community ties. Their health failures were not so rapidly dismissed.

Within weeks of that initial gathering at the health clinic, the number of patients escalated. Spencer Beach, an old friend of mine from the neighborhood, was the first person I knew so afflicted. Spence told me that he had been in and out of hospitals with this mysterious ailment. Greg Norris and I visited Spence a few times, in hospitals and at his home, and saw his health decline rapidly. In those early days, a diagnosis of AIDS was a death verdict. Spencer's funeral was the first of dozens I would attend.

AIDS had invaded the gay community, and no one knew the cause or had seen it coming. Political philistines made painful proclamations. Jerry Falwell preached that it was God's punishment against sinners, and William F. Buckley advocated that gay men be branded—echoes of Germany in the 1930s. The CDC sent inspection teams to examine the walls of gay bars. They were looking for quick explanations and made desperate efforts.

The gay activism that had solidified in the 1970s proved to be a movement that saved lives. After the Stonewall uprising, gay organizations had evolved and a network had been established. Talented men and women from every field were coming out. Sadly, for some men, coming out to friends and family happened simultaneously with the diagnosis of being HIV positive. But when the havoc devastated lives, families, and communities, there were people in place to be advocates and activists.

Our Thursday morning team placed information tables on Sheridan Square, providing the first literature to alert a community to this mysterious new health hazard. Organizations such as the Gay Men's Health Crisis and ACT UP (AIDS Coalition to Unleash Power) established health services and political protests.

Because AIDS was initially considered exclusively a "gay disease," political and media response was painfully slow. The population diagnosed was perceived in mainstream America as expendable. Political fears and institutional homophobia were blockades to a national understanding. It took years before President Ronald Reagan could utter the word AIDS. The death of film star Rock Hudson prompted Elizabeth Taylor to plead with him to put AIDS on the national health agenda.

Larry Kramer authored a play, *The Normal Heart*, a thinly veiled expose of Mayor Ed Koch's criminal silence about the epidemic sweeping across his city. Kramer's central figure was a deeply closeted mayor, who was reluctant to speak out about AIDS, lest his political career be tarnished. Ed Koch never discusses his sexual orientation. Nearly thirty years later, I talked of Ed Koch's silence when I reluctantly appeared in the documentary film *Outrage*. I had long been silent.

I had befriended Ed Koch when he was in Congress and Fortune Society was making some noise. His office was particularly responsive to abuses in federal prisons. The congressman accepted an invitation to be on the Fortune Society's advisory council. Ed was affable and responsive, and politically ambitious. We established a cordial friendship, having dinner at each other's homes and conferring on political matters. After the Susskind program, he asked why I had felt the need to go public, a curious question that reflected more about him than it did about my clear motivation.

As early as 1975, Ed indicated he would make another run for the mayoralty in New York; his effort in 1973 had fallen short of the mark, and Abe Beame had become mayor while Ed remained in Congress. He told me that he was organizing a support team, and invited me to a Sunday night potluck supper at his modest Washington Square apartment. These events continued over several months, and I met many of the men and women who would emerge as leaders in Ed's three-term reign as mayor of the nation's largest city.

I knew several of the people gathered at Ed's from community and Democratic Club meetings. One young man, Richard Nathan, became a friend. His quick humor and charming personality made him a good companion for enduring boring political tirades. Over the months, Richard and I shared many evenings together, discussing the political terrain. Richard, not so closeted, was deputy director of health in the Beame administration. He was so bright and young that almost everyone assumed he would be the next mayor's commissioner of public health. He had tossed his hat in the ring for Ed, who had a primary facing him with a bevy of all-star opponents, including Bella Abzug, Mario Cuomo, Herman Badillo, and Percy Sutton.

Koch was considered a long shot—Manhattan congressmen didn't sit well with the more conservative outer boroughs—but Ed was altering his stands. After a long political romance with Rupert Murdoch, he won the endorsement of the *New York Post*. His future and Richard Nathan's both seemed brighter.

One Sunday night with all the political groupies gathered at Koch's apartment, Richard and I were taking our turns as the cleanup squad in the kitchen. I looked into the other room and observed, "Richard, everyone is leaving; I'm checking out." Richard responded, "I'll walk you home." As we reached for our coats, Ed turned to Richard and with much concern said, "Richard, why are you leaving? Can't you stay?" I thought to myself, "What am I, chopped liver?" Richard shook his head no and informed the congressman that he had an early day tomorrow and would call him.

As we were walking across Washington Square Park, I turned to Richard and inquired, "What was that all about?" In words that could topple an empire, he told me, "I'm having a relationship with Ed." I didn't know how to respond. It was 1976, and congressmen were not known to be gay—nor were mayors. It was political death. What was Ed Koch thinking, running for mayor while having a clandestine homosexual relationship?

As the campaign moved into high gear, Ed received some wise public-relations consultation and was seen everywhere holding pinkies with Bess Myerson, a beloved New Yorker. She was a former Miss America, and Jewish. That could deliver more than a few votes. There were rumors and gossip that Bess might become the first lady of New York City.

History has recorded that Ed Koch defeated his worthy opponents in the heated Democratic primary, which was tantamount to election that year.

We all froze our asses off at the open-air New Year's Day inaugural at City Hall, and Richard and I were among the three dozen close friends invited to an after party at the home of Arthur Schwartz, the food critic at the *Daily News* and the openly gay partner of Herb Rickman. Rickman was to become Koch's Bebe Rebozo at City Hall—you had to get past Herb if you wanted to see Mayor Ed in those later days.

Ed arrived at Arthur Schwartz's with Bess, and everyone was in a celebratory mood, save Richard Nathan, who reported to me, "The gauntlet has been drawn for me. There is no role for me now or ever in this administration." He decided to leave New York and move to Los Angeles, where he established a very successful health-consultancy firm.

I was appointed to two of Ed's transition teams, one of which was interviewing prospective commissioners of correction. I might note that none of our choices were selected for the post. Ed also named me to the New York City Commission on Human Rights, a non-paying assignment but one that gave me access to the media to speak about abuses against disenfranchised and ignored New Yorkers. I was proud of the appointment:

Speech After Being Sworn in as Human Rights
Commissioner by Mayor Ed Koch
on November 8, 1979

There is no aspect of government more vital to this city than the Human Rights Commission—and I am honored and respectful of all that is inherent in being named as part of it.

One of the ingredients that make New York City so great is that it reflects a variety of people, whose backgrounds and differences make this an endowed and unique community. The challenge of this commission is not only to protect this city's varied segments, but also to find the mechanism to celebrate each subculture's uniqueness.

While city government is arduously working day by day through our fiscal crisis, negotiations with labor and management, and other vital rituals to make the machinery of government function, it is ultimately the people of this city and their atavistic richness that make all of that necessary. No agency reflects the spirit of NYC more than the Human Rights Commission, and I feel challenged to be a part of it—as it reflects the humanity of five boroughs.

I have been chosen to succeed a dear friend, Bob Livingston, whose premature death saddened many of us who are in this room today. I am indebted to Bob for the wisdom he shared with me—and I will attempt to capture the excitement and passion with which he assumed this assignment. I can think of no better role model than Bob Livingston to approach the task of being a human-rights commissioner.

Like many others, I am a transplanted New Yorker—one who came here by choice from a small town. In my case, it was from New Jersey, a village in the shadows of Manhattan but closer to Iowa in temperament and pace than to the swiftness of NYC. What attracted me to NYC when I settled here twenty years ago was the variety of people, the variations of lifestyles, language, and color. Many of us have gravitated to NYC, not only for the opportunities but because of the differences of people. It is a city that more quickly assimilates and embraces cultural variations.

Curiously, there always lurks someone or some ones who feel threatened by this wide spectrum of people—challenging you or me because we are, none of us, exactly like everyone else.

I recall my first participation in social protest—back in 1952, as an eighteen-year-old college student in Washington, D.C., when I was one of twenty youngsters participating in a CORE sit-in, attempting to integrate the People's Drug Stores in our nation's capitol. I learned much that summer, being alerted to the perimeters of the battlefield. I viewed the depths of racial hatred that could be expressed—and the irrationality and irresponsibility of ineffective government when any group of citizenry does not receive protection and the fullest opportunity to participate in all aspects of community life. Hatred has a paralyzing affect on the creative fiber of any community.

The struggle for acceptance, protection, and celebration of ethnic and religious minorities became part of American activism in the 1960s. I marched in the marches and I protested in the protests. Inadvertently, I became involved with another segment of the population in the late 1960s. Ex-convicts, unlike other groups that were victims of discrimination, had invisibility. Ex-convicts could lie about their past and thus pay another penalty...leading lives of duplicity and fear of exposure. Laws and public attitudes made ex-offenders a group that never stopped paying their dues. The conflict is subtle, and the failure of government to recognize one whole chunk of humanity alerted me again to the continuing struggle to embrace, rather than repel, people who were disenfranchised. We must be continually vigilant to tap people's potential rather than eliminate them from participation. The Fortune Society, in my life, became a clarion call for the rights and opportunities of ex-offenders.

As ex-cons were becoming visible, another group of New Yorkers were shedding their invisibility—and the community composed of closeted men and women suddenly announced that they would no longer live in shame and shadows. Slowly and painfully, I became enmeshed in that movement and recognized the liberating euphoria of self-acceptance, of abandoning the duplicity and allowing the inner voice to be heard.

I can vouch for the deadening effects of self-denial, for whatever the reason—and no city can flourish when many of its people are only half citizens, restricted by law or by ignorance.

The battleground then is legislative and educational—one without the other will allow for only hollow victories. We must remove laws of restriction and work to change antiquated attitudes of people who feel threatened by our wide range of humanity.

This sometime splintered city must learn to do more than coexist. We must recognize the excitement of our differences.

I pledge myself to work for a prouder city—and I see no aspect of government in New York more essential to the spirit of celebrating our citizenry than the Human Rights Commission.

It is an exciting time to explore the possibilities.

Ed's first term was a great disappointment. The liberal congressman was slowly moving to the right. He was not the man I had campaigned or voted for. As he approached his reelection bid in 1981, Herb Rickman asked me to be chairman of a citywide group of gays for Koch. That election coincided with a statewide referendum calling for increased funds to build more prisons. I had become a spokesman against the referendum and was debating the issue all over the state. Mario Cuomo, who had been elected as lieutenant governor under Hugh Carey, was the state's spokesman in favor of the referendum. In my many debates with Cuomo, though I disagreed with him on the prison bond-issue, I came to realize that perhaps I had picked the wrong man to support for mayor.

I told Herb Rickman it wouldn't make sense for me to head a citywide support group for Ed, since I was a visible spokesman against prison construction and Ed was in favor of it. Richman told me that shouldn't make any difference, and I argued that it would make a difference to me—that building prisons went against everything I stood for. He responded, "You are making a very, very, very, very, very big mistake." I informed him I never had so many *verys* imposed on me.

Shortly after Ed was reelected, I was not reappointed to the Commission on Human Rights. A statement was released stating that I had had poor attendance at the monthly meetings. Jack Newfield, a friend and a solid journalist, noted that I was actually the one member of the commission with perfect attendance.

Years later, when AIDS was the center of discussion at many health conferences, Richard Nathan met playwright-activist Larry Kramer, who was Ed Koch's archenemy because of the play he had written and all of the protests he led against the Koch administration. Larry was an organizer of ACT UP, a noisy protestor against Koch's response—or lack of response—to AIDS.

The story gets blurry here. Richard gave me one version, Larry another. Either way, the two men talked at the health conference and agreed that they both knew me, and Richard admitted to Larry that he was the much-rumored former secret lover of Mayor Ed Koch. Koch at this time was seeking a fourth term and facing a primary fight with Manhattan borough president David Dinkins (who I enthusiastically supported). Larry Kramer returned to New York after the conference and called several journalists to tell them that Richard Nathan was Ed Koch's former lover and that the one man who could validate it was David Rothenberg.

I arrived at my office the next morning and was greeted by a half dozen reporters, all seeking confirmation of Nathan's affair with Koch. A mayor accused of having a homosexual relationship was a sitting duck and big headlines. I feigned ignorance to the newspapermen, who included friends like Jack Newfield, and then called Dick Nathan in California and asked him if he was out of his mind. "You could become the Judith Exner of New York politics."

Richard argued that he had had no idea Kramer would call the press. I promised him silence. I was not enchanted with Ed Koch's incumbency but felt that coming out was a personal matter, and that I didn't have the right to reveal the private life of another individual. (There have been political arguments against that position, citing closeted right-wing elected officials, like former Idaho senator Larry Craig of men's-room foot-tapping fame, who vote against all legislation that benefits or protects gay people.)

A few weeks later, Richard called me and asked for my availability to dine. He was being subpoenaed to appear before a representative of federal prosecutor Rudolph Giuliani (who was preparing to run for mayor and assumed that his opponent would be the incumbent, Ed Koch). Giuliani's man, Richard later told me, grilled him for hours. The crux of it was that Richard had received a small consultant's fee from the New York City Department of Health. Richard had been a consultant for many city and state governments—that's what he did—and this was a task Koch had not even known about. Giuliani was hunting for political ammunition against Koch, which would include revelation of his past lover.

Richard was a wreck when we had dinner following the inquisition. He foresaw a smear campaign, one that was ultimately averted when David Dinkins upset Koch in the primary and then defeated Giuliani, who was running as a Republican, in the general election. (Four years later, Giuliani would unseat Dinkins.) Later, much later, Richard informed me that he and Ed had established a cordial friendship and dined together on rare occasions. I asked him if Ed was cognizant of my stonewalling about his and Richard's relationship. He said, "We've talked about it a great deal." I found that interesting, because the few times I had run into Koch he had been blunt and dismissive, and on one occasion he'd even feigned he didn't recognize me.

Richard Nathan died in 2000, and I was named cotrustee of his estate with his California attorney, Fred Hertz. Dick had left instructions that his money should be distributed for civil-liberties, environmental, and gay causes. Of the latter he had often said, "What about that kid in Oklahoma who doesn't have the support system those of us in New York and California had?" He wanted us to search out the neediest of groups to support. Fred and I managed the Richard Nathan Trust Fund and worked assiduously to locate small groups around the nation: Latinos in San Antonio, gay Mormons in Utah, gay labor activists in Kentucky. It was an exciting venture and a tribute to Richard's humanity. He should be remembered for his courageous work in the health field and his legacy to reach disenfranchised Americans.

His clandestine affair with Ed Koch attracts more media interest posthumously, but it is his body of work that I celebrate.

My early work with AIDS was a clarion call for action. In both the civil rights movement and working with ex-prisoners, I had seen the intolerable perception that some people were not important enough—that their lives were of secondary concern. In politics and in theater, I was often surrounded by men and women who had a sense of entitlement, and they were impervious to the other America. Much of my rage against traditional mores is that very condition: some Americans are considered less important because of the labels imposed on them. It was all of a piece to me. African Americans, Native Americans, Latinos, former prisoners, and gay people may be different in their makeup and sensibilities, but they share the heavy foot of oppression, whether members of each group recognize it or not.

America's subcultures, the hyphenated Americans who exist outside the Hallmark picture dream image, provide a richness and diversity that give a vital pulse to our nation. I am never comfortable in any environment where everyone is the same.

In the early days of the AIDS epidemic, we faced ignorance. The instincts of the health officials at that first meeting were that political activism was essential to challenge the fears. But the president was silent. The mayor of New York City was cautious. And the influential *New York Times* was absent. Our team, those of us who were giving political insight to the doctors, reminded the group of an outbreak at an American Legion convention in Philadelphia a few years earlier. Delegates attending the convention had been struck with an enigmatic disease that resulted in four deaths. It was a front-page story across the country, subject of TV reports and magazine features. AIDS, on the other hand, had reached more than one thousand fatalities, and in its first four years was the subject of a single, inside-page story in the *New York Times*.

The *Times* had a long, homophobic history that had to be challenged. In the sixties, freelance journalist Cliff Jahr had authored a travel feature for the Sunday edition, a saga about a trip-to-nowhere on an all-gay cruise ship. The morning after that story appeared, Iphigene Sulzberger, the dowager empress of the family that owned the *Times*, sent a terse note to the managing editor stating that such stories were not acceptable. As a result, it became unwritten policy that the words *gay* and *lesbian* were verboten at the paper of record. The gay movement was making thunderous noise in the late sixties into the seventies, but the *Times* had to slip-slide past more than one newsworthy story.

I met with closeted reporters, critics, and editors at the *Times*, who shared with me the institutional homophobia at the paper, a policy that limited their coverage of genuine news.

The newly formed Gay Men's Health Crisis sponsored a historic fundraising event, the type of benefit the *Times* Style section would ordinarily recognize were any other group at the helm. It was a sold-out, all-star event at Madison Square Garden, with Leonard Bernstein conducting the opening number and Liza Minnelli singing while eighteen thousand men and women cheered. Television cameras were in evidence, more interested in celebrity coverage than reflecting on the cause, but they were there. The *Times* did not cover it because it was viewed as a "gay story."

In fact, it was more than a benefit. It was a demonstration, organized by a large section of New Yorkers, that lives were being lost amidst silence and indifference. One man bellowed that the absence of the *Times* was tantamount to the silence in Germany when the press failed to record the roundup of Jews.

A letter was drafted to the publisher of the *Times*, noting that they were missing a major health story because of institutional homophobia. We received a quick response and were invited to meet with Sydney Gruson, associate publisher of the paper. He had close ties to the Sulzberger family, so a meeting with him was an indication that our letter was being taken seriously. If there had been no response to our letter, there were plans to picket and boycott the paper.

The meeting with Gruson was a historic gathering, and the implications were vast. With me were NGTF president Ginny Apuzzo, Judge Richard Failla, and writer-activist Andy Humm. Sydney Gruson was a sophisticated man, not ill at ease with gay and lesbian spokespersons.

In contrast, some of our early confrontations about AIDS with elected officials had been pitiful and embarrassing. One city councilman, clearly uncomfortable in our presence, did not view us as people or citizens or voters. He constantly alluded to the sexual behavior in which he imagined all gay people participated. It took great restraint not to shout at him, "Don't heterosexuals have a sexual component?" When we were talking to him about health, housing, and jobs, he saw only sex.

We had met with conservative rabbis, ministers, and priests, who predictably protested against our "lifestyle." At one such meeting, I was short on patience and observed, "My lifestyle is going to work five days a week, attending endless community meetings, looking for time to see a movie or read a book. What part of that is objectionable?"

Those misconceptions and displays of ignorance were what made the meeting with Gruson so essential. Newspaper and TV coverage of the gay community in those early days, post-Stonewall, focused exclusively on sex. The combination of our invisibility at the *Times* and the sensational, sexualized reports in the tabloids created a distortion. That gay people had a sexual component was true, but we kept alluding to the fact that we were all present as a result of heterosexual intercourse. That plain and obvious fact often embarrassed our antagonists. I realized the problem was not their fear or disapproval of homosexuality, but of sex in general. They saw us only as sexual beings, not in our totality.

At the conclusion of our meeting, Gruson informed us that he would arrange a luncheon with Abe Rosenthal, the ferocious and much-feared managing editor of the *Times*. Rosenthal was generally considered one of the most influential men in the city. A meeting with him confirmed that the *Times* was hearing our protests.

As a veteran publicist, I knew that a story in the *New York Times* would give a green light of acceptability to the local and national news assignment desks. The way the *Times* handled any story had a rippling effect on the rest of the media. I recalled many days visiting local and national TV desks, observing editors circling stories in the *Times* and going for the phone.

Word had to get out. America was losing some vital resources in an atmosphere of silence. ACT UP was handing out buttons, flyers, and T-shirts that shouted SILENCE = DEATH. Some prominent citizens with AIDS were being identified. So were priests and actors, doctors and lawyers. The fashion industry, dominated by gay men, remained stonily closeted and silent until AIDS began surfacing, and then they, too, became involved. Tardy—but involved.

We discussed all of these factors as we prepared to lunch with Rosenthal. We created a list of possible stories that would humanize the health crisis. That was the important starting point. Our strategy was clear: We didn't want to bombard Rosenthal with a collection of complaints. We would outline the problem and offer pragmatic suggestions. We wanted the *Times* to introduce its readers to the medical and political implications of AIDS.

We were ushered into the private dining room, where *Times* editors traditionally meet with presidential candidates, foreign leaders, and Nobel Prize winners. Rosenthal was not alone. He had invited several other editors. We were armed for battle, prepared for resistance.

He stunned us with the opening: "We need your help. Tell us what you know and what we can do." That almost took the wind out of our sails. But we made our points, not the least of which was that the *Times* needed to do some self-examination. We asserted that they had talented writers and editors who could cover AIDS and other gay-related stories. I said that I knew several closeted gay reporters. Rosenthal argued that the *Times* would never fire anyone because of their sexual orientation.

"Perhaps not," I stated, "but their perception is that they could become the next correspondent from Casper, Wyoming."

The editor laughed and proclaimed, "You've done your homework."

We suggested they had to create room for men and women inside the "Gray Lady" to not feel threatened, and to give them room to excel. Among the initial stories we proposed was a feature on the "buddy system" that GMHC had inaugurated, where volunteers were assisting homebound men with AIDS. It was and is a dramatic human-interest story. We also called their attention to an upcoming regional conference of parents of gays and lesbians. PFLAG would provide a new perspective on gay issues: the rippling effects of social denial and how it fractures the family. The health crisis had become a game of Russian roulette for many parents.

News travels fast. After the luncheon with Rosenthal, I returned to my office and was greeted by calls from *Times* reporters. One man said, "Things are changing. Thanks."

After those stories appeared in the *Times*, TV news reporters increased their coverage of AIDS and began giving serious consideration to the gay community. The increased coverage prompted influential political people to campaign for financing, treatment, and research. AIDS became the media's major health issue, gaining cover stories in national magazines. The press was playing catch-up, bringing along with them hesitant political leaders, baffled religious monarchs, and households confronting the possible death of a loved one.

Shame and fear of human sexuality puts blinders on people who shape policy. Because AIDS was initially considered a gay disease, false and dangerous judgments were responsible for neglect and possibly the deaths of too many people.

My role in fighting ignorance and misconceptions about the formerly incarcerated fueled me for this battle on behalf of people with AIDS. I functioned best as a grassroots agitator. Others are better equipped for expanded roles and larger battles.

TWELVE

Candidate and Transition

I became a candidate for political office in 1985, in a city council race in lower Manhattan, an infinitesimal speck on the political tapestry of America.

But I was running as an openly gay man in the midst of an AIDS epidemic, and this usually ignored city council race had rippling implications. The Sunday *Daily News* magazine profiled me on its cover; *New York* magazine, which had ignored my coming out a decade earlier, featured me as "the Great Gay Candidate." Manhattan congressman Ted Weiss reportedly assumed the role of Cerberus, assuring my opponent that no national figure would support my candidacy.

In 1985, a candidate not hiding his homosexuality was newsworthy, the kind of icebreaker the media thrive on. If I were to announce as a candidate in the second decade of the twenty-first century, the news would hardly produce a blip on the screen.

My motivation for taking this presumptuous and daunting political turn was prompted by the AIDS epidemic sweeping through New York City amidst political and media inertia. One sentiment that kept surfacing in the early eighties was that no one in the corridors of power was responsive to the medical crisis, to the overload of patients in hospitals and the mounting death toll. It was not on the priority list of any elected officials.

The deaths were overwhelming. The funerals and memorial services were coming at the rate of two and three a week. So many decent men died too early. Friendships I assumed would nourish and sustain me in my later years were suddenly gone. Many were friends and colleagues twenty years younger than I.

Actor Rob Savio's mother called me after his funeral and asked if I would merely say his name on my weekly radio program so that people knew he had been here. I did much more than that. I talked of Rob's early success as an actor; our friendship, which began in the theater; and my last day seeing this once-handsome man as nothing but skin and bones.

Witty, intelligent Brian Riordan was a friend I first met in a men's support group, where I asked him why he was wasting his obvious talents as a bank teller in Queens. Shortly after, I arranged an interview for him with a successful literary agent. Brian's skills were evident, and he became a respected and successful theater agent, representing such talents as Alec Baldwin, Laura Linney, and many others. Brian took me to dinner one night and told me he had tested positive. We talked about fighting it, but in time he began fading, and his death was a tragedy. Together with his beautiful family, I mourned and cried.

Michael Cohen loved movies as much as I did. He would check with me every Friday so we could determine which flicks would gain our attention over the weekend. Going to the movies with Michael was a religious experience—we weren't allowed to talk and share our perspectives until the conclusion—until his six-foot frame began to stoop, and his energy dissipated. On his last night, I sat with his mother and a few friends, knowing it was the end. Such vigils were not uncommon in New York City.

Stark Hesseltine, a theatrical agent, invited me as a guest to his restful abode in East Hampton. One summer he told me my work at Fortune Society was too important, and I should have a retreat from the pressure and tension. He built a small guesthouse in the backyard, handed me the key, and said it was mine when I needed to get away. In his last weeks, he would see no one—a choice I understood. But he sent me a note of "thanks for the friendship" before he died. His lawyer called me after his death and informed me that Stark had left me a generous gift in his will. At first I didn't want to accept it, to benefit from the death of a friend, but his longtime associate told me that that was what Stark had wanted and I should allow him that.

I marched in protests with Vito Russo. We always found each other: while the more vocal enthusiasts were defying police blockades with shouts of "They say stay back; we say fight back!" Vito and I would huddle and lift our banners but talk about old movies. He always had the latest film dirt. At one rally, while cops on horseback were pushing us into a wall, Vito turned to me and said, "Thelma Ritter had eight nominations and never won an Oscar. Now that's injustice." I couldn't stop laughing, much to the consternation of NYPD horseback riders and defiant protestors. His book, *The Celluloid Closet*, became an Oscar-winning documentary, and his early death was shattering to me.

Every week another friend called me to say good-bye. I visited Ken Dawson in the hospital. I couldn't recognize this handsome man in his final days; his body was so ravaged. The nurse had to identify him for me.

There were so many others: Norman Kenneson, Reed Jones, Phil Carey, Bobby Drivas, Tom Stoddard, Bobby Christensen, Steven Chernesky, Michael Grumley, Robert Ferro, Mark Goldstaub, Louis Falco, Fritz Holt, Robert Latourneau, Leonard Frey, Peter Vogel, Larry Josephs, Don Castellanos, Michael Callen, Richard Failla. When I was asked to recite names as the famous AIDS quilt was unfolded on the Hudson piers, I couldn't recite all the names. Years of emotion overtook me.

We had organized endless meetings, applied pressure where we could, but the sentiment was that we needed a candidate to include

AIDS on the political agenda. Funding for health care geared toward the AIDS crisis had no passionate spokesperson in elected office at any level.

I was part of a group developing a political strategy. Ginny Apuzzo, Peter Vogel, Tim Sweeney, and Ken Dawson were all community activists. Peter and Ginny had strong Democratic Club ties in Brooklyn. We laid out a blueprint. Who could run for office, who could win, and what was needed for staging a serious candidate?

The body politic suggested the following:

1) The candidate had to have a visibility in several areas outside of AIDS and gay activism. Our choice could not be labeled a "single issue" candidate. Futile political efforts had been made in the past by gay candidates, but their efforts had been symbolic rather than substantial. As single-issue candidates, they had had little impact on the political scene. Then there had been no AIDS crisis to suddenly create a sense of urgency.

2) The candidate had to run to win. We would have to raise money for a real contest to be realized. We determined that a Manhattan candidate would have the best opportunity to win.

3) The candidate had to run against a vulnerable incumbent, since there were no open seats. Almost all Manhattan council members gave lip service to progressive issues, but a few had clearly indicated they had lost touch with segments of the community they represented.

Carol Greitzer was a sixteen-year incumbent in my district, which covered Greenwich Village, Chelsea, and a curiously gerrymandered sliver of the East Side. Greitzer had begun her political career joined at the hip with Ed Koch. At the outset, both were viewed as liberal and innovative, and she was one of the few women in office when she ignited her political career. She had slowed down during the intervening years. As I noted frequently in public forums and in a weekly column I authored, she represented a district with some of the most creative and exciting men and women in America, but she had a lackluster presence, hardly reflective of the energy that existed in the Village and Chelsea—and she had hardly uttered a concern about AIDS.

It became clear to all that Greitzer was "soft" and past her political prime. That was my district, and it was put to me, most forcefully by Peter Vogel, to consider running for office.

I had volunteered in numerous political campaigns, stuffing envelopes and handing out literature, but I had never entertained the notion of running. The irony was that the very reason I would run was why I had never considered being a candidate. As I noted in my unpublished *New York* magazine essay, when I was an undergraduate and a member of Denver's Young Democrats Club, a fiery young state legislator named Bob Allen suggested I remain in Colorado after graduation and consider a life in politics, but I knew his suggestion was absurd. Because of my secret, the suffocating closet, I had to live in a large city, preferably New York, where the crowds would serve as protection against disclosing secrets. Denver in the fifties was a "cow town," where cowboys and farmers would hit the city on the weekends. I loved Denver, but knew it was too small to protect me. You couldn't walk downtown without running into a half dozen people you knew. Gay men and women in that era made residential choices based on survival, which explains San Francisco and New York City.

Representing the Fortune Society, I had wandered through City Hall and Albany, and even the United States Senate and House in Washington, D.C. I had developed friendships with more than a few incumbents and staff members at all levels. My years as a spokesman on criminal-justice issues evoked some visibility. Local news stations frequently sought me out for comments or sound bites about prison, crime, the courts, or the entire criminal-justice system.

I agreed to step forward. I was not concerned about challenging Greitzer. I had been identified with more than one issue. Most importantly, from the inception of AIDS, I had been a visible presence in the city, forcing AIDS to be recognized as a legitimate concern, challenging political people and the media.

Victory in the 1985 September Democratic primary was tantamount to being elected. Apuzzo and Vogel were my political gurus, blueprinting a two-year strategy for me.

My first assignment was to engage a campaign manager. Dave Fleischer, a bundle of energy and wunderkind community organizer, filled the bill. Money had to be raised, and I had to be coached on complicated land-use issues. Real estate and development are Manhattan's equivalent to oil in Texas. If I didn't know real estate, it wouldn't matter what I knew or did about AIDS or city jails. I was a quick study and learned the ABCs of Manhattan land use quickly. Excellent tutors walked me through the reality of urban politics.

Money is always a factor in a successful campaign. Fleischer arranged hundreds of house parties during the next twenty-four months. We raised more than $250,000, a record at that time for a city council race. Nightly events and endless talks to small groups were the grassroots heart of the campaign. The average gift was a little more than twenty-five dollars per person, and we had support from inside and outside the district.

Dave found a storefront on Bedford Street, in the West Village. Our showcase headquarters became a beehive of activity. On volunteer nights, tables and chairs filled up the sidewalks and spilled onto the streets. Italian grandmas were stuffing envelopes along with gay men, lesbians, ex-cons, and an array of political groupies. Young men and women who had never been politically involved caught the fever. More than five hundred volunteers participated at the height of the campaign. A quarter of a century later, I still meet men and women, now approaching middle age, who inform me that their first political race was "Rothenberg for Change."

Greitzer, as a long-time incumbent, hadn't anticipated a serious challenge. Few incumbents in New York City confront real opposition. Suddenly there was a competitive race, and the media focused on it. The issues I put on the table and my announced sexual orientation created more than casual interest.

I was a good candidate, but I knew from the get-go that this was not my natural ambience. You learn early on that every room you walk into, you are the reason that people have gathered. It can be an aphrodisiac, that flattering realization that everyone assembled wants to savor your opinion and get close to you. But the thirst for approval has to be unquenchable. Within weeks I had to hold my breath and dig deep into myself as I entered another apartment for a fundraiser, another hall for a debate, or another meeting with union and/or business leaders.

As a theatrical press agent, I had been the holder of the coat, the person in the background, comfortable making acidic comments about the assemblage. With the Fortune Society, I had learned to express myself passionately on the subjects of the criminal-justice system and the prisons. When you are the candidate, you are the "one." There can be no slips, caustic asides, or passionate outbursts.

Every presidential race is followed by an avalanche of books detailing the angst of various candidates. The experience of scrutiny is no less at a local level. The intensity is paramount. Every word, each gesture is analyzed. It takes an alligator skin to be impervious to continuous judgments.

I was startled by the presumptuous questions. As an openly gay candidate, I had anticipated some challenges in that arena. What I hadn't expected was for conservative or self-serving gay activists to make inquiry of my relationships and how my sexuality manifested itself. I told one gay reporter that I apologized for not having slides. He responded in print with a series of attacks.

I recalled campaigning with Congressman Ed Koch when he ran for mayor in 1977. He basked in the face-to-face combat with voters. Over coffee, after such a session, I recognized that Ed was charged up, fulfilled by the public nature of his candidacy. His gas tank was filled by the public attention, the endless scrutiny. Ed's famous comment to one and all as he walked the streets was "How am I doing?" I often wondered why he didn't ask, "How are you doing?" That made me realize I lacked something essential in combative politics.

My motivation as a candidate was fueled by the funerals I attended and the hospitals I visited. I had to temper my pain and hurt when I spoke publicly about AIDS so that I would remain within the boundary lines of politics. I was warned to not sound like I was on a crusade.

It was apparent I would win the voters in the Village and Chelsea, but the heavily populated East Side was Koch territory, and he was pulling Greitzer along. I suspect he viewed my candidacy with caution, knowing that I had stonewalled for a decade about his sexual peccadilloes. Richard Nathan still loomed in the background. Newspapermen pulled at my sleeves regarding Ed's secrets.

It isn't news to anyone that politics is a compromising arena. If you have a passion about an issue, you can be quickly disillusioned. In the middle of the campaign my neighbor, attorney Bill Kunstler, embraced me with one of his famous bear hugs and bellowed in his barrister's voice, "I had to register to vote because of you. I never vote for those Tweedledums and Tweedledees." And then he warned me, "This is no place for you. You'll have to compromise to survive or they'll kill you. You're a heel nipper. You should be on the outside. It won't work for you to be on the inside." Ominous words indeed, but

I was beginning to understand what he was preaching. I like the description of a "heel nipper," the conscience prodding the power brokers. That was a role with which I was comfortable.

At one candidates' forum, several incumbents and would-be challengers were presenting their views and answering questions. A man in the audience sought political insight on the drug problem. I listened as my colleagues gave evasive answers and safe responses, and then I volunteered, "Decriminalize drugs. If we continue to take people with *habits*, who should be called *patients*, and put them into a prison, we are contributing to the escalation of crime, because prison is a school for crime." There were some mumbles and quick efforts to move on to new topics.

Moments after the panel concluded, two incumbents cornered me, disapproving of my "militant" stand on drugs. Their response was staggering, because both had secretly revealed to me that they supported my candidacy; though they could never publically oppose an incumbent, they were rooting for me. I wanted to know why they disagreed with me. They didn't. They just feared the public wasn't ready for "decriminalization," and by taking a stand I would be forcing other candidates to assume a position. I argued that there must be times when a political leader should lead and bring the public along. They viewed me as naïve, and the final words, clearly stated with a finger pointing in my face, were "Don't push it."

I did win some endorsements: the *Daily News*, the *Village Voice*, the *Amsterdam News*. The *New York Times* applauded my candidacy and suggested that I had a future—but obviously not at present. They found no reason to unseat my opponent.

Campaigns have unexpected moments of dismay and horror, often matched with great satisfaction. One morning, volunteers clutched me by the arm, snake-dancing through the crowds at a street fair, chanting, "Keep the dream alive." I appreciated their enthusiasm but was embarrassed to be pulled along as if I were on a leash. At one point I asked, "Where is the organ grinder?"

At the other end of the spectrum was what occurred on the Saturday morning Dave Fleischer pushed me into Penn South. This vast building complex, created by the International Ladies' Garment Workers' Union, had a high voting turnout and seniors who professed to champion liberal causes. My assignment was to invade the premises and go door-to-door introducing myself and handing out literature. It is a fairly degrading process. Doors are slammed in your face, dogs growl, pussycats cringe, and seniors peek out from behind chained portals proclaiming they don't want to buy any.

Yet there is that rare moment when the sun shines. I knocked on one door, and it was opened by a tall, stately gentleman I immediately recognized: Bayard Rustin, in all of his splendor—Rustin, the man had who engineered and energized Martin Luther King's famed march on Washington, D.C. I felt like a teenager without my autograph book. I blurted out an introduction and handed him my literature, babbling something about what a pleasure it was to meet him. He smiled, took the flyers, and said, "I know who you are, and I'm going to vote for you." I left the building in a different stratosphere. I said to myself, "If they tally the quality of voters, I'm a shoo-in. Bayard Rustin knows who I am. Who would have thunk it?"

I had the third largest number of votes of any candidate in the city's thirty-eight council races. Unfortunately, my opponent had the second greatest number of votes, which indicated that the turnout was in record numbers for this one well-publicized battle. I garnered nearly forty-five percent of the votes. Impressive, I was told, for my first time out. I was not to make history as the first openly gay elected official in New York, but I did pave the way, and many others have followed. Tom Duane, four years later, defeated Greitzer. Christine Quinn followed Tom in the city council after he became a state senator. It's hardly news anymore, and that's the way it should be. In

New York City, at least, being gay, black, Latino, or a woman isn't enough. You have to bring more to the table to energize your base.

Dave Fleischer's most creative, nonpolitical gift to me was a Passover seder he choreographed in the spring before the primary election of September 1984. It was held at my apartment, and I was a guest, not the host.

David was more than acquainted with my agnosticism. I had had flirtations with religion all my life. The Hebrew schools and then the Christian Scientists on Sundays with my grandmother only made me more suspicious of organized religion. I recall a Friday night service when I was ten, where the rabbi utilized the entire service to excoriate those not in attendance. Even in my prepubescent innocence, I asked my mother why he didn't talk to those of us who attended the service rather than berating Jews in absentia. (Those weren't my exact words. My vocabulary probably prompted, "We're here, Mom. Why doesn't he talk to us?")

In college, I attended Unitarian services, mostly because Denver's Reverend Rudy Gilbert's Sunday sermons focused on social injustice and political malfeasance. Those were the motivating factors for my attending the Baptist Judson Memorial Church in Greenwich Village. I had heard the Reverend Howard Moody at a Democratic Party event and was so inspired by his Adlai Stevenson like intonations that I be - came a faithful attendee of his religious domicile in the heart of NYU.

If my Jewish presence at a Baptist church seemed unlikely, it wasn't as if traditional Baptists could figure out the Judson Memorial Church, where Reverend Moody shared the Sunday pulpit with openly gay Reverend Al Carmines. Al not only brought a unique ecclesiastical perspective to the hallowed grounds, he also wrote popular musical plays, many of which were successfully produced off-Broadway after being premiered at Judson. I was a frequent guest speaker at Judson, the most memorable time being for a salute to children. I invited a few Fortune alumni, men and women who had been reared in foster homes and youth facilities and were now successful and loving parents, having broken the cycle of abuse and neglect. We invited clowns from the Big Apple Circus to join us in the celebration. The clowns led the entire congregation, and the many children with hundreds of balloons, into Washington Square Park. The balloons went aloft, and we sang traditional, uplifting folk songs, celebrating the youngest people in our midst.

Religion like that had meaning to me because it didn't offend my spiritual life.

Dave's creative seder incorporated my sentiments about traditional rituals. The two dozen men and women in attendance were from all over the world. They each brought food that reflected the geography of their youth. The four questions were asked, the wine was served, and Elijah was invited to enter. We included the ingredients that were readily recognizable to veterans of Passovers past, but the new flavors were more exciting.

Passover, celebrating the Jews' flight from Egypt, is about freedom. Dave suggested that many of the guests reflect on their journeys. One was a young woman who had fled apartheid in her South African homeland. She understood the sentiments of the Passover because she was living it, centuries after the Jews had sought escape. A young gay man whose Orthodox Jewish family had disowned him because of his sexual orientation had fled to New York City, where he'd found acceptance. A couple of college students who had been raised in Eastern European countries under Communist domination told of how their families had escaped to the West and finally to the United States. As we went around the room, each young person sharing his or her iconoclastic autobiography, I had a sense of Passover unknown to me before. It was a deeply spiritual experience and gave me an understanding of the passions of Passover.

I have had many close friendships with priests, rabbis, and ministers of various denominations, including Islam. These men and women are less insistent on ritual but see their faith and religion as a plank leading to social justice and to fulfilling human potential.

On reflection, I often challenged myself about faith and the uncharted mysteries of life. My suspicion and aversion to organized religion is contradicted by the fact that the most inspirational leaders in my life have been men of deep faith. Mahatma Gandhi and Martin Luther King are my philosophical mentors—and Rudy Gilbert and Howard Moody have been among my guides to spiritual strength.

I have often commented that religion interfered with my faith. Perhaps I'm most suspicious of traditional religions that insist we be in constant negotiation with the superpower, the gods or god of their choice, while simultaneously being impervious to the pragmatic needs of those on this planet. It has always seemed far easier to make plans for the unknown than to confront the reality at the doorstep. When religion is irrelevant to the here and now, the rituals and rules are more than hypocritical; they are irrelevant.

After my impressive showing in the city council race, most political activists assumed I would run again. I told Tom Duane privately that the race was his if he wanted it. I had decided I would not be a candidate again, but I was not ready to announce it publicly. In fact, in 1986 the Village Independent Democrats implored me to be their candidate for state committeeman in the Democratic Party, not an assignment I desired. The VID was in a battle with organizers of a new group attached to Ed Koch's more conservative and established club. I felt indebted to the VID, agreed to run, and took eighty-five percent of the votes. Everyone around me insisted that was evidence that I had a political future, but I knew that my political future was behind me.

The city council race left me flat broke. During the last months of the campaign, I had taken a leave of absence from the Fortune Society. I checked in two or three times a week, but I was off the payroll, modest as it was. The Fortune staff, enthusiastically behind my candidacy, had kept the organization going on a day-to-day basis. Things were in good order there. Fleischer had made sure all campaign bills were paid, so while my personal finances were in troubled waters, I owed no money.

It was time for some life-changing assessments. I kept humming Sondheim's song "I'm Still Here," from *Follies*, in which the old Broadway veteran sings, "Then you career from career to career." I brought together the leadership at Fortune Society and suggested it was time for me to move on. Fortune could continue without me. The inevitable flatterers suggested it would go under if I left, but I knew that those sentiments, if true, would indicate that I had failed. Building a foundation makes the structure of an organization strong. I was confident the pieces were in place: Each component had been determined by the needs of the men and women who entered our doors.

In 1986 Fortune was well situated, with a staff of nearly forty people and a solid foundation. It had to grow, but my best effort was as a groundbreaker, an organizer at a grassroots level. Fortune needed leadership and skills that were not my forte. I certainly wasn't tired of the struggle, but I recognized my limitations: I had done all I could to shape and develop the organization. Mary Follett would serve as an interim director and Vinnie DeFrancesco would be the day-to-day enforcer.

A year later, JoAnne Page became my successor. She was the perfect choice: her vision was beyond my grasp. Under her leadership, the Fortune Society grew in ways that were beyond my administrative capabilities.

One of the things I noticed watching other organizations that grew in the sixties was that the founders became possessive or challenging of their successors. Projects that begin with passion have to move into maturity; personalities must come second to determined goals. I was secure that Fortune would survive. It had to, because the new drug laws were escalating imprisonment. The need was greater than ever.

What was ahead for me at the age of fifty-two? My overlapping vocational life had consisted of a quarter of a century working in the theater and working with ex-convicts, often at the same time. That's what I knew. So in early 1986 I put up a shingle at 1501 Broadway, the Paramount Theater Building in the heart of Times Square, and waited to see if anyone in the theater remembered me.

I was a different man from the wide-eyed, starstruck youngster who had worked with Max Eisen in the late fifties. My years at the Fortune Society had presented me with a calmer, more mature perspective. I viewed with bemused fascination the hysterics displayed by colleagues in the theater. Drama queens were in full throttle. In my daily routine at the Fortune Society I had often confronted life-and-death situations and other dramatic real-life incidents. I approached the theater with a newfound serenity.

In little time, producers and general managers were presenting me with off-Broadway plays. My old friend Greg Dawson, now an owner of the Ballroom, a successful cabaret, invited me to represent many of his incoming artists, including Margaret Whiting, Anita Ellis, Blossom Dearie, and eventually Peggy Lee.

Greg also sponsored an innovative improvisational group, Artificial Intelligence. The clever Nancy Cassaro was the driving force of the talented young performers, and her humor and intelligence appealed to me. We began laughing together the day we met. After we'd worked together for one gig at the Ballroom, she invited me to a workshop tryout of a concept the group was developing: the recreation of a real wedding ceremony held in a church, with the audience invited to a reception hall for dinner, dancing, and a view of the feuding families. They were calling it *Tony n' Tina's Wedding*. This innovative, hysterically funny farrago ran for more than two decades and has played around the nation. It has also inspired copycat shows, one with an audience involved in a bar mitzvah, another at a grandma's funeral, and several wedding variations, including a Jewish ceremony and one with a gay couple.

The February 1988 debut of *Tony n' Tina's Wedding* gave me a bona fide hit in the theater. A year later, I met three young men, Chris Wink, Matt Goldman, and Phil Stanton, who had found off-Broadway producers for their unique comedy show. Blue Man Group opened at the Astor Place Theatre in October of 1989 and hasn't taken a breath since, continuing in New York while playing around the globe, from Las Vegas to Buenos Aires to Berlin and Tokyo.

In addition, I was representing performers at the Ballroom, the Oak Room at the Algonquin, and Michael's Pub, a popular nitery owned by a gargoyle of a man, Gil Weist. Gil Weist stories are legendary in New York's nightlife, and I was witness to the gathering tales. Gil had Woody Allen's musical combo on Monday nights, and for the remainder of the week he highlighted an array of stars that included Joan Rivers, Mel Tormé, Joe Williams, Frank Gorshin, and many more.

Gil was most famous for his rudeness and inhospitality to his performing artists. This was revealed to me one evening when I knocked on the dressing-room door of singer Maureen McGovern, who was headlining that week at Michael's Pub. "What's up?" she asked, and I said I was merely stopping by to wish her the best and say hello. "Oh, David," the songstress said, "how nice of you. But there's no need for both of us to be here. I have to be. Call me when you want." I laughed all the way home at her counsel.

Gil worked the lights at the bistro, saving one salary. He often taunted the performers as they prepared their entrances. As one singer was being introduced, Gil leaned over to her and whispered, "You're probably the worst single act I've ever booked here." She staggered onto the stage in befuddlement.

Greg Dawson arranged for me to meet Peggy Lee, who was rehearsing her new show at the Ballroom. I watched from the back of the room as she instructed her lighting man to focus the pinpoint spot on her thumb as she snapped her fingers in darkness, a dramatic introduction to her signature song, "Fever." It was fascinating to view this pro in action, who knew the wattage of the bulbs like she knew the notes of her song. Once again, I recognized that divas didn't become stars by accident.

Peggy Lee was a beauty and had a deliciously purring voice, but she worked at her career and never took her talent for granted. The four-week engagement went well, and on the final night, she embraced me warmly and asked if I would represent her when she returned to New York. We continued our partnership for the next fifteen years, until her death. I came to enjoy her personality the same way I loved her singing style; I treasured the talent and the relationship. In her last engagement at the New York Hilton, she was in a wheelchair and living in a suite upstairs. Following each performance, she would greet the elites of show business who came to pay homage. I always joined her as she greeted Liza or Madonna or K. D. Lang.

My favorite Peggy Lee memory is when she once called me at midnight from California. "David," she purred, "I want to sing some Frank Loesser songs when I return to New York."

"And?" I asked.

"Well, I need some Loesser sheet music."

"Easy enough," I responded. "I'll call the Loesser office and have them send whatever you need." I then added, "You know, Miss Lee"—she was always Miss Lee to everyone—"I've never heard you sing my favorite Frank Loesser song."

"Which is?" she asked.

"It's called 'Spring Will Be a Little Late This Year.' It was introduced in an old Deanna Durbin film."

With that she said to me, "Oh, this one ...," and began singing the beautiful ballad in the familiar, sultry Peggy Lee style.

I wanted to call everyone I knew and say: "Listen to this! Peggy Lee's singing a lullaby as I lie in bed at midnight." A time to treasure.

My show-business life was flourishing in its second reincarnation. I had been invited to Chicago to see the Steppenwolf Theatre Company's searing drama *The Song of Jacob Zulu* by Tug Yourgrau, set in South Africa. The title character was a political revolutionary whose acts of violence were a desperate attempt to dismantle apartheid. The African a cappella group Ladysmith Black Mambazo served as a musical Greek chorus for the play, which moved to Broadway and was nominated for a Tony Award in 1993.

Working with Joseph Shabalala and his brothers and cousins, who comprised Ladysmith, was a great pleasure for me. All the African movies I had seen represented Zulus as warriors, yet here were the gentlest men I had ever encountered in the theater. I had great fun showing them around New York City when they settled here. In gratitude they prepared a Zulu feast, and I was one of the invited guests. Working in the theater can make you a world traveler, and on rare occasions, the world comes to you.

When I hinted that I'd retire when the twentieth century concluded, most of my friends and colleagues didn't believe me. I had been working on a few Broadway shows. Alex Cohen engaged me to represent his final plays in the theater. I'd experienced the new wave of theatrical productions, with fifteen producers unable to make a decision; Alex, on the other hand, sought everyone's input, and then he made the decision. It was refreshing to be back with an old pro. David Gersten, who was working with me, left a meeting with Alex Cohen and observed that he now knew how the old-time, legendary producers succeeded: they knew every aspect of the business. Alex had been a stage manager, a company manager, and a press agent, and he knew how to create and sell a show.

Alex hired me for a short-lived play, *The Herbal Bed*, followed by Ronald Harwood's fascinating drama, *Taking Sides*, starring the unpredictable Ed Harris opposite the brilliant Daniel Massey, who played Wilhelm Furtwängler, the great German orchestra conductor tried as a Nazi sympathizer.

What proved to be Alex Cohen's last play in an illustrious Broadway career was also my swan song. Noel Coward's *Waiting in the Wings* follows a group of retired actresses living in a nursing home not unlike the famous Actors Home in Englewood, New Jersey. Casting the show was a joy. Every actress over fifty was considered. Alex called me one day and gleefully announced, "I've just talked to Hedy Lamarr. She might be interested." Hedy never happened, but some fine stage actresses did sign up: Elizabeth Wilson, Helena Carroll, Rosemary Murphy, Patricia Conolly, Dana Ivey, Helen Stenborg, and Bette Henritze. The luminous Rosemary Harris was chosen as one of the leading women, but a marquee name was essential for the play to succeed. Alex had been trying to lure Angela Lansbury to accept one of the lead roles, but she had turned it down, stating that she was waiting for a musical version of *The Visit*.

Lauren Bacall agreed to do it. Like Bette Davis and Peggy Lee, she arrived with an avalanche of warnings from people in the business. She was a tough cookie, one guy told me. I wasn't concerned. I was familiar with divas. They all just needed a professional team and they'd be fine.

Bacall proved to be the exception. She baffled me. She had lived a charmed life but was angry at everyone. With Bogey, she traveled in elite company both in Hollywood and politically. I never understood from where the bitterness and meanness emanated. Everyone walked on eggshells around her.

I told Alex that when *Waiting in the Wings* drew its final curtain, so would I. He and I both said that working with Lauren Bacall would be sufficient reason for anyone to retire.

Alex died before the play's conclusion.

Bacall's meanness had been one clarion call for me; Alex's death was another. I was ready to move on. It was called retirement.

I host a radio program on WBAI, playing my favorite recording artists: Johnny Hartman, Peggy Lee, Dinah Washington, Billie Holiday, Lena Horne, Lou Rawls, Nancy LaMott, Tony Bennett, Eva Cassidy, and Frank Sinatra, to name a few. Interviewing actors, playwrights, authors, and politicians, discovering new talent and celebrating them, have been my greatest pleasures. Reading an unknown author, Richard Russo, and hailing him as an important new writer was gratifying. After each Russo book was published, we extended our relationship. When he won the Pulitzer Prize for *Empire Falls*, I was thrilled. I am often in awe of the people who have been my guests on the air: Mario Cuomo, Edward Albee, Joyce Carol Oates, Lawrence Block, Jerry Herman, Linda Lavin, Christine Ebersole, Hendrik Hertzberg, John Lahr, Alan Bennett, Margaret Atwood, David Dinkins, Harry Belafonte, Jonathan Miller, Pat Conroy, and so many others.

Radio remains fascinating to me. I'm part of the last generation that preceded television. Until I was in my early teens, radio was our home entertainment. As a child, I had a small radio on the table behind my bed. After lights were out, I would lie in the dark and be transported around the globe. Monday nights on *Lux Presents Hollywood*, Cecil B. DeMille would introduce Paulette Goddard or Henry Fonda, and they would enter my bedroom. There were chills and thrills with *Inner Sanctum* and *Suspense*, quiz shows such as *20 Questions* and *Quick as a Flash*—during which I shouted out answers—as well as comics who brought me laughter. Joan Davis and Jimmy Durante filled my bedroom with merriment until I heard my mother yell, "It's time for sleep. Turn the radio off!"

A young me and a younger Greg Norris, my friend for more than forty years.

Former New York City mayor Ed Koch appointed me to the city's Human Rights Commission in the late 1970s . . . but our friendship faded when he took a sharp turn to the right.

Testifying at a congressional hearing with one of the men I most admire, former U.S. attorney general Ramsey Clark. Representing Fortune: me, Vinnie DeFrancesco (behind me), and Carlos Bristol.

Mayor John Lindsay and Oscar winner Jeremy Irons were two of the luminaries who showed up at Fortune Society events.

Comedian Richard Pryor visited Fortune Society one morning . . . and did two hours of stand-up comedy before joining me in my office.

Onetime New York City mayor David Dinkins, with me when I was in a political frame of mind. David proved that you could be a decent man and successful in politics.

At a retirement party for me: former *Essence* editor Janice Bryant, me, comedian Randy Credico, and Joy Behar of *The View*.

Top: Rod Taylor and Vinnie DeFrancesco, two men who came to the Fortune Society nearly forty years ago—with a lot of prison time behind them—each found a new path. They have been taxpayers for four decades, defying all the odds and obstacles imposed on them.

Right: Legendary film actress Fay Wray, of *King Kong* fame, visited backstage at *Waiting in the Wings* and told me her real name was Fay Rothenberg. I said that could have made me King Kong's cousin.

Top: Actor Jerry Orbach was always great fun to pal around with. The longtime Broadway star and *Law and Order* leading man was one of the most beloved actors—by his fans and particularly by his colleagues.

Left: Caz Torres, who reclaimed his life at the Fortune Academy and has demonstrated that it's possible to overcome adversity and abuse.

The cast of *The Castle*, a play which I conceived and directed. A unique cast with more than sixty years of prison among them: Angel Ramos, Vilma Ortiz Donovan, Kenneth Harrigan, and Casimiro Torres.

The Fortune Academy, called the Castle by the residents, where we are witness to men and women finding new beginnings in their lives. What goes on there is more dramatic than any film or play I have ever seen.

Two-time Tony Award winner Christine Ebersole was an early and strong supporter of the play *The Castle*. Me, Caz Torres, Vilma Ortiz Donovan, Angel Ramos, Christine, and Kenny Harrigan.

My sister, Carla Romaner (older by two years and ten months), whose friendship has been a rich part of my life for more than eight decades.

I hosted a sports program on KVDU as an undergraduate at the University of Denver, but I fell into WBAI by accident. During the Vietnam War, my production of *Viet Rock* caught the eye of the counterculture hosts on WBAI. The station was located in a converted town house on East Thirty-Ninth Street and looked less imposing than my recollection of KVDU. Everyone was bustling and protesting around WBAI, which I learned was part of the Pacifica network, started by Lew Hill as a way to encourage antiwar and civil rights advocacy. Hill also insisted that the stations in the network be listener-sponsored and commercial-free, the only route to remaining true to the principles of pacifism and societal inclusion.

In the late sixties, when the Fortune Society began, several WBAI radio producers hosted forums and gave voice to the formerly incarcerated. I then proposed that I'd host a program, *Both Sides of the Bars*, to engage guests from the criminal-justice system head-on with men and women who had been incarcerated. The show played on WBAI for four years.

Activism against the Vietnam War increased the listening audience and the listeners' contributions. The station moved to the Upper East Side, into a church that also had a performance space, and people became champions of the station as they listened to folk-rock singers. Hosts such as Bob Fass and Larry Josephson were building massive followings. Fass, an impressive iconoclast and unique radio personality, introduced many of his listeners to Bob Dylan, whom he championed before Dylan achieved iconic status.

There was always acrimony at WBAI. Money was a problem. Though I didn't get into the heat of the battle, it occurred to me that if everyone paid at least a dollar for these extraordinary concerts, it would help meet the station's costs. Purists fought the pragmatic, arguing that the performance space should remain free. The purists won, the church costs couldn't be met, and the station found new headquarters in a rabbit warren on Eighth Avenue and Thirty-Fifth

Street. It was always my contention that the station could have maintained the spacious church building if financial pragmatism had prevailed. But it was the sixties, and everyone was out-left-flanking everyone else.

After four years on the air, I arrived one afternoon to broadcast and was informed that my show had been cancelled. No warning or reason. You're history, I was told. "Farewell to WBAI," I thought.

My life in the theater was fulfilling and profitable. Work with Fortune was all-consuming. Yet WBAI kept inviting me to be a guest on various shows. A new program director, Samori Marksman, had appeared on the scene. This most remarkable man kept asking me if I would consider returning to the station.

I've often said that Samori Marksman, the closest thing to a saint I have ever known, was not a man you wanted to refuse. Born in the Caribbean, on Grenada, he carried with him an intellect matched by a compassion and intensity that defined what leadership could be. Samori took this station, inhabited by the wildest collection of protestors, malcontents, geniuses waiting to be discovered, and lost souls, and brought a maturity and direction it longed for.

I considered returning to the air, pleased that Samori thought me a possible asset. I told him I didn't want to host a criminal-justice program, because I would be preaching to the choir. Rather, I noted, I wanted to be WBAI's answer to Martin Block, the disc jockey all teenagers in Teaneck had listened to when I was a schoolboy. It was my considered opinion that I could share my political and criminal-justice comments between songs by Sinatra and Ella. You have a larger audience when you play good music.

More than anything else, I knew that retirement would allow me to reconnect with Fortune. It would prove to be another adventure in my life, one I could never have anticipated: at seventy years of age, merging my two passions, the theater and the Fortune Society, together again, like bookends.

THIRTEEN

Retired

In 2001, I became a retiree—officially and for all practical purposes a senior citizen. Betty Bacall had become irrelevant. Stories of her acrimony amused my friends. There are always irritants in life, and then you turn a corner and they evaporate.

"Wasn't there anything redeeming about her?" one curio asked. I then waxed theatrical. Legends always stopped by to see Bacall. Most memorable was at a Wednesday matinee, when ninety-two year-old Fay Wray attended a performance at the Walter Kerr Theatre. I volunteered to accompany King Kong's leading lady backstage after the curtain fell.

I discovered her seat location before the proceedings began, and introduced myself. "Miss Wray, I'm David Rothenberg, and I will escort you backstage to see Ms. Bacall and the others in the cast. Photographers might be there." Wide-eyed, she excitedly asked, "What did you say your name was?" I repeated it, suspecting that age had impaired her hearing. She beamed. "I'm Fay Rothenberg," she said. Between screams at RKO, it turned out, Fay Wray had wed a Dr. Rothenberg. I mused for a moment, thinking that I could have been King Kong's brother-in-law.

Following the play, the photographers clicked away at Fay and Bacall, two remnants of Hollywood's past. Suddenly, Fay broke away from Bacall's clutches, surrounded me with a bear hug, and instructed the fleet of photographers, "Take a picture of the Rothenbergs." It's one I still treasure.

Tales of Bacall always conjure up memories and comparisons with other stars—legends, if you will—Bette Davis, Elizabeth Taylor, Miss Peggy Lee, and Eartha Kitt, all recognizable in a glance and entitled to any ad proclaiming, "What becomes a legend most?"

People have an insatiable curiosity about "up close" tales of fabled celebrities. As more time passed, my stories elevated from gossip to folk history. Openmouthed, people asked, "You actually had a date with Elizabeth Taylor?" "Peggy Lee called you at home at midnight?" "You really took Eartha Kitt to the Y for a workout?"

I kept assuring eager listeners that toiling with stars didn't place you in their orbits forever. Take Joan Fontaine, for example. We were together morning, noon, and night for two weeks in summer stock: breakfast together, drive to an interview, return for lunch, blah, blah, blah. Within a fortnight I returned to New York City and went to some event, and there she was, *la Fontaine*, the Oscar-winning actress, who had been my constant companion for two weeks less than a month prior. I walked toward the cinematic queen to renew our friendship, smile enveloping my puss as I greeted her. *Nada. Niente.* Not a hint of recognition on her part. I mumbled words about summer stock; she smiled dismissively at me. I was as much a part of her life as the furniture in Skowhegan, Maine.

In retirement it occurred to me that I was becoming a dinner guest in order to name-drop. Before the salad was served, the hostess was instructing me to "tell that story about Charles Laughton and Elsa Lanchester." Dessert was preceded by "Remember you told us of that phone conversation with Tennessee Williams?" "Tell everyone about having lunch at Sardi's with Charles Boyer." Not to mention Stan Musial, George Raft, Judy Garland, Jackie Robinson, Eleanor Roosevelt, JFK, Maurice Chevalier, Richie Pryor, Richard and Elizabeth, Eleanor Roosevelt, and on and on. All the people with whom I had had a moment or a season. It was celebrity time in America. Talk to a screen goddess for a second and you achieve God status yourself for that moment.

I was doing a one-man show at dinner parties before I ever actually performed. The material was there; I merely needed a reason to gather it all together. Instead of giving away my stories for free, I decide to do a benefit performance. I organized my tales and announced on my Saturday morning radio show that *Namedropping* was on its way. It would be a benefit for the Fortune Society, held at the Fortune Academy residence, the Castle. My director was Marcia Jean Kurtz, a talented actress whom I first met when she was in the cast of *Viet Rock*.

Strangers arrived. They laughed and they applauded; they demanded an encore performance and then another. Jonathan Banks invited me to present it as a Monday evening series at his intimate midtown Mint Theater. The *New York Times* and the *New Yorker* magazine assigned critics, and they approved of my tales. You couldn't kill it with a stick. *Namedropping* has yet to be put into mothballs. It surfaces a few times a year, with an occasional updating as a story emerges from the recesses of my mind, as an incident or a legend is recalled.

Mostly I wanted my retirement days to be with the Fortune Society. In Manhattan, retirement can be a full time job. The options are insurmountable. Theater to see, books you've promised yourself to read, and endless museums and concerts are available. I wanted it all, but first and foremost I wanted to be where I saw young men and women exploring the possibility of a new life. How better to spend your remaining years?

The most rewarding times in the past had been the small groups. As an administrator, you exhaust yourself fundraising, hosting visiting dignitaries, directors of other programs, and foundation executives; it is easy to drift away from the real reason you exist. I had always made sure I was in close contact with the new arrivals at Fortune, people striving to reclaim their lives. But as Fortune became a larger organization with more staff, my time with administrative necessities increased.

This time around I was Grandpa... enjoying the pleasure without the burdens. I suggested to JoAnne Page that I teach a weekly class, not unlike the one I taught at Rahway State Prison, where I would recite a story from that day's newspaper and prompt responses from the students. I would also invite outside guests, men and women whose experience would shed new light on the classroom.

JoAnne noted that the greatest challenge was with the Alternatives to Incarceration program, or ATI, made up of mostly teens. Fortune had structured this program as an exciting alternative to prison. Advocates would enter court on behalf of an individual with an open case, arguing that he or she would benefit more from six months at the Fortune Society than from being encaged. Several judges, having lost faith in the prison system, were enthusiastically responsive. They were particularly anxious for first offenders and/or teenagers to be spared jail or prison.

ATI needed the involvement and cooperation of the district attorney's office, traditionally a more punitive group. In some instances, the politically savvy DAs can be responsive to problem solving rather than insisting on punishment, and the ATI program at Fortune had nearly two hundred young men and women involved, mostly teenage African American and Puerto Rican youth.

Like so much at Fortune, the ATI evolved organically. In the early 1970s, Judge Alvin Schlesinger alerted me that he had a teenage Puerto Rican gang kid who was facing five years upstate. "There's something about this kid," he commented. "There's a spark there. Prison could kill it. Can I send him to Fortune and hear what you all think? I can delay sentencing."

José Torres was at our office the next morning, in full leather costume with enough chains hanging from his apparel to be an ad for an East Village S&M shop. The spark was there but so was the baggage. Fortune in those early days responded to the desperate needs of people reentering society from prison. A teenager filled with piss and vinegar, not yet afflicted with labels—his spirit not yet suffocated from the prison experience—was a different breed, a new challenge.

José had an appealing personality, and we all took an immediate liking to him. Nevertheless, the obstacles were vast. We immediately discovered that the eighteen-year-old could neither read nor write, nor even tell time. He admitted that he traveled to our office from the Bronx on the subway by counting on his fingers the number of stops he was instructed to count. He joked that he was glad there weren't more than nine stations because he would have to take off his shoes and count his toes.

He was charming but had almost no clue about the world outside of his turf in the South Bronx, where his gang lived and fought. Though he was a total illiterate, José was clearly a bright kid. His mind was fertile. His smarts were used to navigate the streets, to buck the system. He was in a trap that could destroy him, and he didn't know it.

José agreed to be tutored, to absorb the alphabet, to learn how to intelligently travel in the city, and how to tell time. He had always been so embarrassed by his limitations that he manipulated and conned people so they couldn't detect his shortcomings. More than anything, he enjoyed the attention he received at Fortune. Like many of the kids we would encounter, José revealed that attention at home was restricted to parental hysteria when he was arrested. He received no accolades for positive achievements, few that there were.

After a few weeks, he began arriving each morning with Juan, his lifelong friend and coconspirator in the gang. José and Juan would be sitting, propped up against the door, when I opened the office. Without any prompting, they would grab a broom and sweep and straighten rooms that had been left in disarray from support groups the night before. They were marking territory, just as Harry LaCroix had when he'd lived with me many years earlier. They felt it necessary to justify their presence at Fortune.

The three of us always had an hour together before other staff people began appearing. It became our coffee-and-donuts quality time together. Our routine was consistent. The postman dropped the mail off early, and Juan and Jose grabbed letter openers to unseal the two hundred plus letters arriving each day. Over coffee and donuts or bagels, we got to know each other. They were comfortable in my office, chatting away.

Support groups are vital, and tutoring sessions are essential, but the informal coffee session in the morning, doing routine chores, was when the conversation moved spontaneously. José and Juan opened the mail and I sorted it—one pile from prisoners seeking "reasonable assurance" for parole consideration, another from prisoners searching for legal guidance, and another for mail from students and other civilians needing general information. I shared comments of interest from some of the letters, which would prompt José and Juan to reveal portions of their lives. Those are the real confidences that traditionally emerge in office settings around America.

As their comfort level increased, they were more forthcoming with their family and school tales. I posed two questions to them that resulted in long answers that became the nucleus of real work that was necessary in their young lives.

"How did you two become such buddies?" They shared with me that in the first and second grades, they would meet in the principal's office or in a detention class after school. By the time they were nine years old, they had been declared "outlaws." They only received attention for their obstreperous behavior, which enraged teachers and principals. They were feared by students and teachers. Other gang members we later met at Fortune were the kids they'd recruited in detention.

My second probing question was more complicated. José and Juan were so clever, especially José, so it seemed incongruous, almost impossible, that they could be so bright and yet illiterate. Wasn't it frustrating to be in that trap?

José reflected on his childhood without embellishment or resentment, merely recollecting what his life had been. His family's apartment was overcrowded. In addition to several siblings, there were always other relatives in the two-bedroom apartment, cousins, uncles, and aunts, and activity that continued all night long. Music, fights, and drinking were in his home every night. He never questioned it. That was what it was.

When José became a first-grader, the classroom was the quietest room he had ever encountered. He would immediately fall asleep, exhausted from the nightlong revelry that punctuated his home life. Annoyed teachers would scold him without questioning or exploring his exhaustion. By the second and third grades, if he suspected a teacher might call on him for an answer, exposing his ignorance of the topic, he would act out, ensuring his expulsion from class and sometimes from school. José didn't boast about these situations or make apologies. He was trying to understand what had happened.

The classroom had become a place to sleep, and it evolved into a room of humiliation. That was how and why he teamed up with Juan. It never occurred to the schoolteachers or any adult in their lives that there was cause and effect in their behavior. No one insisted that education was necessary. School was where there was discipline. There were no hints that learning could be enjoyable. Their futures were outlined for them in the first grade.

In time, José and Juan were not the only members of their gang hanging around at Fortune. José was the only one mandated by a judge to be there, but each week another teenager accompanied him to the office. Juan was his main man, but then came Chico and Pedro and later Oswaldo and Chino and Carlos and others. Nearly two dozen of their fellow gang members became part of the Fortune family. We had to respond to their specific needs, not the least of which was tutoring, since most of them had reading levels not much higher than José's.

Within six months at Fortune, José was reading at a survival level. His math scores were impressive. Judge Schlesinger dismissed all charges. We suspected that with no sword of Damocles hanging over his head, José might conclude his stay with us. The opposite took place. He recruited what seemed to be the entire South Bronx for Fortune. He was rounding up the troubled and the needy. I would often quote to him Emma Lazarus's words on the Statue of Liberty: "Give me your tired, your poor, your huddled masses yearning to breathe free..."

José and Juan stayed around Fortune for a couple of years, improving their education and skills, and then they began looking for employment. The children were ready to leave the nest. Their wings were ready for flight. They had become young men ready to face the challenges of a swirling, complicated, madcap metropolis.

About fifteen years later, I was walking up Seventh Avenue to my Times Square office, when a car came to a screeching halt. Two large Latino men exited the vehicle and came charging at me. They had broad grins on their faces that told me a daytime assault was not about to happen. Like two little kids, they jumped up and down and smothered me in bear hugs. José and Juan were on their way to work. They asked me a million questions, but it was their total joy that was evident. They informed me about their families and their jobs. They were husbands, fathers, and taxpayers.

After we exhausted ourselves with catching-up stories about mutual friends, they drove off and I resumed my walk. I realized that tears were streaming down my face. Sometimes it takes a decade and a half to see the fruits of your labor. Frequently, you never have that great gift.

Mel Rivers once told me, "You have to do what you think is best or right. You can't sit around and wait for thanks, which might never come. Just do the best you can."

When we first met José and Juan, they were teens on a path that promised prison, a life on the outer ridges of society, and perhaps early deaths. We rerouted them. Their stories and thousands more like them never make the six o'clock news. But they're out there.

That was the start of what evolved into ATI, a structured alternative. All of the programs at Fortune have been created in response to the needs expressed by the men and women who walk through the door.

I was in my late sixties when I retired. That's quite different from thirty-five years of age, which I was when the Fortune Society began, when teenagers viewed me as an older brother or cousin. Running an ATI group was not virgin territory for me, but the age gap between me and the participants presented a new experience. My first group with a dozen teenage youth was daunting. Their body language was expressive: arms folded, no eye contact, and a silence that shouted, "We'd rather be anywhere else in the world." I introduced myself and asked if they would go around the room and say their names.

The mumbles were audible, until one lad blurted out, "Why do you want to know my name?"

"So I can know you as a person. But you can give me a number instead."

That provoked a couple of chuckles.

I gave them none of my background at Fortune. I was an elderly white man who had entered their space. No credential would impress them. I had to break down the walls. I picked up a newspaper, read a few paragraphs, and asked for their reactions to the story.

One grumbled. "Why do you want to know what we think?"

"Because we can all learn from each other. You have experiences I don't know about, and I can learn from you . . . just as I might know a few things you could learn from me."

The discussion began. The room's air was clearing. Slowly…very slowly.

I knew it would take more than a few sessions to break through. Consistency was important. Just showing up sends a message to young people who have been lied to, betrayed, and ignored. I had to take a few major steps. I invited guests to join the group…especially some who had done time. That made an impression. I hustled for tickets for a Wednesday matinee of a Broadway musical. Of course, none of the guys had ever seen a Broadway play, never even considered the possibility of attending such a show. They were hesitant to show interest, but the chance to get out of groups and out of the office was incentive enough.

The first group to go to Broadway was intentionally small. You can't give attention to sixteen kids, but four affords you the opportunity to become better acquainted. Two of the four had never been to Times Square, though they had been born and raised in Brooklyn. They wanted to see where the ball dropped on New Year's Eve. They knew their block, the police station, youth houses, shelters—but not Broadway.

The five of us took the train to Times Square and lunched at a fast-food joint, where I discovered their atrocious eating habits. Bad food was their history: burgers, potato chips, soda, and pizza—rarely sitting down at a table for a shared meal—were their regular diets. Fresh fruits and vegetables were not part of the deal. Cigarettes and drugs were more readily accessible than a bowl of oatmeal or a green salad.

The musical we attended was *Hairspray*. They sat wide-eyed, punching each other at each funny line, shocked at the suggestive sexual innuendos.

After that shared afternoon, I became Dave to the four of them. "When are we going again? What else can we do?" More than that, they filled my ear with tales of neglect and fear. It was startling how little it took to open the airwaves.

The guys moved on, but ever after, they would remember going to the theater, to a Broadway musical, as a major event in their lives. I received a phone call after the Tony Awards were televised, and it was one of the young men, who excitedly told me he'd seen *Hairspray* on TV. His girlfriend and her friends couldn't believe he had seen the show. He just wanted to share that with me.

I was reminded of what I had learned a long time ago from Harry LaCroix and Charlie McCleese, both teenagers for whom I became legal guardian, to keep them out of jail. These kids are so starved for attention that it only takes a trip to a show to gain a morsel of trust. That is not to suggest that the show turns their lives around, but it is unsettling how a minimum of attention can loosen their resistance. The responsibility of such a realization is awesome.

Years earlier a teenager named Willie Bosket had visited the Fortune Society. Newspaper articles had branded him as the poster boy for teenage evil. Books were written about Willie and his father and their alleged atavistic antisocial behavior. But around the halls of Fortune, Willie was no better and no worse than many of the youths we met. He had become one journalist's story, dramatizing a generation of rage.

It was not much different with Sal Agron, labeled "the Cape Man." Sal achieved legendary status and went to prison as a teenager for his role in a gang fight that ended in the death of another youth. The tabloids hung nicknames on Sal and another young man, who was dubbed "the Umbrella Man." They became the symbols of all that was wrong with their generation.

The Cape Man, in fact, became a headline merely because the tragedy took place on West Forty-Fifth Street. If the gang war had unfolded on 145th Street, the tabloids would have ignored it as they did every other gang conflict north of Ninety-Sixth Street, which had long been the dividing line between white and brown New Yorkers. All of this resonated as a living echo of the turf war exposed in the musical of the fifties, *West Side Story*. That Broadway hit demonstrated youthful hostility and ethnic difference. Ironically, it was an adaptation of *Romeo and Juliet*, a reminder that fractious battles are ubiquitous and timeless.

Sal Agron corresponded with me from his prison cell, and we met on a few of my visits to Green Haven Prison. When he was eventually released, he became another parolee at Fortune, trying to find a place for himself on the streets.

Sal Agron and Willie Bosket were created by headlines in tabloids, figures brought to the public larger than life and given iconic status to frighten the readers. Neither could outrun the whispers and finger pointing when they entered a room.

Willie was bright and charming. I had been told of his ferocious temper and the vicious acts he was accused of committing, but I saw an angry, frightened man-child. Sal eventually left New York City and had an early death. He was a shy, almost epicene, rail-thin young man.

I have no illusions of the harm that enraged young men can commit. I've been witness to uncontrollable, often irrational rage, but I have also seen, up close, the vulnerability, the possibility of being more than a bundle of anger and disappointment. Rarely does society structure itself to repair the broken. One description of our criminal-justice system, the prisons, and particularly the youth houses is: "They are Band-Aids on gangrene."

I often repeat a line from Marc Connelly's Pulitzer Prize winning play, *The Green Pastures*. De Lawd (the Lord) high in the heavens is instructing one of his angel aides, "Make sure that we take care of the planet over there. And don't forget the wing of the sparrow." When we are caught up with the overwhelming odds posed against the young men and women who have been in trouble forever, we frequently ignore the possibility that a hand reaching out could be the first step in effecting change.

My friend Maria Perez, a counselor at the Fortune Society, surprised me with a story. When she was first released from prison and started attending groups at Fortune, she wasn't sure she was ready to buy the hopeful signs that were in evidence. She quoted something I had said in a group setting: "You are not the worst thing you have ever done. You are much better than that." Maria began reflecting and realized she had been defining herself by her crime, her imprisonment, her past drug history. She was ignoring the totality of her being and buying into society's labels. It took that one remark, made to a group, to start her positive engine to purr.

You never know which hand reaching out will provide the stimulus. Willie Bosket and Sal Agron were suffocated by the labels imposed on them. Juan and José, based in anonymity, had the time to find their potential.

Retirement at Fortune gave me a master's degree in human services. Without the worries of making payroll, I could observe ebullient young men and women flirting with the possibility of a new life. It used to drive me up a wall when I would meet with those who fund nonprofits, government and foundation people, but particularly government-agency representatives, who were absorbed by statistics, by their definition of the "success" rates of anything they funded. Their concern was making the funder appear positive rather than exploring how dollars could move mountains. Retirement volunteering steers you clear of that perennial frustration. I had the grandfather's pleasure of bringing youngsters written off by society to a Broadway musical, a museum, or the planetarium, or of guiding them to a library or a computer class where they could catch up with the rest of the population. Stanley Eldridge had explained that the library was where he caught his breath, where he could read and muse in comparative calm. Caz Torres, a resident of the Fortune Academy, pointed out that he was addicted to reading before he was addicted to drugs, and that books made him realize there was something else; he just didn't know how to find it.

My weekly radio program is now in its fourth decade on WBAI. Men and women from Fortune often visit me in the studio while I am on the air. More than a few released prisoners arriving at the Fortune Society note that listening to me on Saturday mornings was their information ticket for a new start.

When you sit in a studio with a mike, you can only estimate the number of people who are measuring your words. A man alone in a prison cell, with little notion of what life will be upon release, hears you and considers a new possibility. That is a huge responsibility, one that I do not underestimate. When I hear the hatemongers on talk radio, I cringe because they are oblivious of the lost opportunities. Conflict and divisiveness might ignite the ratings, but they ignore the potential of the medium as a healing element.

In 2002, the Fortune Academy opened on 140th Street and Riverside Drive, thanks to JoAnne Page's vision and tenacity. It would become the catalyst in the lives of hundreds of men and women who would have been homeless when released from prison—a model community residence that made reentry a dramatically positive experience.

It would also bring me back into the theater, full throttle. At the ribbon cutting I had no idea this was in my near future.

FOURTEEN

The Fortune Academy

D riving up Manhattan's West Side Highway, motorists have for years eyed an imperial structure in West Harlem. The five-story Gothic edifice, now the Fortune Society's innovative residence known as the Castle, is a commanding presence on Riverside Drive and 140th Street.

Built in the early twentieth century, the Castle was originally a Catholic girls' school, St. Walburga's Academy. In the late 1950s, the school doors were shut. For a brief period in the 1970s, the building became a yeshiva, but that was short-lived; the castle-like structure became an eyesore and eventually a crack house. As the community regained its dignity in the 1990s, the building was a source of concern.

It was at that same time that JoAnne Page had a mission for the Fortune Society: to locate a building that could provide decent and supportive housing for men and women released from prison who would otherwise be homeless.

Homelessness has always been the Achilles' heel of reentry. Reports to the public of the high recidivism rate (two out of three released prisoners, nationally, return to the cages within three years) rarely disclose the barriers facing those in reentry. In New York City, thousands of parolees needing housing are thrust into drug-infested shelters. Job restrictions are overwhelming. As one man stated, "It's always a recession for us."

The New York State Division of Parole suggests that housing and jobs are necessities to meet its requirements, but there is no actual setup to provide help. At best, a parole officer might recommend a program, such as Fortune, to deal with the parolee's overwhelming odds against survival on the streets. Quite simply, the system is geared to guarantee recidivism, ensuring the keepers of the prison cells that their jobs will be secure. When crime dropped in the cities, parole violations accelerated, ensuring a continued inmate population.

Housing, like jobs, was always a problem we confronted at the Fortune Society. In our early days, Kenny Jackson, Mel Rivers, Fran O'Leary, and I frequently had released parolees sleeping on our couches. Guys would say to us that if they had to remain in the shelters or SROs, they'd end up back in jail. Some even indicated that a prison cell would be preferable to a bed in a shelter dormitory.

There is little government oversight of this crowded, unhealthy, substandard housing. Several improvised, profit-making residences scattered around New York City violate every health standard, with little or no accountability. Drugs and booze are in ample supply. These places are breeding grounds for survival crimes, frustration crimes, drug-related crimes, and anger crimes.

Few in government or in the media make a connection between the housing crisis for released prisoners and the high recidivism rate. They are content to convey the impression that inherently evil or bad people continue to commit crimes.

The need for permanent housing like The Castle was evident on the day Fortune Society was born, back in 1967. Naïve and frustrated by the stories I would hear, I was determined to find out for myself. In the early 1970s, I checked into the Greenwich Hotel on Bleecker Street, a privately run hellhole for hundreds of homeless men, almost all recently released from jail or prison. I was placed in a room with paper-thin walls—a partition, actually, that raced halfway up to the ceiling. Meshed wire covered the remainder of the space as a bleak protection from invasion. A small table with a single drawer completed the furniture. The room wasn't nearly as hospitable as the cell I was introduced to when visiting Rikers Island a few years earlier.

The community day room boasted a few sofas with stuffing erupting from them, and a small black-and-white television set. Some residents aggressively offered me drugs, weed, heroin, and pills I couldn't identify. Someone asked me if I wanted to buy a gun, and several sexual propositions of various contexts were presented. I quickly returned to my room and slept with the bed against the door after several efforts were made to break in.

After I rose in the morning—discovering a bathroom atmosphere out of Gorky's *Lower Depths*—I ventured into the lobby, searching for anyone who could provide guidance or direction. A volunteer nurse from St. Vincent's Hospital told me she could only direct ailing men to emergency rooms. Several men waiting to speak with her had self-made bandages revealing cuts and infections.

The building had an internal atrium where tens of men gathered, walking in circles as if in a prison yard. Most of the population over-flowed to the streets and nearby Washington Square Park, where they panhandled, dealt drugs, or sat in a comatose state. More than a few were sustained on Thorazine.

Of course, the community was outraged about the collection of men dominating the neighborhood, most of whom were black and Latino and surviving illegally. The protests were about the negativity but gave little consideration to the conditions of the welfare hotel.

The hotel was a big moneymaker for whatever corporation ran it. It received the clients' welfare checks directly. Neither the city nor the state insisted on health or safety standards, and the atrocious living conditions were what the population had come to expect as their due.

When the men and women at Fortune learned I had checked into the hotel, they came down hard on me. "You idiot!" Kenny Jackson hollered. "You could have been killed. You don't know how to survive in there." That was the whole point, I argued. If people can't survive there, it must be exposed. Subsequently, I wrote of this experience in an article published in the *Villager*, a weekly New York City newspaper.

The revelations were startling but hardly created a political ripple. The population affected was expendable. We at Fortune knew that decent and safe housing was essential if society were determined to fight crime, but apparently, that was not a good selling point at election time. Though the costs of a prison cell are higher than a bed at the Castle, the clanging of prison doors still seems the most effective campaign strategy in political TV ads.

Years later, when I was a candidate for political office, I visited buildings similar to the Greenwich. One of them was around the corner from Macy's: the old, stylish Martinique Hotel, which had become a blight on the area. By the 1980s, it was a crime-inducing machine. I sat in a single room with a woman who had three children. A mattress on the floor was where the two oldest slept; the one-year-old slept on the cot with his mother. She used an illegal hot plate to heat canned foods, the family's diet.

Children raced up and down the hallways, which smelled of urine. The noise was continual. The young mother I met with was overwhelmed. Her husband was in prison. She, not yet thirty years of age, had a look of defeat on her face. She saw no way out. Of course, she was no one's constituent. Voting or elections were hardly her concern, and she was of little interest to incumbents.

As I observed the kids running in and out of rooms, mostly searching for food, I commented, "I don't want to meet these kids in twenty years. They are the next generation of prison inmates. You can see them being molded."

Caz Torres, who was a resident of the Castle in 2005, heard me recall the conditions at the Martinique. He told me that his mother had been sent there by welfare in the 1980s and that as a twelve-year-old he had been in and out of the hotel. He confirmed what I had suspected: The kids stole to eat. They infested the stores in the neighborhood, stealing and selling to feed their siblings and mother. They smoked weed and drank wine to blot out their misery.

JoAnne Page, the CEO of Fortune, was determined to challenge the societal absurdity of substandard housing for the formerly incarcerated who are homeless. For years, she had teams of sophisticated real-estate friends explore sites where men and women out of prison could be housed in a safe environment. From the outset, her prevailing theme was, "If you are going to change your life, you have to feel safe." Shelters and many neighborhoods did not guarantee safety for people on a reentry journey.

JoAnne undertook a Herculean challenge, knowing that whatever site she found, there would be community resistance to having a collection of ex-prisoners in the neighborhood.

When JoAnne first learned of the fortresslike building, she began a series of negotiations to secure and finance the residence. Then began the internal rehabilitation of the building, scooping it out and restructuring it for our specific housing needs. This labor of love took five years, from 1997 to the 2002 opening, when the Fortune Academy became a residence for sixty-two men and women, all recently released from a city, state, or federal institution, and all of whom would otherwise be homeless and forced to a shelter or the streets.

As expected, "not in my backyard" was the initial cry at 140th Street. The large twenty-four-story apartment building across the street from the Castle was the home of many community and political activists, a modern complex of working, middle-class Harlemites. They had endured the building as a crack house but were not ready to consider five dozen released prisoners in their neighborhood, directly across the street. The residents had a spectacularly big voter turnout, so their concerns about the Castle were heeded by local elected officials.

JoAnne turned her attention to the opposition of the plan. She garnered a team to meet regularly with the local precinct council and with the neighboring building's tenant council. Members of the Fortune staff who were former residents of the area addressed the concerns of the doubtful. Two of the men had grown up on the block and knew many of the old-timers still living there.

Local politicians were cautious at first. They recognized the vital need for such housing but were mindful of constituent hesitancy. At a community-board meeting, former inmates testified, stating, "We are your sons and brothers. When we were shooting up and selling drugs at the abandoned building, you looked away. Now we have a new life and plead that you will allow others the same opportunities that have been afforded us."

The Neighborhood Advisory Council was formed.

The Fortune Academy opened with a ribbon-cutting ceremony on a cold winter day in 2002. Many elected officials, including former mayor David Dinkins, appeared in support. Yet there were pickets and protests on that chilly day. With my friend Sam Rivera, I was up and down the street, talking to a handful of protestors, explaining the goals of the house and promising that Fortune Academy would be a good neighbor, alleviating their concerns.

Once the Castle opened, the fears abated. It is always the unknown that terrifies people, a device too frequently used for political goals. The large backyard was utilized on summer afternoons for cookouts, and the neighbors were invited. More than a few people in the area joined us on Sunday afternoons for hot dogs, grilled chicken, and potato salad. We were becoming part of the neighborhood.

On the first Halloween, we converted the Castle into a haunted house and invited the children from the block. A couple of hundred mothers brought their tots for some scares and some treats. We repeated the event the following year, and the year after that; within three years, it became a major Halloween event in West Harlem (unreported in the downtown press, though a fascinating story). The Fortune Academy residents created a variety of surprises and dressed as ghosts and ghouls to entertain the tots. JoAnne commented, "At first, they were frightened of us; now they trust us with their kids."

Within a couple of years, the community board asked permission to hold their monthly meetings in the community room at the Castle. The Castle became a routine pit stop for elected officials and community activists. Its residents helped set up the room and acted as monitors for the events.

One of the components established by Joanne Page was a Thursday night meeting for all residents. She invited me to join her in those early months, and I have rarely missed one of those gatherings in the intervening years. They afford me inspiration and hope, as I pay witness to people reclaiming their lives.

Seeing how people live and adjust to a community is very different than sitting in on group raps about drugs and alcohol. JoAnne tells them, "If you are going to live in the community, you have to solve some of the problems you are facing here." What are the problems? Mundane, but for many of the residents a new experience. The music down the hall is too loud; people are smoking in the hallways; residents aren't picking up their waste after eating in the dining room. Most of us grew up with such situations, but they can be alien to people raised in training schools and youth houses. Life at the Castle is more than not going back to drugs and prison: it is about learning how to live in society—and to enjoy it.

The residents also have focus meetings each morning before they go out into the city. It is an effort for them to greet each day with positive direction. A second compulsory meeting takes place Monday through Thursday nights at nine p.m., when they review their day and discuss how they are confronting the obstacles of reentry into society. Since most residents are on parole, they have a curfew, which the house honors.

The Thursday night gatherings allow the executive team at Fortune to meet with the residents. Frequently, outside guests are invited. The New York State Division of Parole sent four members to exchange views with parolees. That two-hour session was an unprecedented learning experience for everyone. Few members of a parole board ever meet with released parolees to gain a different perspective of the restrictive reentry process.

Candidates for Manhattan's district attorney all visited the Castle on a Thursday night, including Cyrus Vance Jr., the man who is now Manhattan's DA. That too provided new insights, not only for the residents of the Castle but for public figures hoping to lead the city on criminal-justice issues. I always argued that it makes sense to ask the patient where it hurts before you begin operating.

Several of my theater friends have sat in on sessions. The folks at the Castle immediately recognized *M*A*S*H*'s Mike Farrell, who listened intently to the unfolding tales of the week's struggles. Christine Ebersole, a two-time Tony Award winning actress, has been particularly supportive, not only attending Thursday night sessions but also performing a fundraising concert in the community room. Theater people recognize the drama, often intense in the room, as far more compelling than most calculated reality TV shows.

Playwright Edward Albee accepted my invitation to attend a Thursday night meeting. DA candidate Judge Leslie Crocker Snyder was a guest at that same meeting. At one point Edward whispered to me, "Is it okay if I ask a question?" "Of course," I responded. The judge gave a curt response to Edward's question. After the gathering, she pulled me aside and asked, "How much time did that old guy do, and what was his crime?" I responded, "His crime was writing plays. Three of them won the Pulitzer Prize."

The rules of the house are not complicated: no drugs, no alcohol, no violence or threat of violence. The residents mostly control the culture of the house, which reflects their determination to reconstruct their lives. At some intervals, the house culture is questionable, usually when there is a turnover. When a dozen people graduate into their own apartments, a dozen new residents replace them. People come to the academy with their prison faces and prison postures. They look around at the comfortable surroundings and see people at ease and hugging, the antithesis of their years behind bars. It takes time to shed the coats of institutional life.

Newly arrived residents live in four-person rooms on the top floor, which is known as the Emergency Section. After they demonstrate that the Castle is where they want to be, they are eligible for the next level, called the Permanent Phase, where they move into a one- or two-person studio apartment, complete with kitchen and private bathroom. The Castle is the antithesis of a shelter residence.

Fortune Academy policy makes clear to all who apply that the Castle is not just a bed...this is not the Hotel Fortune. It is a place for people who want to change their lives. The numbers seeking that opportunity are overwhelming. They come to the academy after years of drugs and prison, hungry for a new start.

JoAnne Page chairs the Thursday night meetings, often joined by Barry Campbell or Stanley Richards and me. Both Stanley and Barry have been incarcerated. Stanley, who is now the COO of the Fortune Society, was a Bronx street kid who discovered while in prison that education was his ticket to opportunities. He is a bearlike presence who commands attention with his quiet intelligence and physical being. His good nature conceals a background of drugs, streets, and prisons.

Stanley often reflects that he thought he had no options in life, but then he gained his GED and absorbed college courses. The college programs were later eliminated by New York's governor George Pataki, under pressure from conservatives who argued that convicted felons should not be given college opportunities. Pataki agreed, stating that the costs were too high. JoAnne, appearing on Bill

O'Reilly's program on Fox, pointed out to the fiscally conservative TV personality that cost was the reason cited for the elimination of college programs in prisons. Then she noted that it costs $100,000 to construct a single prison cell, and nearly $50,000 a year to house a prisoner, but the argument is against subsidizing a few dollars that will give an inmate tools to reshape his or her life. All statistics indicate that prisoners who take college programs have the lowest recidivism rates. The reasons are obvious. As Stanley Richards often states, he saw doors opening that he never knew existed.

Barry Campbell, JoAnne's troubleshooter at Fortune, is more mercurial, constantly discovering his great abilities. He is equally comfortable talking with gang street kids as he is persuading elected officials in the corridors of power. Had Barry been white and privileged, he would have been a CEO of a large company or a professor at a university. He continually surprises with his insights.

From the outset, JoAnne's soft voice commanded respect. It is fascinating to watch a roomful of men and women, who collectively have hundreds of years of prison time under their belts, listen attentively as she draws them out. Street people often talk about giving or gaining respect being a big part of confrontations and battles. They are really talking about acts of courtesy. Respect is much more complex, something not casually given. Joanne has gained respect because of her wisdom and concern.

There have been moments of dramatic tension and revelation at the Thursday meetings. There is also much laughter. Visitors always remark that the experience is unique and rewarding. They want to return and bring friends, because they recognize hope.

People wearing the prison face show caution, fear, and suspicion of the surroundings, which contain an atmosphere more akin to a college dorm than a rescue effort for men and women who might otherwise be in a shelter. The physical upkeep is important, so self-pride can be maintained. If you have lived your life in drab and impersonal institutions, it takes an adjustment to live in a building that is clean and reveals a personality reflective of its residents.

In the early months of the Castle, one young resident appeared to be in a constant state of pouting and disapproval. In our subway rides after each meeting, Joanne and I would comment on what took place, and we often remarked on the sadness of the young man named Solio. He seemed reluctant to participate or to share any part of himself. But he listened. JoAnne always advised, "Give them time. If you do drug and prison time for years, it doesn't turn around until you replace it with something new and hopeful. There is always that period when folks are letting go of the past but haven't found something new to hold on to."

After several weeks, Solio's perpetual frown was neutralized. He volunteered comments. We discovered he could smile. Then he didn't stop smiling. He was starting to recognize the possibility of something in the second half of this life besides prison and being unhappy.

We christened it the Solio Smile. Ever after, we observed men and women arrive at the Fortune Academy door and frightened, only to slowly learn how to find pockets of joy. We could see it on their faces, and we recognized the Solio Smile in many different people. It was like those slow-motion botany films that show how a flower blossoms.

One Thursday meeting remains with me. A resident shared an incident that was the starting point of a life changed forever, the rebirth of an extraordinary man.

Thomas Jones never uttered a word for the first six or seven meetings after he first surfaced at the Castle. There were mumbles on the side but no words for all to hear. Then he entered one night in a blaze of rage. He had found a job, but on his way back to the Castle, some kids were tossing a bottle of ketchup that went awry, and the red juice sprayed all over his trousers. TJ bellowed, "These are my only work pants. I have no other pants!" Then he admitted that after he'd recognized the damage, he'd realized the teenagers were all girls. So he just left, yelling at them as he passed them.

The next two hours centered on TJ's pants. JoAnne challenged him: "What if the ketchup tossers had been boys or young men?" TJ expressed his macho credentials, suggesting that he was a man and those were his work pants, so he would have had to respond to such disrespect.

Joanne then asked, quietly but firmly, if TJ was willing to go back to prison over the pants. "No, of course not," he responded. "But those are my only work pants."

JoAnne and I both stressed that he had firmly established that those were his only work pants, but that he must weigh the value of the pants versus surrendering freedom. An ex-con on parole fighting teenagers would result in police contact, and any police contact can be considered a violation of parole, even if new charges are not filed.

The question we both emphasized was simple: How much did he cherish his freedom? Other residents chimed in. Those who were now veterans of the Fortune Academy shared stories of similar incidents. It was clear that living in New York City, any civilian would constantly face situations that could escalate and threaten his or her parole. "Guaranteed," one person stated, "someone will push you on the subway." How you respond to that in prison is very different from how you respond in Manhattan. A wise resident pointed out to TJ, "Up in the mountains, in prison, we were geared to retaliate. That's what you do so you don't become a victim. Out here, we have to find new ways of dealing with these things. In prison, it is about establishing a reputation. Here, it is about keeping freedom."

TJ stubbornly said, "But I'm a man."

We acknowledged his manhood and asked if he wanted to be a man at the Castle or behind bars. And are you less of a man because you walk away from strangers, some kids who are fooling around?

It was evident to all in the room that no one prepares prisoners for different behavior when they come out. Prison prepares people to survive in that curious and violent subculture, where men fight over a stare or a push. Resident Larry White told the group, "We put on coats of survival when we are locked up. No one guides us to strip ourselves of those coats of armor that get in the ways of functioning out here." That, of course, is the unique mandate and challenge of the Castle.

At the end of the meeting, JoAnne simply asked TJ to think about it.

I asked TJ's counselor to surreptitiously get his pants measurements. On my weekly radio program, I relayed the story of this man with one pair of soiled pants and his learning how to function on the streets. It served as an example of the thin line that determines if an antisocial act will or will not take place.

WBAI listeners responded, and at the next meeting we presented TJ with seventeen pairs of slacks. We told him they were from strangers—folks who had never met him, just like the kids who dirtied his trousers.

He said, "I don't understand you people."

JoAnne Page told TJ to consider this: "Strangers ruined your pants. And people you never met responded to that incident." He began to understand, and more importantly, he began examining himself and his priorities. He later told me, "I knew how to stab people; I never learned how to talk to them." Thomas Jones began a transition.

At later Thursday meetings, TJ became a catalyst, asking tough questions of JoAnne, Barry, and me, always searching for answers and clarifications. After a year at the Castle, he enrolled in a human-resources training program to become a counselor. He was an outstanding student and was hired by a drug program. I started to have long rap sessions with Thomas, and I learned that when he'd gone to prison for the last time, he'd been totally illiterate. He took odd jobs in prison to earn money, and he bought a dictionary, and then he taught himself to read. I realized that the determination was there, and that he had something else, a real spark. In spite of his reading limitations, he was a deep and probing thinker. Like so many other men I had met, his inability to express himself had led him to compensate with bursts of anger. Now he was moving steadily away from all that.

When a job opened at the Castle, TJ applied and was hired, becoming a counselor in the building he had entered three years earlier. He began work with a full wardrobe of trousers.

FIFTEEN

The Castle: A Play

Hamza Hakim's arrival at the Castle was as dramatic as a meteor flying overhead. His enthusiasm was infectious. Hamza was clear that the second half of his life would be a substantial departure from his earlier years. The streets, drugs, and prison were his past. His future was unexplored territory, and he embraced it with the energy of a schoolboy. His optimism and humor were evident from the outset.

I first met him in the Castle's TV lounge on the day he moved in. He greeted me: "I'm Hamza Hakim; I just finished twelve years in a federal penitentiary. Do you live here?" He was so open that it was disarming; he had not a hint of the prison face and institutional fears so evident in most men returning to society.

Hamza announced he was selling musk oils for pocket money until he found employment. The small bottles he was displaying had an intoxicating aroma, and I made a purchase of a small sample, his first sale in the free world. He became involved with every opportunity offered at the Fortune Society, and quickly emerged as the go-to guy for residents and staff, resolving petty conflicts and listening to the doubts and fears of his family of residents.

When he learned I hosted a radio program, he invited himself to the studio for Saturday morning broadcasts. He became a regular, settling in comfortably at WBAI and frequently offering listeners the perspective of the formerly incarcerated on a variety of issues. He also realized that my radio gig afforded me press tickets to new Broadway and off-Broadway plays. When I mentioned I had an extra ticket for each show, he yelled, "Me! Me!" He wanted to do and see everything in the free world. His spirit was contagious, and his sense of humor was sharp. He once told me, "I can't make up for those lost and wasted years, but I can make the time left count for something."

In essence, that was the very reason for the Castle: to provide a launching pad for rediscovering life. Many people arrive at Fortune motivated, desiring something new, but burdened with the baggage of institutional life and a street past filled with drugs and booze.

Hamza had a full realization of the mission of the Castle.

He and I attended dozens of plays together, nurturing a unique friendship. In prison he had become a Muslim, and he was devout in his religious observance. We had endless discussions about religion and faith, arriving with very different perspectives, but neither of us seemed bothered by the philosophical chasm.

In fact we had some of the most stimulating exchanges I ever had with a Castle resident. We acknowledged that we shared a spiritual journey that manifested itself in two distinct ways. Hamza loved being challenged and respected my view of traditional religion—my agnosticism, if you will. As our friendship developed, a visitor once asked if it were possible for a devout Muslim and a gay agnostic Jew to be friends. Hamza laughed and said to me, "I'm not going anywhere; are you?"

I have always been fascinated and dismayed by people who surround themselves with mirrors of themselves, creating their own ghettos. Life is an adventure when you are in a mixed bag, an environment celebrating diversity.

Hamza shared a great deal about his family, his loving mother and sister, and how the streets pulled him away from them. Their support was uncompromising. He agonized over the pain and heartache he had caused them when he was young and restless.

After one play we attended, I listened to him recall some episode from his past, and I commented, "Your life is more dramatic than some of the plays we are seeing." That single line sparked an idea. We would develop a theater workshop at the Castle.

A play had been the inspiration for the Fortune Society, and my love for theater, particularly for plays of social drama, had never waned. Here was an opportunity to blend my passions once again and to provide a rich opportunity for some residents.

Over the months, my mind churned about this new project and how it would evolve. Hamza's life was moving on. A year later, he was hired as a counselor at Fortune, working with teenagers in the Alternatives to Incarceration program. Eventually he moved out of the Castle. He had met a lovely woman who shared his religious faith, and they were planning to marry. She lived and worked in Philadelphia, and they were making arrangements for her to move to and work in New York City after their betrothal. It was important to him to maintain his faith in marriage, and I celebrated with him those wonderful steps in his newly realized life.

Several months into our friendship, he had confided to me that because he was devout in his faith, he had been celibate and would remain so until he met a woman who would be his wife. He was a handsome and manly figure, and that revelation surprised me, but it reminded me of his unique character and commitment to being a new man. He was serious about his faith and reclaiming his life, and he approached marriage with responsibility and excitement.

Though his work and plans for marriage were time-consuming, we kept exploring the possibility of creating a play, dramatizing his life and perhaps involving others at the Fortune Academy.

On a hot July day in 2006, Hamza chaperoned a group of Fortune teenagers to a modern amusement park, well supplied with rides and crowds. He phoned me the next day and lamented, "I'm getting too old for that sort of thing. The trip really wore me out." That was extremely uncharacteristic for this vital forty-two-year-old man. I assumed he would snap back within a day with newfound enthusiasm.

He failed to show up for work the next day. His answering machine was taking messages. I kept calling, concerned about his health. For a moment I feared he was going to chuck it all in, give up. That's always in the back of your mind. Long ago, Pat McGarry told me, "Once I tripped over a matchstick and bled for three years." He was referring to one drink that led to three years on skid row, interrupted by trips to Rikers Island.

For three days, there was no word from Hamza, which was totally out of character. Everyone with Fortune and his family began checking with one another. Finally, a Bronx hospital administrator called the Castle to report that Hamza had died of a massive heart attack on the way to the hospital after calling 911. The hospital had mixed up his ID with another patient's, and he had been unclaimed for seventy-two hours.

Fortune Society held a memorial service, a painful and necessary pulling together, in a room filled with ex-cons and dozens of street kids Hamza had counseled. Hamza was remembered with eloquence. Several of the teens, tough kids who strutted with macho authority, disclosed their emotions with tears. These were young men and women who rarely received adult attention, and they told us that Hamza had been a man who believed in their possibilities. It was a cathartic experience . . . the emotional volume was high. His new wife thanked everyone at Fortune and then turned to me and said, "David, Hamza loved you so much. Our entire family thanks you for your friendship."

When Hamza lived at the Castle, one of the residents with whom he established a close bond was Casimiro Torres. Their rooms were adjacent to each other, and they frequently cooked together and over a shared meal considered the possibilities of a new life in a square world. Caz and Hamza were on a similar journey.

I was only slightly aware of Caz when he arrived at the Castle. He did little to draw attention to himself. He sat in the corner during Thursday meetings, slouching in his chair. His body language indicated he was not totally comfortable in the room. He had a scruffy look, the classic appearance of a man with a long history of drugs and incarceration. He was tentative, unwilling to commit himself—the antithesis of Hamza.

One week, Caz made a comment during the community meeting. It was not particularly insightful or profound, but he had entered the dialogue. I knew that that was often a major step for a man considering a reconstruction of his life. After he spoke, I whispered to Joanne, "It talks, too."

As the weeks passed, Caz participated more frequently at the meetings. His body language altered, as did his physical appearance. His hair was combed, his face shaved, his clothes pressed and clean...and he sat up, indicating that he was alert to the passing comments. The transition was slow, but evident.

He approached me one evening and informed me that he was writing a book, his autobiography. He asked if I would look at it. "Why not?" I thought. "Everyone and his grandmother are writing a book; why not this guy?"

I read his story.

The horrors of Caz's childhood were not unfamiliar territory for me. Bob Brown, Stanley Eldridge, Eddie Morris, Chuck Bergansky, and many other Fortune alumni had introduced me to tales that resonated with a Dickens-like initiation of poverty and child neglect. Caz Torres's early years easily fit into the pages of *Oliver Twist*.

Those stories overlap from person to person. Each one who survives it is branded with the pain, which is exclusively their own. That child abuse is so widespread does not make it a cliché. Each child endures it in isolation and terror. As I read Caz's recollections, I found myself grieving for the child he once was. My background of suburban comfort and parental love was so distant from his life, and yet there he was, a man fighting to overcome the crocodiles of his dreams. This tall, increasingly self-confident man was moving past the adversities and blockades that had dominated his early years. He wrote of his brothers and sisters, particularly his brother Nino, a year older, who was his continual companion through an avalanche of abuse.

Caz's mother had nine children from three different fathers. Caz never knew the man who fathered him. He learned that the man was from Puerto Rico and was in the navy. His mother was obviously a complicated figure in his life, offering love and yet, as an alcoholic, not providing for her brood. Her home was always filled with addicts and gangsters.

Caz wrote that the men in the house often picked up him and his brother Nino, ages five and six, made a ring in the basement, and had them fight each other. The men took bets on who would win, and the two lads were encouraged to battle each other as the men cheered them on. After the scrapes, the two boys would tend to each other's bloody wounds and sleep huddled together on a mattress in a back room.

Eventually, authorities took the children away from their home. Placed in training schools for unwanted kids, they were subjected to unbearable physical and sexual abuse from staff members. The boys grew up in these facilities and learned how to survive amidst nineteenth-century punishment programs. When Caz and Nino hit the streets of New York, they stole to survive. Caz admits that at the age of ten he was introduced to weed and alcohol, and "from then on, that's how I managed my pain."

Reading his stories, I wanted to wave a magic wand and undo all the suffering that boy had endured. He had managed to survive, and that boy became an imposing man and my friend. I marvel at his intelligence, quick wit, humanity that transcends all reason, and capacity to forgive the damage that was done to him. As a counselor at the Fortune Society, he is revered by the men and women assigned to him.

In time I talked with him about my theater conversations with Hamza and thoughts of dramatizing his experience. Caz's chilling childhood tales suggested he, too, had a story screaming to be told. Our discussion then became the Fortune Society version of an old Mickey Rooney Judy Garland movie, when the kids get together and say, "Let's do a play."

Caz and I began looking around at the residents of the Castle. Who among them had made it clear they were ready to assume a new life and had taken steps to achieve it? We sought people who had made a commitment, abandoning the false crutches of drugs and booze. Everyone in the Castle had a story that could be dramatized, but none of them needed a spotlight put on them, however dim, if they had not yet examined the lives they had led and explored where they wanted to go. Jack Abbott, among others, had demonstrated that to me years earlier.

Kenny Harrigan was clearly a man to approach. A tall, handsome guy with a winning smile, he was right out of central casting. He was quite outspoken at Castle meetings, once stating that he had had to leave a visit to a relative's house because weed was being smoked. "I love my family," he told the group, "but I will not endanger my freedom. You have to leave." He added, "If they really love you, they will not put you in that position. I am on parole and can't be around users. You just walk away." Kenny was a faithful churchgoer, had become an active volunteer, and had entered a positive relationship with Sharon White, a woman who had done time and was as motivated as he for a better life. Their relationship was a source of strength for both of them. Kenny had attended a human-resources training program and was working as a counselor.

When I learned of his background, it stunned me to discover he had served sixteen years straight on a twelve-to-life sentence for burglaries that supported his drug habit. No violence had been involved, and he had never carried a weapon. It is clear that sentencing for African Americans is disproportionate to that for white addicts. Most of the men and women doing time in New York on drug charges are black or Hispanic—close to 90 percent, which is hardly reflective of the percentages of drug use or sales. Kenny Harrigan was a man with a drug problem and needed medical attention, not prison, where he endured knife wounds, a physical breakdown that involved two operations, and the loss of a kidney. Had he been white, he probably would have been sent to a rehab center. As it was, he spent his prison time in the law library and the chapel.

The female population in prison is about one-tenth of the men's, a figure reflected at the Castle. But the experiences for women are different for a variety of reasons, and we knew it was important to share that perspective in our play. Vilma Ortiz Donovan was an easy choice. Vivacious and outgoing, she is incandescent, all out-front emotions—a clear presence in any room she enters. She expressed herself passionately at the Thursday meetings. After she left the Castle and moved into her own apartment, she returned for the meetings, as do many of the Castle alumni. One night, listening to the predictable complaints about house rules, she asked for the floor and outlined the opportunities for everyone there. And she added, "I grew up in this room."

I began to realize that the Thursday nights were like a very private series of auditions for me. A play was formulating right in that room.

A suburban kid who grew up on Long Island, Vilma states in the play, "I'm the one who shouldn't have ended up in prison, but we make choices...and good or bad, we live with them forever." She was from a large family, and apparently her emotional needs were overlooked. Like many rebellious teens, she found salvation and escape in the drug culture. She ended up in New York State prisons twice. After her first release, she wanted to go straight, but she now recalls that she wanted it all right away and wasn't prepared for the streets. After her second incarceration concluded, she came directly to the Castle. Vilma marvels that when she entered the Fortune Academy, staff and residents greeted her: "Welcome home, Vilma." She knew that she was in the right place. She is a wonder now, working full-time at Fortune and going to college at nights. She is a reminder that anything is possible.

Angel Ramos sounds professorial when he speaks. Few would suspect he was in prison for more than thirty years, from the age of seventeen until forty-seven. Thirty years in cages preceded his release, and he came directly to Fortune and the Castle. He had entered prison an illiterate—a fact that reflects many lives in those places—and taught himself to read and write. I first became acquainted with him when another inmate at Attica, someone I had known for years, suggested that Angel send me his poetry.

During the second decade of his incarceration, Angel began attending Quaker meetings. He found their sessions attractive, and he looked forward to their quiet moments of serenity. The Quakers were his bridge to society, and he arrived at the Castle motivated but frightened. He admits that the changes in society were daunting; he had to learn to become acquainted with new technology. In the play, he informs the audience, "The world was very different, and I had to move slowly. Everything in my youth prepared me to end up in prison."

Angel grew up in East Harlem, and his family would at best be called dysfunctional. His mother was on prescription pills, and his stepfather was a recovering alcoholic. He reflects that he tuned out of school by the third grade and grew up on the streets. At thirteen he was into petty crime, and by fifteen he was selling pot. A fight with a friend when he was eighteen years old resulted in his friend's death. Looking back on his life, he describes himself as young, smart, angry, making money, and just running around acting crazy. "All the pain in my tiny little soul came pouring out." Like many long-timers, Angel grew up in prison, but he was blessed to find the Quakers. At the Castle, he was anxious for the next step. In addition to appearing in the play and film of *The Castle*, he worked at Fortune as a counselor before becoming a full-time college student.

It was my conceit to create a play based on the four lives and to present it in the meeting room where we gathered each Thursday. If I announced it on my radio program and created flyers to distribute to friends, I guessed that we could perform it for a few weekends and raise money that could be used for special events.

From the outset, I told the cast they would be paid seventy-five dollars for each performance. I am from the school that says "actors must be paid."

We began simply. I asked Caz, Kenny, Vilma, and Angel to each write a one-page biography highlighting their life's high and low points. When they had completed the school-like assignment, I interviewed each one separately, using the biographical sketches as a starting point. At Fortune, I rarely know the crimes for which individuals have been convicted. I always remember Sam Rivera's "the crime is what I did, not who I am." But this was a different exercise, and Caz reminded me of something I had learned long ago: the convictions hardly tell you the story.

I absorbed their lives and shaped them into a presentation, using my lifetime of theater to dramatize their stories. Recalling some of the most effective dramatic evenings, from *Don Juan in Hell* to *The Vagina Monologues*, I knew the narrative needed no props or onstage distractions. It had to be the three men and one woman commanding the audience's involvement with the sheer power and drama of their lives. If it worked, it was theater.

More than once, when describing a unique theatrical experience not understood by critics or audiences, I have cited the words Joseph Mankiewicz put in the mouth of actor Gary Merrill in *All About Eve*, the best film ever made about the theater. Merrill's Bill Sampson instructs the ambitious Eve Harrington, who is hoping to get her foot in the door of a Broadway production:

> Listen, junior. And learn. Want to know what the theater is? A flea circus. Also opera. Also rodeos, carnivals, ballets, Indian tribal dances, Punch and Judy, a one-man band—all theater. Wherever there's magic and make-believe and an audience, there's theater. Donald Duck, Ibsen and the Lone Ranger, Sarah Bernhardt, Poodles Hanneford, Lunt and Fontanne, Betty Grable, Rex the Wild Horse, and Eleanora Duse. They're all theater. You don't understand them all, you don't like them all— why should you? The theater's for everybody—you included, but not exclusively—so don't approve or disapprove. It may not be your theater, but it's theater for somebody, somewhere.

We purchased four stools, the perches from where the actors would deliver their lines. If the drama was in the stories, audiences would listen and relive the actors' experiences. *The Castle* was not designed for traditional theatergoers or critics. Our goal was for it to resonate for the formerly incarcerated and those now incarcerated. We hoped the general public would respond too.

We needed an opening setup. I suggested the actors enter and introduce themselves thusly: "My name is Casimiro Torres and I lived at the Castle. I was homeless when I arrived in 2005 with sixty-seven arrests and sixteen years in prison." That, I assumed, could immediately capture the audience's attention. Critic Walter Kerr once opined, "If they haven't involved me in the first five minutes, the chances are they will not for the remainder of the evening."

After the quartet introduced themselves, standing behind the stools, they would present historic facts about the Castle, the building where they all began to reclaim their lives. My assignment was to shape their stories, chronologically akin to one another. I broke it down: childhood, alienation, arrests, and prison, followed by the Castle and today.

We rehearsed at the Castle and the Fortune Society offices. The cast had no theater experience, but I pointed out to them that when they'd been running the streets, they'd been acting—to their families, to cops and officials, so their criminal acts wouldn't be detected. That is acting. It was important, also, to instill theater discipline. Be on time, call if unable to make a rehearsal, and be responsible to the craft. All four took the assignments seriously. They were all attending groups or therapy, holding jobs, and going to school. It took real commitment to find scheduling time for *The Castle*.

We placed the printed scripts on four music stands. The cast didn't believe me when I told them that in time they wouldn't need the scripts, which would remain only as security blankets.

After months with a scattered rehearsal schedule, we thought it time to invite an audience. We had been self-contained, five of us in a room. We had no idea what we had. We invited JoAnne Page and other staff members to a classroom on a late weekday afternoon. I asked a few friends, a couple of whom had acting backgrounds. No one knew what to expect, least of all me. I recalled how hesitant I had been years earlier when Alvin Ailey had asked me to watch the rehearsal of his new dance company. I was repeating that ritual— hesitant and at the same time brave, hoping the invited guests would respond to our creation.

I have sat through hundreds of first readings and gypsy run-throughs—so named because dancers in Broadway choruses are called gypsies, and they are usually invited to sit through a new musical, without costumes or sets or a full orchestra, before it goes out of town. A gypsy run-through would have a single piano and a glaring lightbulb on the barren stage. This was how I first saw the

Lunts (Alfred Lunt and his wife Lynn Fontanne) in *The Visit*, one of their greatest triumphs. We all knew that it was a hit, even minus all the accoutrements that would accompany it when it opened on Broadway. In fact, I recall the play with greater clarity from the empty-stage run-through than from the fully realized production, which I attended weeks later. It was the words and the acting on which the audience focused.

Thus, in the great tradition of the theater, we had our gypsy run-through in a classroom on Twenty-Third Street before two dozen friends and colleagues. There were four stools, four music stands, and four actors. Nothing else. I stood in the back of the room as the cast made their entrance from the hallway.

From the moment it began, from Caz's opening words, the room was electric. Those in the audience who had done time were shaking their heads, nodding up and down in recognition, giving silent affirmation as their lives were reflected on the improvised stage. When the actors concluded, after repeating their opening passages of introduction, they took their bows. There was a long moment of silence. And then, as if the audience had been choreographed or directed, they stood and cheered. Several in the room were wiping their eyes.

The Castle had come to life. It takes an audience to make a play.

We scheduled performances for two successive weekends in the community room at the Castle. Insecurities resurfaced. How would strangers respond? I announced the show on my radio program; the cast members lured family and friends. They came and they cheered on the first Saturday and Sunday. I then invited my old friend Eric Krebs, for whom I had done publicity on many shows he had produced at the John Houseman Theater.

I had initially met Eric in Los Angeles, where he was operating a theater in addition to the Houseman in Manhattan. I had gone to LA with Carol Levine, whose advertising company was adjacent to mine in our Broadway offices, to see the opening there of *Tony n' Tina's Wedding*. Carol was the ad rep for the play, and I was the publicist. Carol became an important colleague and friend in my life. Her wisdom and kindness were in evidence, and she and I laughed through more than one rocky theatrical experience together.

She suggested that while we were in LA, we should have lunch with Eric, who I had never met.

It was the start of many years and several shows working together—Carol, Eric, and myself. Eric asked me to contact him when we all returned to New York, and I became the publicist for most of his plays. More than that, a friendship was created amidst the professional turmoil of seeing a show evolve in production.

Eric had his hand in many pots. Carol's and my main task was to tell him after going to a gypsy run-through: "Close it. Don't let another person see it." He often listened, and we always laughed.

Eric Krebs, like Carol Levine, was generous to a fault. He was always rescuing a lost soul. Even after I retired, I remained in close touch with both of them. They were friends more than business associates.

Carol was a two-pack-a-day smoker, and we all knew that was an invitation to disaster. Her passing from cancer was traumatic for her family and friends. She had been the woman you called for advice and direction. Visiting her in her last days was unbearable; seeing this strong, confident woman reduced to skin and bones was another of life's cruel tricks. There are people you meet who appear as strong as the earth, and you assume they will be there for you forever...and suddenly, they are not.

Again, I was a eulogist at a memorial service I didn't want to attend—held, appropriately, in Eric's Houseman Theater. I had begun to think that my new career was giving eulogies for people I loved. The toughest thing about growing older is outliving people who have been a beacon of light in your life.

So you continue and meet young energetic folks for whom life is all ahead of them. Working with Caz Torres, Vilma Ortiz Donovan, Kenny Harrigan, and Angel Ramos on *The Castle* was the offsetting tonic. Young lives with energy and hope and new direction are the ingredients to make each day count.

Eric accepted my invitation to see *The Castle.* About five seconds after the play concluded, he said to me, "This is the kind of theater I want to do. I want to present *The Castle* off-Broadway."

First things first. I was stunned and cautious. I had to talk to the cast, for this was a collaborative effort. Did they want to continue?

The four actors quickly agreed. They were committed to the play and to a new adventure.

Chase Mishkin accepted Eric's invitation to a second performance. Chase is a seasoned Broadway producer—I had worked with her on a couple of shows—and she immediately became Eric's partner in the off-Broadway presentation of *The Castle.* She is not only smart about the theater, she is nice, not a word used too often about producers.

We began at the New World Stages in April 2008. The building in which we were to play had recently been converted into five theaters for off-Broadway shows. Before that, it had been a popular second-run movie house, famous for charging only a dollar for a ticket. Caz had often slept all night there as a runaway teenager.

Angel Ramos would be making his stage debut on the second anniversary of his release from Attica after thirty years behind bars.

Among them, the cast had been in prison for more than seventy years. This was unprecedented in theatrical history. My years as a theatrical publicist insisted that the appearance of the quartet was a perfect feature story.

I was painfully naïve. The press, which loves crime, was not as enthused about men and women who had reclaimed their lives. I had always been aware of this but assumed the presentation of *The Castle* might transcend the prejudice.

A reporter for the *New York Times* called about interviewing the four cast members. His editor killed the idea. The *Times* sent a fifth-string critic, who gave a gratuitously favorable review that ran deep inside the *Times*'s theatrical section. That was the last time the Arts and Leisure section of the most influential newspaper ever reported on the play. When we were invited to perform in Albany before state legislators, it wasn't of interest. Our playing at maximum-security prisons, easily some of the most dramatic performances I have ever witnessed, went unrecorded. The *Daily News* and *Newsday* never reviewed the play. The *New York Post* critic did attend, stood and cheered at the conclusion, and later informed me that his favorable review had been killed. A producer from ABC TV filmed the cast for hours and two weeks later told me the network wouldn't run the feature.

Angel joked, "Perhaps one of us should get rearrested. They would make that a big story."

In spite of media silence, *The Castle* was having an impact off the usual path of theatrical entities. We received numerous invitations to play in colleges, churches, and most significantly city jails and state prisons. The impact and implications of formerly incarcerated persons returning to prisons where they had served time were illuminating. At one prison, a man stood during the question-and-answer period that follows every performance and, pointing at Caz, stated, "I know you. I did time with you. You were just like me. If you can be up there, I can be up there."

Officials at the men's prisons always warned us not to expect any response in the Q&A period. We learned to ignore that. True, the men would look around after the play's final lines, but after the first man found the courage to speak, the floodgates would open. The main question, asked in various ways, always seemed to be, "How do we get to where you are?" Most prisoners want to travel a new path, but as Caz says in the play, "I always knew there was something else; I just didn't know where to find it."

Performances at the women's prisons are an emotional shock-wave. The women are much freer than the men with their responses. They cry throughout, applaud in the middle of speeches, stand up and cheer at the end of a single statement. When *The Castle* is performed at a women's prison, it usually runs fifteen minutes longer.

At one of the performances at the women's section on Rikers Island, the starting time was delayed because of sound difficulty. I walked through the crowd apologizing for the delay. One woman asked, "What is this?" I was surprised they hadn't been clued in; they had no idea about what they were about to view. A beautiful young woman named Maria asked me if she would be able to dance to it. "Check with me after," I said.

During the Q&A, I called out to Maria for her response. She stood and cheered to me, "Now, I can dance forever," which was probably the best review a play could ever receive.

Most exciting for me is to be at the Fortune Society when a young man or woman approaches and tells me, "I saw you at the play when you did it at the prison I was in." They come for a new beginning, inspired by a play.

Having been involved in more than two hundred Broadway and off-Broadway plays, including the life-altering *Fortune and Men's Eyes*, I can say that *The Castle* has been the most gratifying theatrical experience of my life. It is a gift to men and women who have been written off by society and see a glimmer of hope. It reaches into the dungeons and says, "You too can have a new life; look at us. We're just like you."

The Castle, of course, is the other bookend to the story the *New York Times* didn't grasp. Forty years ago, *Fortune and Men's Eyes* was the starting point for a social-change movement and the creation of the Fortune Society. Four decades later, off-Broadway was the venue for a new play with four formerly incarcerated persons.

Unfortunately, in today's media, preoccupied with celebrity, the Hamptons, and exposure of sexual behavior, this was not an area of interest for the daily papers.

Media indifference aside, *The Castle* continued to perform. And who would have anticipated the next stage? Marty Feinberg, a friend of Eric Krebs, joined us at a performance at a women's prison. He later informed Eric that he wanted to make a movie of *The Castle*, which is exactly what happened.

The four cast members have all moved out of the Castle into their own apartments. In the play, Caz relates how he needed his time at the Fortune Academy so he could learn how to be a husband to his wife, Allison, and father to his daughter, Cassie. He is succeeding at both.

Vilma has her own apartment; she is a college student and a supervisor at the Fortune Society. She remains ebullient, enjoying each new phase of her life. In the play she reveals, "My high now is the life I lead today, without drugs, without alcohol." She appears to be enjoying every moment.

Angel Ramos became a regular cohost on my Saturday morning radio show at WBAI. He has his own apartment, and after serving as a counselor for two years at Fortune, he enrolled at John Jay College of Criminal Justice. In *The Castle*, Angel observes, "I love my life today, but if I spent too much time brooding about the past, I would be denying myself the pleasures I now seek. I am not forgetting where I came from, but part of being the new Angel is placing the past in the past."

Kenny Harrigan has been a tower of strength. During the end of our fourteen months at the New World Stages, he was diagnosed with cancer of the jaw and began taking radiation treatments and chemotherapy. He fought off the demons and returned to Fortune as a counselor in the ATI program. He and his wife, Sharon, live in upper Manhattan. Their wedding, which I happily attended, was the first ceremony of its kind at the Castle. Kenny has one simple line in the play that I have always found powerful. After talking about all of the barriers in prison, with little help to ready you for the streets, he simply states, "So I worked on me and did some soul searching." Kenny continues to fight cancer, and his courage is heroic.

I've come to understand why the play is so significant and resonates with so many formerly incarcerated and currently encaged men and women. I often quote lines from the play to make a point when debating or discussing criminal justice issues. The lives of Caz, Angel, Kenny, and Vilma are dramatic, and the courage they have displayed in sharing their demons and their dreams makes me hopeful and proud.

I have become close to the four people in the cast in different ways. We have shared a journey that is unprecedented for people who have been in prison. Despite the seventy years among them, they are now consummate artists as well as taxpayers.

When Harry LaCroix lived with me decades back, I experienced paternal feeling. It is a mixture of pride and protection, one I have felt again now, working on the play. Caz Torres wrote an essay and presented it to me, reflecting his feelings about our evolving relationship. I cried when I read it. This was his message to me:

> I have often wondered what kind of man my father was and what he looked like. He left when I was two years old, and as hard as I may try, I cannot remember what he looked like. Sometimes I look in the mirror and wonder...do I look like him? Have you ever heard someone say, "You're going to be tall just like your father" or "You have your father's eyes"? Well, nobody has ever said that to me.
>
> After all the years I have spent in prison and doing bad things, I sometimes can't help but think that maybe I did get something from my father. These types of thoughts would always come to me either in a prison cell or a crack house or

maybe during those cold nights I spent on the subway. As small and pathetic as it may have been, it was my identity, or at least who I thought I was. It wasn't until I was 38 years old that I finally met my father. Of course, I had no idea he was my father at the time; even so there was something about him that drew me to him right away. I began to observe him, listen to him, and, more importantly, I began to talk to him. There is something about him that speaks of kindness, a noble heart, and not just a willingness but a determination to fight for others. Amazing. Secretly this is how I have always wanted others to see me and always who I want to be!

But all I knew of my father was bad, and I just couldn't shake that. Besides, I wanted an identity so bad that I took whatever I could even if it was bad, all the while reading my Superman comic books and asking God for help.

My father has the noble spirit of Superman and the kindness of a saint.

My father is not tall like me nor do I have "his eyes." My father is a little, old Jewish man who wears glasses and funny shirts.

My father has taught me many things. He taught me that I am not the worst thing I have ever done.

He has told me that I am a good man, a kind man, and even noble at times.

I am just like my father.

What father wouldn't be proud?

In June of 2012, Caz found his birth father. Or rather, his father, Luis Torres, found him. The senior Torres searched for his three children for four decades. He had married and had begun a new family, with a daughter and son, Connie and Wellington Torres. When they were of age, Luis informed them they had siblings somewhere. Connie began searching but Caz's name never appeared. She felt it a lost cause and for several years did not google. But she tried again in 2012, and Caz's name appeared as a member of the play *The Castle*.

Connie called the Fortune Society and was put in touch with her brother. Two days later, Caz received a call from his father living in Florida. On Father's Day weekend, Caz flew to Orlando and was greeted at the airport by his father and his sister. Upon his return to New York City, Caz proudly showed me photos of him, embracing his dad.

There is now a second company of the play, *The Castle Two*, in which four alumni, four lives, dramatically share their stories. Rory Anderson, Chris Carney, Thomas Jones, and Victor Rojas, have between them served more than sixty years in New York prisons. In the play, Thomas Jones tells the pants story, and it is always well received.

When *The Castle Two* gave its first performance at the Fortune Academy, Eric Krebs asked the first questions after the play. "You men have revealed extraordinary lives, filled with punishment and rejection. How does it feel to receive applause?" A great question, and one that they were not ready to answer. In rehearsals we had prepared for a variety of questions that might be posed...but not Eric's. The four men agreed that they need time to absorb this new experience of being applauded, of being given signs of acceptance and approval. Applause is a new part of the journey.

The Castle Two, like its predecessor, continues to perform in prisons, drug programs, colleges, churches and synagogues, and criminal justice conferences.

SIXTEEN

Snapshots

Bob Brown pulled me aside one day at Fortune and told me he had something on his mind. Quietly, he asked, "How do I tell my daughter that I once killed a man?"

It was the 1970s, and Bob had come to the Fortune Society after serving twenty-five years in prison. He had been rescued in his last years by a chaplain who was, more significantly, a clinical psychologist. Bob worked with him during his last years at Wallkill Correctional Facility and labored to come to terms with who he was—abandoned at birth, shuffled from foster homes to orphanages, with no self-identity. By the time he had hit the streets, he was a man-child waiting to begin his life. He had conventional dreams and goals, none more important than establishing a family. He married quickly, perhaps too soon, and became the adoring father of Phaedra Brown. He couldn't pour enough love upon this bright and beautiful little girl. When Bob asked me about sharing his past with his daughter, she had turned six, and her every conversation focused on "Why?" or "How?"

I told Bob I would call Eda LeShan, a child psychologist I had met while she was hosting her own PBS TV show, *How Do Your Children Grow?* Eda was impressed with the work of the Fortune Society, and we achieved a natural alliance. When I told her of Bob's question, she laughed and said, "They don't teach that one in psych classes." Then she suggested that Bob and I come up for dinner one night and, in a cordial atmosphere, discuss the issue.

When other parents at Fortune heard of this planned dinner, they wanted in. Fran O'Leary had just reconnected with her two daughters and was going through big changes. Rod Taylor had become a father to Rod Jr. and suggested that he knew little of fathering since his dad had been in prison during Rod's own childhood. Danny Keane and Eddie Carabello, both recent fathers, had a multitude of parenting problems. Few of the people who came to Fortune had parents on whom they could model themselves.

Eda's dinner became a weekly potluck supper where the subject of parenting was explored. Everyone shared in Bob's decision, which was to tell Phaedra that he had been in prison—when she was age-appropriate. That was translated to mean that when she started asking questions, he would provide answers. No evasions, but he would not initiate the discussion; he would respond to the natural questions a daughter asks about her father's past.

Eda and I agreed that those parenting groups were powerful and rewarding.

Nearly twenty years later, JoAnne Page and I decided to have a small party at the Fortune offices. We invited as guests of honor the children of the participants in the parenting group. Phaedra Brown, a magazine editor in her late twenties, attended and paid homage to her late father. Dante Carabello, a handsome young man, recalled his time as a six-year-old running around the Fortune offices. Rod Taylor Jr. told us he was there as the guest of his best friend, his dad.

None of the children of Fortune had known about their parents' participation in the parenting class, but by telling us who they were and sharing their love for their formerly incarcerated parents, they made me realize how monumentally successful Eda's potluck suppers had turned out to be.

Alex Cohen loved parties, galas, pulling in the icons. It could be exhilarating or cumbersome.

During the run of *The School for Scandal*, cognoscenti were ready to celebrate British royalty. The two sirs, John Gielgud and Ralph Richardson, were at the height of theatrical fame. Every night was a celebration. At one party Alex hosted, he arranged for small tables, place cards for all, at some Manhattan East Side restaurant. I was seated with three women at a table for the internationally acclaimed— and me. I found myself facing Judy Garland, Vivien Leigh, and Dame Margot Fonteyn. There was enough theatrical glitter at the table to light up Manhattan.

Sadly, at the supper table, these three artists, whom I admired and revered when I was an audience member, were less than appealing. Curiously, they ignored one another; twenty-eight-year-old David was the focus of their collective attention. They fired questions at me, seeking some autobiographical data, as if I had to justify my placement with the goddesses. Judy was blotto, slurring each word as she clutched my arm. Vivien seemed of another world, more Blanche DuBois than Scarlett O'Hara. Dame Margot was imperious, practically on pointe while sitting at the table. I couldn't wait for the last morsel to be consumed.

For days, everyone I knew wanted reports of the meal. Word had filtered out concerning my dinner companions. Alas, dropping their names was far more satisfying than being placed in their collective company.

Alex was more successful in reaching my celebrity curiosity when he reported to me that the first family, President John F. Kennedy and First Lady Jacqueline Kennedy, would be attending the *School for Scandal* opening in D.C. following the sold-out Broadway run. "Call the vice president and the Supreme Court chief justice," he suggested to me. "Invite them to the opening."

"How do I do that?" I bravely responded.

"Call them," Alex barked at me.

And that's what I did. I can't recall what service provided me with the appropriate numbers. There I was, talking to a woman who answered the vice president's home phone. "I'm David Rothenberg," I proudly announced. "Would the vice president and Mrs. Johnson be our guests at the *School for Scandal* opening next month?"

"This is Lady Bird," the woman informed me. I was startled, having assumed I had the ear of a secretary. She told me she and Lyndon would love to attend, and indeed they did appear at the opening of the play.

Next call was to the home of the Supreme Court chief justice. I went through the obligatory introductions to the presumed servant at the other end of the wire. She informed me, "This is Mrs. Warren. Well, I certainly will attend. Let me call over to the Supreme Court and confirm the judge's schedule."

I cautioned, "There is time. No need to interrupt the Supreme Court."

"Nonsense," she responded, "they're not doing anything over there." Within moments I had a report that the Earl Warrens, along with the Lyndon Johnsons, would be in attendance at the National Theatre premiere.

On opening night, it was relayed to us that British ambassador David Ormsby-Gore was in the audience with England's Labour Party leader, Harold Wilson, who was in town to meet with JFK the next day. A Labour victory in the upcoming British election would make Wilson the next prime minister.

Alex, after appropriately seating the president, vice president, and chief justice, told me, "Go get Wilson to come backstage after the show to meet the cast. I'll get the president."

"How do I do that?" I challenged Alex. "Go ask him," was Alex's sage and obvious response.

So there I was, escorting Harold Wilson down one aisle while Alex moved along the other with JFK and the missus—and we all ventured onto the stage from opposing wings behind the closed curtain, where the cast had been assembled to meet political royalty.

I marched over, arm in arm with Mr. Wilson, and said, "Mr. Wilson, I would like you to meet Alex Cohen, our producer, and the president of the United States." Alex, picking up the cue, turned to JFK and said, "Mr. President, this is Harold Wilson and David Rothenberg."

On the following day, the press reported that Harold Wilson visited the White House and met President Kennedy for the first time—a meeting of two great allies and the leaders of the free world. In fact, the press was not accurate. They had met the evening before, when I had introduced them.

I told everyone I had made a cameo appearance in political history.

My career shift from the theater to the Fortune Society produced unlikely dramatic events. I often claimed that most days at Fortune were more dramatic than most of the plays I represented or saw.

For instance:

It was a Labor Day weekend in the early seventies. Cell phones and answering machines were still in the future. My phone was ringing as I entered my apartment. The frantic caller was from the police department and told me that a man on top of the World Trade Center was threatening to jump. He had told the guard on the roof that he would only speak to David Rothenberg of the Fortune Society. The police caller had no name to identify the would-be suicide. The NYPD was sending a car to pick me up if I were willing to go to the top of the World Trade Center. I quickly consented.

Within moments, a car arrived. I told the detectives that I had no experience with suicide attempts, and asked for guidance. They began giving me a quick course in life-saving persuasion. A phone call came to the police car from Channel 5 TV. A reporter, Steve

Bauman, whom I knew from past events, asked if they could wire me when I went to the top of the Trade Center. This was decades before reality television, but Steve wanted to go live with my efforts. I quickly vetoed that, knowing that this was unknown territory for me and I didn't need the intrusion of the media.

The police rushed me to the roof, and as I approached the man, who was unfamiliar to me, he climbed down, falling into the arms of a religious leader who had also been summoned. Upon seeing me, the man winked and moved on in the custody of the police.

I learned that he was the brother of R. Merrill Speller, whose murder in Trenton's Vroom Building was witnessed by Danny Hogan. I found it overwhelmingly sad that this Mr. Speller was so isolated he could only reach out to someone he had never met, a confidant of his slain brother. After the incident, Mr. Speller was institutionalized. Years later, I read that he was arrested for threatening the life of President Ford.

In later years at Fortune, I became aware of several suicide attempts, a few of them successful, by men and women who were filled with so much self-loathing they couldn't endure life on this planet.

Joe (not his real name) was very bright, and he often confided in me about his frustrations in adapting to street life after years of encagement. He lost his temper easily and was very rough on himself. I often suggested that he be more forgiving of Joe. When things were going well, Joe was able to charm the world. When he faced a minor setback, he went into a cave of sadness and self-reproach.

One day Joe called me at home and announced that he was at a subway station on the Lexington Avenue line, preparing to jump in front of a train. I knew enough to realize that his calling me suggested he wanted to be talked out of it. But that didn't guarantee that he wouldn't kill himself. I had to keep talking to him as I heard subway trains rushing by.

We talked for twenty minutes. I attempted to reassure him that whatever sadness and rage he felt at the moment would pass...and that if he would only meet me, we could identify hopeful and positive alternatives for him. My voice was going dry as I pleaded with him to go to Fortune, where we could talk. He argued against that, stating he didn't want others to judge him. He kept asking why he should live. I could only respond that it would break my heart to lose such a friend. I have no idea if that is what suicide watchers are taught, but the words came from the depth of my being.

At last he agreed to leave the train station. I quickly called Stanley Richards and Barry Campbell at Fortune and implored them to be on hand. I felt drained and didn't know if I could successfully convince Joe that his life mattered. Stan and Barry's collective wisdom, street smarts, and compassion were what Joe needed.

We met with him for exhausting hours. He went through changes during that long afternoon...came out smiling and ready to begin another day. We do it one day at a time. Joe didn't take his life. But he went after himself slowly, returning to drugs as his escape from reality. He ended up back in prison. I have no idea what the future will be for him. I can only hope that as he matures, he will be less harsh on himself. He'll return to the streets and will have to face his demons, one day at a time.

I don't remember being disillusioned at the age of four when I learned that those Christmas gifts were from my parents and not some bearded mystery man. My sister, Carla, and I discovered the packages in the back of my parents' closet and realized the truth. I thought it was *neat* that my mother and father were giving me the toys. Who could relate to a stranger who invaded every home and forced his way down the chimney? We didn't have a chimney.

My big disillusionment came at fourteen, and the villain of the piece was baseball's New York Giants.

I was a sports fan, through and through, and for me the sun rose and set on the Giants. My first hero was Mel Ott, succeeded by Bobby Thomson and later Willie Mays. I wanted to be a sportswriter some day, so I gathered statistics and war stories about old-time players. Of course I purchased the *Sporting News* every week, the Saint Louis based publication that fed you all the baseball news. When I noticed an ad for a fan paper called the *Trading Post*, I immediately sent away for a copy. From the *Trading Post* I learned there were varieties of fan clubs for different players and teams. Alas, nothing for the Giants.

My dad had an old mimeograph machine in the basement, and I determined I could publish a Giants fan newspaper—mimeographed, of course—and start a club for those who shared my enthusiasm for the men on Coogan's Bluff. I ran an ad in the *Trading Post* and said that for two dollars a year you could receive my Giants fan newspapers. Nearly two dozen people sent me the two dollars, which would pay for paper, postage, and travel to the Polo Grounds.

I created Giants quizzes, amassed historic facts from the baseball guides of past years, and in the first issue published an interview with a young, left-handed pitcher named Monte Kennedy. I cornered Kennedy outside the ballpark, and he agreed to a fast interview. Within a few months I had nearly seventy-five subscribers from around the country. I was in business.

At dinner one night, a phone call came to our Teaneck, New Jersey, home. The operator said it was "long distance from New York for David Rothenberg." Back in the forties, a call to New Jersey from New York was executed by long-distance operators. My father announced that the New York Giants were calling me. On the line was sportscaster Steve Ellis, informing me that the Giants organization had heard of my publication and was impressed. They wanted to meet me. It was arranged for me to visit headquarters one day (after school, of course). My father drove me into Manhattan.

Ellis and his team were clearly startled when a five-foot-two fourteen-year-old walked into their office. My voice had just started to change, and I must have sounded like an un-oiled rocking chair.

They informed me that the Giants wanted to broaden my concept. In the after-game program, *Giant Jottings*, they would announce the fan club and newspaper. They would have it printed by a professional. I was told I could write for each issue, and they would bring me to spring training, as their guest, to meet and interview the players.

I left the offices in a state of elation. I went home and wrote my first article; I mailed it to Steve Ellis, and it was published in the initial edition the Giants printed. On the air, they reported that more than twenty-five thousand had responded to their announcement of a fan club and newspaper.

And that was the end of it for me. After that, they didn't return my calls. My father, clearly upset, tried to get a response. We didn't want anything other than a fulfillment of promises that would include my going to spring training for a week. I wrote several letters to Steve Ellis and the Giants' owner, Horace Stoneham. I listened with mixed pride as they reported the swelling members of the fan club.

In retrospect, I think they could have benefited from announcing that a teenage fan had inspired the entire operation. They were probably afraid we would sue. Nothing was in writing, and we didn't want to sue—my dad never even mentioned that. All that my dad wanted for me was the recognition by the Giants of my inspired concept.

I have always argued that you can't know someone by a one-time interaction. But it certainly doesn't stop you from having an opinion. I've gained quick impressions from single meetings with a variety of people. Dinner with Charles Laughton and Elsa Lanchester was certainly a memorable occasion. Bob Ullman had informed me that we would be working on Elsa's new one-woman off-Broadway show, which her husband, Charles, was directing. I was excited about working with an actress made famous as the Bride of Frankenstein and an actor I always identified as the Hunchback of Notre Dame.

Having dinner at the Algonquin was a first for me. I sat across from Bob, with Charles Laughton on my left and Ms. Lanchester on my right... a fabled Hollywood couple dining with me at the historical Oak Room. Less than a year into a show-business career and a young-looking twenty-five years of age, I was impressed. The salads had no sooner been served when I realized that Charles's hand was on my knee, slowly moving upward to my inner thigh. I began tilting over, realizing that a real scene could erupt as a man, an internationally acclaimed film star, was groping me with his wife sitting on my other side.

I consumed my food sitting at a forty-five-degree angle. It was the only time I ever spent with Charles Laughton, but he made a deep impression on me... and my thigh.

As I discovered Elsa's unpredictable quirks, I realized they were both mad as hatters, and my guess is that she probably wouldn't have been surprised at her husband's frisky table manners. In fact, when I arrived at their hotel suite the following morning, Elsa greeted me warmly. I was there to coordinate a series of interviews for the Hollywood character actress. When I told her there would be photographers, she asked, "How do I look?" and then proceeded to throw up her skirt as if she were dancing the cancan. She had not donned any undergarments for the morning session, and I stood there, startled, exposed to her womanly privates. "Put that down!" I squealed, and she obeyed.

I realized they were both determined to shock me. They were successful.

Elsa was a perfect lady with me during the run of the show... and Charles returned to Hollywood after the opening night. But you can be assured, though our meeting was brief, I have held definite opinions about Charles Laughton and Elsa Lanchester. They are both wonderful actors, but when I see them on-screen, I can't help wondering what poor unsuspecting waif or intern on the set was shocked and frightened by their antics.

Of all the celebrated people I have encountered, none baffled me more than Andy Warhol. My old friend Yvette Schumer invited me to dinner one night. There were only four of us, including a male chum of Yvette's and the fabled Warhol. I felt privileged, hoping to gain some insight and wisdom from the internationally acclaimed artist, avant-garde filmmaker, and guru for an entirely new art movement.

He talked incessantly. At first I thought he was putting us on, because his comments were so mundane, clichéd, and often unintelligible. I was numbed into silence... bored, but fascinated by how extremely uninteresting Andy was. As he spoke, my face must have looked like that of an audience member watching Mel Brooks's classic musical number "Springtime for Hitler" from the funniest movie I ever saw, *The Producers.*

When I began plotting a getaway, Andy asked where I lived, and when I told him, he said we could share a cab and he would drop me off. In the taxi he turned to me and said, "You mentioned you were working on a Tennessee Williams play."

"Yes," I responded. "It's the second Williams play with which I have been associated."

"Poor Tennessee," Andy lamented.

"Aha," I thought to myself. Now perhaps I would gain some Warhol insight about one of the finest living American playwrights. "Why 'poor Tennessee'?" I asked.

"He's so out of touch with the times," American's media darling explained.

"How so?"

"Tennessee is still doing alcohol and pills. He has not moved into experimental drugs."

And that was it. Andy Warhol's assessment of Tennessee Williams was based on the playwright's apparent reluctance to experiment with the latest drug fad.

Andy fell into silence, a blank look on his face, exhausted from his shared observation of the man who had penned *The Glass Menagerie*, *A Streetcar Named Desire*, *Cat on a Hot Tin Roof*, *Night of the Iguana*, and *Sweet Bird of Youth*. When we reached my apartment, we shook hands good-bye. Shaking hands with him was like clutching a wet fish.

I kept thinking that I must have missed something. I assumed I had caught him on an off night, bottled up for whatever reason, and as I read of him over time, I kept looking for a clue, a reason that the media and the critics were in awe of him. I kept recalling Gertrude Stein's line about Oakland: "There is no there there."

In Jerzy Kosinski's insightful novel *Being There*, the central figure, a man devoid of personality and purpose, becomes acclaimed for his neutrality about everything, and the outside world sculpts him to be what they want him to be. When I saw the film version of *Being There*, I was fascinated by Peter Sellers's bewildered look as the enigmatic man whose casual comments propel him into international acclaim. I kept saying to myself, "He's playing Andy Warhol."

But the legend continues. Long after Warhol died, art critics and social commentators kept citing his achievements and role in art and social commentary. His dull Polaroid photos of famous people sell for millions of dollars. I am always as bewildered as I was by Peter Sellers in the film. I want to shout, "The emperor has no clothes!"

There is a postscript to this. Years later at the Fortune Society, a counselor came to me and said that a woman—a new arrival, recently out of prison—wanted to meet me. I was then introduced to Valerie Solanas, the woman who had shot Andy Warhol and who was the subject of a fascinating movie about her rage against him, in which she was played splendidly by Lili Taylor. Ms. Solanas was as blank-faced as Andy, revealing not a hint of emotion.

I recalled watching the film and wondering how Andy could have evoked anger in anyone. But apparently, in his own bailiwick he was able to incite the ambitions and dreams of a small army of lost souls.

I have always referred to Andy Warhol as the Big Enigma.

Jean Bach, my friend for more than forty years, knew practically everyone. She was the producer of the Arlene Francis radio show, and her husband, Bob, was the producer of the Sunday night hit TV show *What's My Line?* But it wasn't their prestigious media positions that drew people to them. Jean Bach was the liveliest, most attractive, wittiest woman in any room she entered. Jean and Bob's parties at their well-appointed Greenwich Village town house were where you wanted to be.

Jean was a jazz aficionado. In her late years she produced an Oscar-nominated documentary called *A Great Day in Harlem*, a fascinating inspection of the musical greats who once posed on the steps of a Harlem brownstone for a photo that first appeared in *Esquire*. At Jean's parties, an assortment of performers would get up and croon. I heard Blossom Dearie, Mary Lou Williams, Margaret Whiting, Mel Tormé, and Annie Ross, among others, warble in the Bach living room.

I was also a frequent weekend visitor to their country home in Bedford Hills, New York, and shared wonderful Saturdays with them and their fabled guests. Perhaps the afternoon I treasure most was when I sat in their back lawn alongside Johnny Mercer, having him exclusively to myself, and he nostalgically regaled me about songs and movies and personalities. Jean was puttering around the house, and Bob had been called off somewhere. WNEW radio was playing in the background, and it seemed as if every third song on the air prompted Johnny to say, "I wrote the lyrics for that song in forty-nine" or "that was in a movie I worked on."

Other weekend guests included Germaine Greer, Ed Koch, Blossom Dearie, Bobby Short, Julia Meade, Tommy Flanagan, Brendan Gill, Lenny Lopate, Annie Ross, Dorothy Loudon . . . authors, playwrights, actors, and musicians.

Jean and her longtime friend Bobby Short would have an annual "anniversary" party celebrating their decades of friendship. The buffet sit-down was often packed with music legends and held at a smart East Side place like the Carlyle or the Plaza. At one memorable fête, I found myself on the buffet line with a stunning woman whose easy charm seduced me. We talked and laughed as we picked our food and found a table, where we continued our chatter. Considering the surrounding cast of music legends, we exchanged views on various artists, some of whom were sitting at nearby tables.

She seemed particularly interested when I told her I hosted a weekly radio program on WBAI and had the opportunity to play my favorites. She insisted I report on who that list would include. I named Johnny Hartman, Dinah Washington, Peggy Lee, Lou Rawls, Joe Williams, Carmen McRae, Billie Holiday, Tony Bennett, Sinatra, and of course Nat King Cole. "Why of course?" she asked.

I proceeded to wax eloquent to my gracious co-guest, explaining to her what was so special about Nat Cole and how he influenced me and touched me on several levels. I gave her details of when I heard "Unforgettable" for the first time when I was in college, sitting alone in an Italian restaurant in Denver with jukebox selections at the table. I recalled the range of emotions that only a teenager could gain from the sentiments of a ballad. I told her that listening to Nat Cole was like rubbing my face on velvet.

It was at this juncture that Bobby Short and Jean Bach, making the rounds, stopped at our table. Jean said, "I'm glad you two discovered each other." We both laughed at once, realizing we hadn't even introduced ourselves. I was so caught up in her charm and beauty that I had ignored basic introductions. I turned to her and said, "I'm David . . . David Rothenberg."

She smiled demurely and said, "I'm Maria Cole."

I had been explaining the virtues of Nat King Cole to his widow. She laughed and hugged me.

It was a single meeting, but I was charmed forever by Maria Cole.

People always look startled when I begin a sentence, "When I was in the army . . ." Their usual response is, "You . . . in the army?" Indeed I was, for two years in Fort Benning, Georgia, at a time when Martin Luther King's voice was just beginning to be heard. I was close to Columbus, Georgia, and saw apartheid up close.

After basic and advanced training, where I became an expert in heavy weapons, I was assigned to the public-information office of the Third Division. Within months I was editing the division newspaper, the *Marne News.* I had just six months left when the Third (or "Marne") Division was sent overseas, so I was assigned to Fort Benning's main post and became editor of their newspaper, charmingly called the *Bayonet.*

I covered most of the sporting events at Fort Benning and was assigned to a lieutenant, a six-month ROTC sports god. Jim Brown was arguably the best running back in National Football League history. He was doing his military obligation, but it was clear that his heart and body were readying for the next football season. At Benning he participated in all sporting events, particularly track. I suspect he was not enamored by the segregated southern lifestyle.

We traveled to Fort Bragg, where our Benning trackmen were competing in an all-eastern army meet. Jim was running in a few events. We arrived at the barracks, and strangely, they assigned us to share a double bunk. That a private first class was to share living quarters with an officer was an indication of Bragg's confused procedures. Nevertheless, Jim seemed unbothered by the lack of protocol. He took the upper and I had the lower.

On the first night there, I went to bed early and was in a deep sleep when suddenly the world caved in on me. Jim Brown, about six-foot-two and 220 pounds, perhaps the most perfect specimen of male sculpture I had ever seen, was climbing into his upper berth in the dark, unaware of my sleeping presence, and was vaulting upward thanks to the pressure he was putting on my five-foot-six, 120-pound frame. I gasped for breath. He leaped off the upper bunk and put on the lights. "I didn't know you were there," the all-American told me, truly apologetic.

For years I would tell the story that I had been stepped on by Jim Brown.

In 2008, it was announced that a guest was bringing the fabled Jim Brown to the Fortune Society's annual fundraising gala. Jim, who after his illustrious football career became a film star for a decade or two, had also become an activist, dealing with men coming out of prison—a West Coast advocate for many of the same issues we were confronting at Fortune.

I was introduced to Jim at the party and told him we had met once before. He claimed that I looked familiar. Then I told him the story of Fort Bragg, and he certainly remembered the track meet—but I realized that my memory of being a Brown-stepped-on survivor was just one of a multitude of experiences he had lived through. After all, his football career was determined by the number of men he plowed through.

But how many people can say that they were stepped on by a sports god? I can.

Roy Cohn was certainly one of the most evil and odious men of our time. He was joined at the hip with witch-hunting senator Joe McCarthy at the time that the Wisconsin senator had the nation in the palm of his hand with fear tactics and threats. Cohn first won national attention when he partnered with G. David Schine, a handsome hotel heir, and the two marched through Europe like Sherman through Georgia, accusing American embassies of Communist sympathies. Journalist wags often referred to Cohn and Schine as the Loeb and Leopold of American politics in the 1950s.

I first met Cohn when we debated the death penalty on the Barry Farber TV show. The young page led me to the greenroom, where Cohn was in deep conversation with another guest, David Duke, the Louisiana Klansman who would be debating Julian Bond in another segment of the show. Clearly, Barry Farber was looking for polarizing views rather than enlightenment for his viewers, a trend that has escalated in today's media.

Catching a view of Cohn and Duke, I asked the page if there was another room. He suggested I join Mr. Bond, who had had a similar reaction to the Cohn-Duke tryst. I was taken to a small room where Julian Bond had settled in. He and I agreed that we would have enjoyed being a fly on the wall absorbing the exchange between Cohn and Duke, but that actually being there seemed beyond any social courtesy either of us had learned.

During the debate I found Cohn to be cold and intimidating, mostly because he revealed no feelings about the death penalty. At one point, I mentioned that Ethel Rosenberg had been executed even though the FBI knew she'd had no involvement with espionage, because they felt her silence deserved punishment. I asked Cohn about the death of this mother of two young boys, and he bluntly responded, "I would have pulled the lever myself if they had let me."

Years later, when I saw Tony Kushner's prize-winning play *Angels in America*, Ron Leibman, portraying Cohn, uttered that line. I always wondered if Kushner learned that quote from my debate with Cohn or if it was a line that Cohn projected as a matter of course.

During a commercial break in the TV debate, Cohn turned to me and asked, "What are you getting so worked up about? It's only a television show." We were discussing life and death, and he viewed it as show business.

I had several other encounters with him, none pleasant, all enlightening.

We were two members of a panel discussion on WOR radio focused on criminal justice. I arrived early at the studio and learned that two other panelists were sitting criminal-court judges. Cohn was running late, and the live show began. I found the judges candid and supportive of my views about prison and the reentry problems facing men and women coming out of institutions. Fifteen minutes into the hour-long program, the tardy Mr. Cohn arrived with a burst of opinions. Suddenly, the room temperature turned cool; the judges became taciturn. The program became a two-man battle: me confronting the punitively inclined Mr. Cohn. More than anything else, I was fascinated by the intimidation Cohn imposed on the judges. Nothing was said, but it was apparent what had taken place.

I didn't understand their fears of Cohn's influence. I was to learn how deep it went.

I was called in as an advisor for a drug rehabilitation program for teenagers. Encounter Inc. had opened a facility on Sixty-Eighth Street off Fifth Avenue. It was an unlikely neighborhood for a drug program, but the folks at Encounter Inc. had done their work. They had engaged most of the neighbors, and many had become part of an Encounter Advisory Council. Several became volunteers and tutors. What Encounter did not anticipate was the wrath of Roy Cohn.

Cohn lived in a town house on East Sixty-Eighth Street and argued that real-estate values would be affected by Encounter's presence. Most of the neighbors disagreed. A community-board meeting was called at Automation House. I was one of the speakers and presented my strong support of the program, with a snarling Cohn in the front row. He and I had exchanged words in the hallway before the meeting; before then, I had written a letter, published in a weekly newspaper, accusing Cohn of a willingness to sacrifice kids in need because of his own convoluted and inaccurate estimation of property values. The community board voted overwhelmingly to allow Encounter to remain, and the room cheered.

Cohn had taken a bitter defeat, or so we thought. Six months later, Encounter was suddenly and without any warning stripped of all state and city funding. How and why Cohn got to the highest reaches of government, we can only suspect...but he had the last word on the Encounter episode.

Political insiders often stated that Roy Cohn knew where the bodies were buried and would act on it. The cruel irony was that Cohn's concern about the value of his town house never became a reality. His drug-filled body led to his dying a painful death from AIDS.

He was certainly the most evil man I ever saw up close. That didn't alter the fact that he could influence reasonable and successful judges into silence...and have funds cut from a necessary community program for his own selfish and misguided real estate aims.

I mentioned that Cohn and Schine were often referred to as the Loeb and Leopold of politics. Richard Loeb and Nathan Leopold were the central figure in what was called the crime of the century: the murder of a young boy, Bobby Franks. Their motivation had been merely to see if they could commit a perfect crime. Clarence Darrow, through his famous defense, spared the two wealthy Chicago heirs from the death penalty. They both received life sentences in prison.

Dickie Loeb was murdered by another prisoner. Nathan Leopold became a model inmate and was released after decades in an Illinois prison. He became involved in critical scientific studies and moved to an island in the Caribbean. I read that he sometimes visited New York City.

One night in the late sixties, after a performance of *Fortune and Men's Eyes*, a quiet, self-effacing man asked if he could go backstage and greet and praise the actors. I brought him to Terry Kiser. The man said he had served many years in prison and recognized the power of the play. He introduced himself as Nathan Leopold.

He seemed gentler and kinder than any facet of Roy Cohn's character.

SEVENTEEN

Senescence

I am well into my senescence, a state of being from which most people expect senility or wisdom, or a combination of both. Let me reveal some gained wisdom on the subject of age...of growing old.

By almost anyone's standards, I am old. Yet, every time I describe myself thus, I am greeted with a barrage of objections: "Don't say that. Age is only a number," warned one colleague. "You are only as old as you feel," alerted another friend. "You are an active and vital person," I was informed by a third sage. If there is a bromide to describe old age, it has been served to me—disputing the indisputable fact that I am an old American. When an acquaintance recently asked how I was, I responded, "Old and Jewish." And he, in a state of alarm, warned, "You must never say that." I asked, "Which part, the old or the Jewish?"

As I write this, I am in my seventy-ninth year. I have read reports stating that the average life span for American men is seventy-eight years. I hope I can pass the statistical cutoff, but if seventy-eight is the expected life span and I'm at the bar, no matter how many clichés you throw at me, I'm old.

So what's the beef? Obviously, being old—or saying such—is perceived as a negative reflection on yourself. It is, in fact, interpreted as threatening. One man, overhearing my description of myself, called me "self-deprecating." I tried to make light of it, telling him,

"Seventy-eight is the new seventy-four." The sixty-five-year-old found no humor in my jibe.

It isn't news that we are a society preoccupied, obsessed, by youth, and we cling to middle age up to the wall. So much so that being old, or labeling yourself as such, is unacceptable in polite society or even rude society.

We know television commercials assault us with endless products attempting to deny the inevitability of the aging process. Of course, they are only offering creams, salves, and Botox to alter the facial appearance. This has little to do with the evolving changes of the body—the liver, the heart, the kneecaps, the prostate. I holler at the TV ads and manufacturers, "Bring it on!"

Of course, there are disadvantages to growing old, all well documented and drilled into our heads from infancy. But as I recall, youth wasn't such an around-the-clock bargain, with few guarantees of being pain- or angst-free. The faces were unlined and the bodies were sculpted, but the inner turmoil was in evidence, so much so that many of us didn't appreciate the physical advantages. I, for one, am always startled when an old friend remarks that I was "handsome" when I was younger. I often reflect that I wish someone had mentioned that to me while I was in my confused youth, a condition which was not mine exclusively.

Let me put forth some of the advantages of advanced years... or old age. For starters, I have changed many of my habits because of the onslaught of time. I go to bed earlier, wake up earlier. It is true that subway steps seem steeper than a decade ago, and my long walks are shorter. I have noticed illness is not confined to the elderly, but the prospect of the "Big D" hovers over the aged more emphatically than it does young people, for whom life seems eternal. As I recall, we always knew we wouldn't be on Planet Earth forever. We are using up space until the next group comes along and tries to louse it up. I'll keep chugging along, but the end will come to me as it has to everyone else. We have not been promised a limitless stay. Beethoven died, as did Gandhi and Shakespeare and Elvis and Martin Luther King, and we might get misty-eyed about their mortality, but somehow the world managed to go on without them, so I think it will do fine in my absence.

Beethoven, Shakespeare, and King made the world better for those who came after them, using the time they had to their and our best advantage, a feat many since have attempted to emulate. For most of us, a few people will shed some tears, hold some cherished memories, and hopefully be inspired enough to make their own lives more meaningful.

But before I get caught up in the senility-wisdom cycle, I did say I would list some advantages of being old. For one thing, you don't have to waste much time or money on your appearance, since once you hit the streets, you are practically invisible. No one notices you when you are old, so you can dress comfortably and for yourself. No one else cares. I can don an unironed shirt and march off to the store without a nod of disapproval. That might seem glib and superficial, but it is a good starting point for recognizing the pluses of dotage.

A moderation in emotions evolves with age. I am no less angry or indignant about social injustice or incompetence and mediocrity... but I am less disappointed by the shortcomings of other people. I have learned to modify my expectations. When Dick Cheney was vice president of the United States and his every word sent terror through the streets, I was reminded and comforted that this too will pass. I still speak out against political inanities but recognize that nothing is forever, even elected philistines.

When you have lived eight decades, you know that whatever bothers you will pass. When I think of the angst created by elected officials of the past, I realize they are merely historical footnotes to the present generation. I wonder if many young activists have any notion of what the mere mention of Richard Nixon, Roy Cohn, or

J. Edgar Hoover would do to me and my friends. The world moves on, and a serenity replaces the stomach turns caused by those perennial foes.

I stay busy, occupying my time by visiting the Fortune Society a few times a week, spending Thursday evenings at the Castle's weekly community meeting, and becoming acquainted with men and women who are first accepting the challenge of new possibilities in their lives.

I have more time to read, see two or three movies a week, and attend the best of Broadway and off-Broadway shows. And on an odd evening, there is always a game on television, be it the Mets or Yankees during the baseball season or the Knicks during basketball season. Sports seasons are so extended that they overlap, and cable TV assures you there is always a game being played somewhere in America.

More than anything else, I have the people in my life: friends of many years and recently acquired acquaintances. I recently took a young man from the Fortune Academy to see a Broadway play, the first in his life. Over a bowl of soup after the play, he poured his life out to me, revealing that he was one of ten children of a mother who is still addicted and a father long since gone. He wants something more in life, and the Castle is where he is finding it. He talked to me about going to school in the fall and finding a new set of friends. When he said good-bye to me at the subway stop, he leaned over, hugged me, and said, "Thanks for the play, Pop." He did more than make my day. He made me look forward to the next day—and the next time I can invite him to enjoy one of the cultural experiences New York City offers.

Growing older is palatable when a youngster's broad smile is accompanied by "Thanks, Pop." So if it's wisdom you are seeking, just make growing older a part of your life, and look for someone just discovering life. It can almost make you feel young, if that's what you are looking for.

Index